Edinburgh Law and Society Series

Sex Crimes on Trial

The Use of Sexual Evidence in Scottish Courts

BEVERLEY BROWN, MICHELE BURMAN AND
LYNN JAMIESON

EDINBURGH UNIVERSITY PRESS

© Beverley Brown, Michele Burman and Lynn Jamieson, 1993

Edinburgh University Press Ltd
22 George Square, Edinburgh

Typeset in Linotron Plantin
by Koinonia Limited, Bury, and
printed and bound in Great Britain
by The University Press, Cambridge

A CIP record for this book is
available from the British Library

ISBN 0 7486 0408 1

Contents

Acknowledgements

This research was funded and made possible by a grant from the Scottish Home and Health Department and was undertaken with the sponsorship of the Scottish Courts Administration. A summary report on the research was issued as a Scottish Office Central Research Unit Paper, entitled 'Sexual History and Sexual Character Evidence in Scottish Sexual Offence Trials, 1992'.

The views expressed here are ours and are not attributable to either of these bodies.

We would like to thank all the court administrators at High Court, Sheriff Court and District Court level in Edinburgh and Glasgow. A special thanks to John Robertson, the Deputy Principal Clerk of Justiciary, and George McIlwain of the Edinburgh Sheriff Court and Sgt. Middleton of the Edinburgh High Court who kept us notified of the scheduling and rescheduling of trials. Most of all, however, we must thank all the clerks of court who took the time to fill in our forms. In the last year of our research we were assisted by members of the judicial and legal professions whom we subjected to a fairly lengthy interview. They remain anonymous in the text but their views have considerably enriched our understanding and, we hope, our book. Thanks to them all.

We also have to thank all our researchers whose meticulous note taking forms the basis of much of our report. Attending sexual offence trials is grim work and all of us suffered for it. In particular we would like to thank Liz Hammersley who acted as researcher and secretarial backup. Also thanks to Liesa Spiller who compared legal arguments in sexual offence cases with other aspects of law, to Joanna Cherry who perused documents on the consultation process and the Parliamentary debates surrounding the passing of the legislation, and to Nadia Faccenda who trawled court records for sexual offence cases. For secretarial assistance we would like to offer profuse thanks to Alison Mason and also to Terri Inkster for her assistance in the early stages of the research. All of these people gave more than could reasonably be expected.

We have benefited from discussion with individual members of the

Edinburgh University Law Faculty - John MacLean, John Blackie, now Professor at the University of Strathclyde, Professor W. A. Wilson – and owe thanks to Professor Robert Black for his comments on earlier drafts. None of them are responsible for any opinion or error found here. Professor John Murray, Professor A. Busuttil of Edinburgh University, Superintendent Tom Wood (now Assistant Chief Constable) of Lothian and Borders Police, and Sheriff Principal Gordon Nicholson all met with us informally at various times and provided background insights. John Willis, Visiting Scholar to the Central Research Unit, the Scottish Office, commented on our report and shared an outsider's view of the legislation.

Glossary

The following terms are used throughout the text:

advocates depute: Advocates are the Scottish equivalents to English barristers who act as professional pleaders in all courts and prepare legal opinions for solicitors. Advocates depute are practising advocates nominated by the Lord Advocate to examine all cases reported to Crown Office with a view to solemn proceedings and to prosecute cases in the High Court.

application: The procedure in the trial whereby the defence applies to the presiding judge or sheriff to question the complainer on sexual history and sexual character matters excluded by s. 141A/B and s. 346A/B of the Criminal Procedure (Scotland) Act 1975.

complainer: A person who has made a complaint of being the victim of a crime. The English equivalent term is 'complainant'.

The Crown: The state, in the sense that crimes are seen as committed against the body politic. Represented in English law as R [Regina/Rex] v. ... and in Scots law High Court cases as HMA [Her/His Majesty's Advocate] v. ...

Crown Agent: The senior civil servant assisting the Lord Advocate in the prosecution of crime in Scotland.

Crown Office: The Lord Advocate's permanent staff selected from members of the fiscal service and located in Edinburgh.

defence counsel: Advocates who act as professional pleaders in the High Court on behalf of accused persons.

defence lawyers: Also known as defence agents. Solicitors in private practice who give legal advice to accused persons and can represent them in Scottish District and Sheriff Courts.

District Court:	Third and lowest tier of Scottish Court system.
fiscals:	See procurators fiscal.
High Court:	Highest level of ordinary court/court of first instance in Scotland. Criminal trials at this level are always jury trials; custodial sentences over three years may be given only at this level.
honest belief:	see mistaken-belief defences.
indictment:	The document issued in the name of the Lord Advocate containing the full charges against an accused person in the case of offences or crimes which are thought to be serious and to warrant prosecution by solemn procedure.
Lord Advocate:	The principal law officer of the Crown in Scotland who is responsible for the prosecution of all cases and is the Government's chief adviser on questions of Scots law.
mistaken-belief defence:	In sexual offences that turn on the complainer's non-consent, one line of defence is that the accused mistakenly believed the complainer was consenting. While traditionally such a defence depended upon it being objectively 'reasonable' to have made such an error, more recently it has been accepted in law that such a belief, if subjectively genuine ('honest belief') is sufficient even if unreasonable. In statutory offences where consent is determined by the fixed age of consent of the complainer, the parallel defence is that the accused was mistaken as to the age of the complainer.
procurators fiscal:	Also known as fiscals. Qualified solicitors employed as Crown servants who prosecute crime on behalf of the Crown in each Sheriff Court district.
res gestae:	A set of incidents linked in time and place so as to be part of one inter-connected event.
Sheriff Court:	Deals with crimes less serious than the High Court although some borderline charges may be dealt with at either level. Maximum sentencing power is three years' custodial. Sheriff solemn procedure is a jury trial, while Sheriff summary procedure involves non-jury proceedings.
solemn procedure:	The procedure for dealing with serious crime which may lead to a trial with a jury at the High Court or the Sheriff Court.

Solicitor General:	The junior law officer of the Crown in Scotland, depute to the Lord Advocate.
summary procedure:	The procedure for dealing with less serious crime which may lead to a trial without a jury before a sheriff in the Sheriff Court or before a lay justice in the District Court.

1

Introduction

The last two decades have seen a growing concern about the way the law deals with sexual offences. One focus of that concern has been the courtroom, the complainer and the law of evidence in sexual offence trials. The basic issue is the fact that those who go to court as victims of sexual attacks, most obviously rape, are frequently subject to extensive questioning about their sexual lives. Evidence from other witnesses will also be taken about the complainer's sexual activities or reputation, although the use of such evidence has been, and remains highly controversial. Is it ever relevant to admit such evidence? Does it bias judge and jury, especially if used by the defence counsel to discredit the complainer? Certainly such questioning makes the witness box a daunting place. But what about the rights of the accused, perilous as those rights are often judged in other sorts of criminal trials?

Since the early 1970s, many jurisdictions, including Canada, a number of American and Australian states, and New Zealand have enacted legislation curbing the use of sexual evidence. In 1976 the Sexual Offences (Amendment) Act ss. 2 and 3 introduced restrictions covering trials in England and Wales – legislation that has been widely criticised as ineffective. Ten years later, in January 1986, legislation of a rather different design came into force in Scotland[1] (Scotland having a separate legal system from England and Wales.) This is a study of how sexual evidence has figured in the Scottish courts under the new rules. Since the Scottish legislation had the benefit of the experience of all these jurisdictions, it will be of interest to all those concerned that such reforms should actually be effective.

'Sexual evidence' has many facets and goes by many names – evidence of prior sexual activity, sexual experience, sexual history, sexual character and sexual reputation. Here we use the distinction between 'sexual history' – specific information about particular facts, individuals and events, which may sometimes be occurrences after the time of the alleged crime itself – and 'sexual character'. Sexual character, by contrast, involves the typing of a person, usually in moral terms of 'good' and 'bad' and evinces generalised tendencies or propensities. Reputation can be included under this heading too. These notions of sexual character have led a dual life in the legal traditions of Scots and English law in both principle and practice. On the one hand, evidence of this sort has been deemed admissible in principle in sexual crimes, even where it is excluded from all other crimes (but there are some key doctrinal differences that will be discussed between England and Scotland). On the other hand, court practice often goes far beyond what is formally allowed in besmirching the victim's sexual character.

Modern law reform has largely set its face against sexual character evidence while accepting that there will be some relevance for sexual history evidence. But keeping to this distinction is highly problematic, since sexual history evidence can clearly function to connote sexual character. Even when not officially endorsed, sexual character may be implied by innuendo and implication. Hence, some of the main problems of regulating sexual evidence.

Like legislation in other jurisdictions, the Scottish legislation does not bar sexual character and sexual history evidence totally, but lays down specific conditions and procedures for introducing such evidence if it fulfils certain conditions. The legislation is structured in terms of exclusions followed by exceptions. As elsewhere, the defence must apply to the judge or sheriff for permission to introduce the evidence; this is done in the course of the trial. However, the Scottish legislation is unusually broad in scope. It covers not only trials for rape and rape-related offences (such as attempted rape) but also almost every sexual offence: heterosexual as well as homosexual offences, where the crime concerns age-of-consent or legal capacity to give consent as in those crimes covered by the Mental Health (Scotland) Act 1984, as well as crimes of indecency. The only omissions are incest and clandestine injury (sexual intercourse with a sleeping woman) and some crimes such as brothel-keeping. Thus, complainers may be male as well as female, and the accused may be female as well as male. However, rape is taken as the paradigm instance. This wide scope also has the important implication that the legislation applies not only in the High Court but also in the lower courts, notably the Sheriff Court where all the same sexual crimes except rape and the Mental Health Act crimes may be prosecuted and gaol sentences of up to three years may be awarded. (The Scottish Court includes both the possibility of trial by jury as in the High Court (solemn procedure) or trial by sheriff sitting alone (summary procedure).) In Scotland the accused is not offered the option of choosing between judge or jury trial; the nature of the proceedings is determined by the Crown Office, primarily on the basis of the seriousness of the offence. Some of the offences covered could also come up at District Court level.

Another distinctive feature of the Scottish legislation is that it excludes not only evidence or questioning concerning the complainer and persons other than the accused ('third parties'), but also, at least in the first instance, any evidence of the complainer's sexual behaviour with the accused. No other jurisdiction does this. Certainly the English Sexual Offences (Amendment) Act deals only with the question of the complainer's alleged dealings with other people. (However, the fact that Scottish legislation puts the exclusion this widely does not imply the intention to disallow evidence concerning the accused on application.)

THE RESEARCH FOCUS

This book describes the findings of our research, undertaken over a period of three and half years, which studied how the new legislation is operating in the courtroom. In examining the implementation of the Scottish legislation, we had two main aims. The first aim was simply descriptive. We wanted to give a picture of the actual use of evidence about a complainer's sexual life that is currently to be found in the Scottish courts. This meant documenting the ways that complainers are questioned by the prosecution and defence, as well as looking at verbal evidence from other witnesses and also medical and forensic reports that are often introduced and made the subject of questioning. Summing-up statements by the prosecution, defence and judge/sheriff are also important in the way they convey how such evidence has been construed. At this level, the main concern was to give a more concrete reality to the abstract categories of the legislation by showing how often sexual evidence is used, and how construed in the process of attempting to prove or, more usually, dispute the crime. One key question here is how far the court use of sexual evidence follows the patterns and situations envisaged by the law reformers in their reports, consultation documents and also in Parliamentary debate.

Still by way of description, the research also shows how the legislation itself is actually invoked in the courtroom to prohibit or allow sexual evidence. Are procedures being followed, and what happens if they are not? How are the exclusions and exceptions being interpreted? What role do prosecutors and judges take in enforcing the legislation? How is the legislation being used in relation to non-rape offences and in the Sheriff Court?

The second aim of the research was to evaluate whether the legislation has been a success. Here we take a straightforward, instrumental, means–end approach. The legislation had certain ends. It aimed to overcome or ameliorate problems. The horizon of evaluation here is defined centrally by the stated aims of the official law reformers, as shown through the background reports, consultation documents and also through Parliamentary debate. (To take these goals as the standard of assessment is not, however, to regard them as beyond criticism.) Looking at the legislation as a 'means' – an instrument for achieving these ends – involves concentrating on the actual wording and overall design of the legislation in order to assess whether it is helping or hindering the achievement of the goals of the reform. Comparisons with alternative designs in other jurisdictions and also critical discussions about the Scottish legislation, will provide some important points of reference, as too will various queries and criticisms raised during the reform process.

In thus separating description and evaluation we hope to have produced a comprehensive picture of the existing situation that may also be of use to later researchers while, at the same time, making our standards of evaluation and description totally clear. (All references to cases thus include case numbers which can be cross-compared.)

Two other studies provide important points of comparison. For Scotland, Gerry Chambers and Ann Millar's *Prosecuting Sexual Assault*[2] provides a highly critical account of the use of sexual evidence in the Scottish courts before the new legislation was introduced, and points to some potential problems with the new legislation, which had just been introduced as their study was reaching its final stages. Although their account is not so detailed as ours, it provides one important version of the 'before' picture. The other key text is Zsuzsanna Adler's *Rape on Trial*[3] (and also various articles by her) which describes the fate of the English legislation in the courts. Her study is, in fact, doubly significant because her documentation of the drawbacks of the legislation south of the Border was taken into account when designing the Scottish legislation.

The rest of this chapter focuses primarily on the process of reform leading up to the Scottish legislation.

THE SCOTTISH ROAD TO REFORM

The story of the English reform process is well known. Partly triggered by the public outcry over the case of *Morgan*,[4] the Heilbron Committee (Advisory Group on the Law of Rape) was quickly set up to look into a number of problems concerning the law on rape. Their report[5] was completed within the year and espoused the principles that ' ... a woman's sexual experiences with partners of her own choice are neither indicative of untruthfulness nor of a general willingness to consent.'[6] Soon after, the *Heilbron Report* went to Parliament where, after some heated debate in which the reform initiative was very much championed by Jack Ashley, the amendments to the Sexual Offences Act were passed. *En route* were dropped a number of the Heilbron recommendations as to how the legislation should be framed.

There are many contrasts between the English and the Scottish reform process. In England, sexual evidence was considered together with other aspects of rape and rape offences, so that the resulting legislation also provided a statutory definition of the crime of rape itself. The Scottish reform, by contrast, dealt solely with sexual evidence, and this reflected quite a different route to reform. In Scotland, sexual character and history evidence were looked at in the wider context of the Scottish Law Commission's (SLC) general programme of law revision on the law of evidence as a whole. Sheriff Ian MacPhail was commissioned to undertake a critical review of the Scots law of evidence in civil and criminal matters, indicating areas in need of reform. In his report, sexual evidence was discussed primarily in terms of the general issues of character evidence. It was one of the areas clearly earmarked for change. The *MacPhail Report*[7] was submitted in April 1979 and its proposals for change were then presented in the form of a consultation document and circulated. The reform process was under way.

However, law reform on such a scale is a lengthy process and the programme of reform was, in fact, due to begin with the civil, rather than the criminal law of evidence. Meanwhile, there was growing public agitation about rape trials, especially from feminist and victim support movements. The fact that there had been legislation south of the Border fuelled the pressure for reform in Scotland, with the added demand to avoid the weaknesses of the English version. In 1978 the Scottish Conference of the Labour Party had noted with concern the lack of any legislative moves in the direction of the English reform.[9] During the passage of the Scottish Criminal Justice Bill in 1979-80 there was an attempt to introduce some such measures.[10] These pressures came to a head in early 1982 when a number of rape trials attracted a great deal of adverse publicity. Later that year, the Lord Advocate invited the Scottish Law Commission to give the sexual evidence reforms priority. Within the year the SLC had produced an official report specifically focused on sexual evidence (*SLC Report*), whose recommendations for a draft Bill were, in turn, circulated in a second round of consultation. After a fairly smooth passage through Parliament, including a (very lawyerly) debate by the First Scottish Standing Committee, the legislation, with minor changes to the SLC draft Bill, was passed and came into force in January 1986. One clear consequence of this lengthy and integrated reform process, with its many rounds of consultation, is that the resulting legislation in Scotland is much closer to the conception of the law reformers than in England, both in terms of the purposes and the statutory form of words.

However, it is also true that public concern about rape trials clearly played an important role in both places and focused on a wide range of issues besides the question of sexual evidence, including sentencing, police investigation, and prosecutorial decision-making. In the background there was an increasing sensitivity to all aspects of victims' experiences of the criminal justice system and a concern that dissatisfaction might undermine the legitimacy of the state legal system as the way to deal with sexual assaults. Feminist concerns were obviously an equally important influence in raising questions about the adequacy of the system in dealing with sexual crimes whose high actual incidence – by contrast to the official figures – was documented not least through the work of the Rape Crisis Centres. Thus, although the range of problems highlighted around sexual offence trials was diverse, the problems were ultimately linked together through such wider perspectives.

The controversial factor in the *Morgan* case, which was so important in precipitating the English reform, was the 'honest belief defence', popularly denounced as a 'rapists' charter'. This case validated for the first time the defence that a man had not committed rape if he genuinely believed that the woman was consenting at the time, however unreasonable it might have been to believe that. (In fact the *Heilbron Report* accepted that 'honest-belief-in-consent' should stay as a recognised defence to the charge of rape but conjoined with the successful recommendation that the statutory definition of the crime should also include reckless disregard of whether the complainer was consenting.) The honest-belief defence was also at stake in the events of 1982 that speeded up the Scottish reform. In that year there was the case of *Meek*[11] in which the principles of *Morgan* were (with some reservations) inscribed in Scots law. The Scottish case involved a girl on her way home from a country dance who was raped in a field by a group of boys, some of whom had chanced along later and, on appeal, claimed they had thought she was willing as the others were already having sex with her. The appeal failed on its facts (as had *Morgan*) but the principle was established.

The second controversial case of 1982 was an English case – the famous 'hitchhiking case' – in which Judge Richards decided, contrary to all the principles of criminal law, that a victim's 'contributory negligence' was a relevant factor in rape, and accordingly awarded a fine of £2,000 by way of sentence. While it has long been recognised that blaming the victim is often an implicit factor in jury decisions in rape trials,[12] until the Richards decision, no-one had dared to suggest that it was a *legitimate* consideration, and indeed this maverick ruling was later repudiated as totally alien to criminal law. For lawyers, legal sociologists and feminists, the suggestion that the victim was negligent was the crucial factor. However, its notoriety in the public eye was primarily as a scandal about light sentencing.

The third famous case of 1982 was the Glasgow Rape Trial. This was a group rape involving massive injuries to the victim. The victim did not know her assailants beforehand; the physical evidence of her non-consent was incontrovertible. It was the 'ideal' rape case from a prosecution point of view. Yet the public prosecution system dropped the case before it went to court, without notifying the victim, because, due to her still being under treatment for the injuries and the trauma that recalling the events might produce, she was deemed not fit to endure the trial process (itself a telling comment on the ordeal of the witness box for rape complainers). Thus, the real issue here was the prosecutorial decision-making. The only reason why there was ultimately a Glasgow Rape Trial was due to the victim's battle to bring a private prosecution. Because of this case, there was a review of decision-making procedures and it was decided that Crown Counsel could no longer take such a decision without referring it to the Lord Advocate or Solicitor General.[13] But at the time there was another complicating factor that outraged public opinion. For, when it was first aired that a private prosecution might be pursued because the case had been dropped, the official 'off the cuff' (and, seemingly, uninformed) pronouncement made no mention of the considerations about the complainer's welfare.[14] Rather, it said that the case had been dropped because it was 'not good enough' to go to court and it 'did not have sufficient, competent or available evidence', and also apparently because the fact that the victim had been drinking prior to the incident was damaging to her reliability as a witness, and raised questions about her non-consent. The public reaction was, in effect: how could such an 'ideal' rape case be trashed in this way? If this case was discounted, what hope for any rape victim?

Another event in the Scottish calendar of critical moments highlighting the law's handling of sexual assaults was the publishing, in 1983, of a Scottish Office research report, called *Investigating Sexual Assault*[15] by Gerry Chambers and Ann Millar which documented the way that police and prosecutors dealt with allegations of sexual assault in the pre-trial stages, including the factors which determined whether such charges ever came to court. This study apparently contributed to a number of reforms in police practice although, technically, its publication date rules it out as a factor in the Lord Advocate's decision to make sexual evidence a priority for reform.

Thus, perhaps oddly, none of the obvious public controversies about sexual offence trials in 1982 actually focused on the issue of sexual evidence. Nonetheless, these public debates do seem to have played a part in facilitating the Scottish reform. The *SLC Report* notes that:

> many reforms on these aspects of the law of evidence have in recent years been taking place both in England and elsewhere in the world and that, particularly in the last year or two, there has been some demand for reform in Scotland coupled with considerable media interest in the subject of trials for rape.[16]

Perhaps the more relevant event in the law reform calendar was the fact that 1982 was also the year in which Zsuzsanna Adler began publishing her series of articles[17] in academic law journals and in also the more accessible papers such as *New Society*, based on her study of how the English sexual evidence legislation fared in the courts. She argued very forcefully that in practice the reforms were far removed from the spirit of the original *Heilbron Report* and from even the perhaps more limited intentions of Parliament.

The publication of Adler's work may perhaps have served to underline the fact that such reforms had already been undertaken for England and Wales and hence contributed to the speedier implementation of what were, evidently, already well established plans for Scottish reforms. But the far more significant impact of her research conclusions was to focus attention on the problems of effective legislative design: how to find an effective form of words to express and safeguard the purposes behind the drive for reform. The crucial 'design' problem was the wording of the exception provision that determined when sexual evidence could be admitted (on application by defence counsel). The *Heilbron Report* had proposed an exception provision framed in terms of 'fact similarity', so that evidence about the complainer and men other than the accused should be allowed only on condition that it bore some sufficient resemblance to what allegedly had taken place between her and the accused. Although Heilbron's choice of 'fact-similarity' as the criterion of admissibility has been much criticised,[18] the important point is that they had tried to impose a specific clear criterion to determine the kind of evidence that should be allowed on application.

Heilbron had also recommended a statutory statement that character attacks on complainants in rape trials should, as in all other criminal trials, license a counterattack on the character of the accused (which would include possibly revealing past convictions). Both these recommendations were dropped in the passage of the ensuing Bill through Parliament and what emerged instead was the open-ended formula that such evidence should be admitted if the judge was satisfied that it would be 'unfair to the defendant' to exclude it. Adler's study confirmed the many doubts about the large amount of discretion this left to the trial judge, presumably one of the same caste of judges responsible for the pre-existing situation that the legislation sought to alter. For her, any such legislation had to be very tightly defined in order to combat the prevailing sexist attitudes of all personnel in the courtroom.

Thus, the significance of Adler's work was not limited to technical matters of wording. For she also re-articulated at just the right time, and very forcefully, and in a mode that official law reformers could cite as authoritative, a number of key themes of feminist critiques of sexual evidence. From a feminist perspective, the use and abuse of sexual evidence poses a series of overlapping but distinct problems that converge on the notion of sexual character: those stereotypes that divide women into the polar opposites of 'good' and 'bad' women – women who don't and women who do – or that promote the idea that women in general say 'no' but mean 'yes'. Here, feminist concerns seem very much at one with the principles espoused by Heilbron who also emphasised the legal and social bias in the fact that such sexual character evidence was allowed in rape trials but not generally in criminal trials.

However, feminist concerns about the law's official and unofficial stereotyping also insist that more is at stake than the law's fairness and the potentially biased outcomes of criminal trials – even more, the unfairness of society's double standards for men and women in sexual matters. For these stereotypes are also governing images by which all women are judged and controlled. They have wide effects in determining how women conduct their everyday lives. Similarly, the women's movement shares with the victim support movement some fundamental concern about the subjective experience of complainers in sexual offence trials: a mere prosecution witness, kept uninformed of key decisions and dates in the progress of the case, subject to a baffling and humiliating ordeal in the witness box, not only by the defence but sometimes from the prosecution – the sense that the victim is on trial yet, unlike the accused, without a legal representative.

Such feminist concerns clearly played some role in the Scottish reform – too strong a role, according to some. For, although the many rounds of consultation in the reform process clearly sought to achieve consensus, the submissions from the different consulted parties revealed some dissenting voices. On the one hand, there were those who felt that reform was completely unnecessary as there simply was no problem in the Scottish criminal justice system either in principle, since all the existing rules and principles of fairness were adequate, nor in practice since all the existing rules were operating properly. This opinion was expressed particularly by members of the criminal bar and police, some of whom also felt that Scottish reformers had been stampeded by the English reforms and media publicity which, again, arose from English problems. There was also some concern that one area of the law of criminal evidence was being altered out of context. On the other hand, a completely different grouping, mostly but not exclusively represented by Rape Crisis Centres, thought that the legislation did not go nearly far enough and that there should be a complete exclusion of all sexual evidence except where it might show that someone other than the accused was responsible. The exclusion of incest was also seen as a mistake. Behind this dissent lies some even more fundamental differences of principle.[19]

BALANCING AIMS AND MEANS

The stated aim of the reform is to achieve overall, a balance between minimising undue questioning of complainers on their sexual life, while continuing to admit all the evidence necessary for justice to be done to the accused. A number of different reasons were given for restricting evidence concerning a complainer's sexual life. First, the element of 'trauma and distress' caused by 'intimate, or possibly embarrassing questioning' was acknowledged as an important problem.[20] The aim of minimising this distress would, properly, be called a policy goal. Furthermore, the dangers of over-light sentencing and the unwillingness of victims to report sexual offences to the authorities, for fear of the courtroom ordeal or lack of belief in the system to achieve justice, were also mentioned as undesirable consequences of the use of sexual evidence which the legislation might help overcome.[21]

These side-effects of sexual evidence are, however, secondary to the issues of principle which concern the law of evidence itself. Thus, second, the *SLC Report* strongly rejects the validity of any sexual character construction of consent. It is fundamentally wrong to 'permit a wide-ranging enquiry into a woman's sexual history for the sole purpose of establishing that, because she has in the past had sexual relations with A and B, she must therefore have consented to intercourse with C'.[22] While the validity of any such inference had also been strongly denounced in the Scots law tradition, it was feared that in recent years this principle had been eroded in courtroom practice. Third, it also states that it should no longer be legitimate – and this time past tradition was rejected as out of touch with contemporary social and sexual mores – to make inferences about a complainer's credibility on the basis of sexual conduct or prostitution.[23] Fourth, the additional danger is also noted that sexual character evidence, even when not introduced as showing consent, was highly likely to be taken that way by a jury.[24] These principles are obviously very similar to the stand taken in the *Heilbron Report*.

Finally, it should be noted that it is not only the individual complainer whose interests are to be protected by' such legislation. In a system of public prosecution, crimes are seen as being committed against the public at large and the possibility that perpetrators of crimes are evading justice raises important problems about the legitimacy and effectiveness of the criminal justice system in dealing with sexual crimes. If the use of anomalous forms of evidence, of dubious relevance and great potential for prejudicing a jury, is contributing to this problem, then it is not only the individual victim who is at risk but the system of public prosecution as a whole.

The counterbalancing issue of justice to the accused is not discussed in such detail in the *SLC Report*, but respondents to the prior 'SLC Consultative Memorandum No. 46' had expressed fears about erosions of the rights of the accused. There was some concern that the exclusion of evidence concerning the alleged victim could unduly disadvantage the accused in sexual offence trials, while also acting as a point of leverage for wider changes in the criminal law, especially as this reform was being undertaken in advance of the broader reforms of the criminal law of evidence. However, some of the respondents (notably the Scottish Council for Civil Liberties) had argued that matters should not be seen in the 'zero-sum' terms of any gains in rights for complainers necessarily diminishing rights of the accused or vice versa. The *SLC Report* seems to endorse this view to the extent that the criterion of admissibility is to be the relevance of the evidence. This principle is stated particularly strongly in the context of their discussion of the criterion of 'fairness to the accused' used in the English legislation.[25] This formulation, in their view, 'obscures' the main point that relevance should be the criterion of admissibility. At the same time, their emphasis on relevance also makes it clear that the accused's rights are not to be confused with the accused's interests. It is obviously in the accused's interests not to be found guilty but it would be totally unprincipled to accept this as a criterion of admissible evidence. It would mean that absolutely anything should be allowed so long as it helped the accused to go free. As it was put in an important American constitutional case on the equivalent 'shield' legislation in Michigan, the defence has no constitutional right to ask irrelevant questions.[26]

Thus, it is one important aspect of ensuring justice to the accused that none of the normal rules of evidence should be distorted by the new legislation on sexual evidence. To the extent that the reform generally can be seen as essentially seeking to discard past anomalous rules covering sexual offence trials, thus abolishing any bias of principle or practice against the complainer, by the same token, there was a concern that the accused not now be placed in a different and less favourable position here than in other criminal trials.

As summarised in the Consultation Paper circulated by the Scottish Courts Administration in preparation for putting the legislation to Parliament in 1984:

> The Government fully understands the public concern about this matter and the ways such cases are handled in court. They wish to see the law of evidence changed so as to provide that, while the court would continue to admit all the evidence necessary to ensure that justice is done to the accused, the exposure of the complainer to intimate, and possibly embarrassing, questioning is reduced to the minimum possible. It is clearly not easy to achieve that balance, but the Government thinks that the general scheme of the Scottish Law Commission is right ... in that they combine a general prohibition on

> the admission of certain questioning with a discretion to the court to
> allow specific exceptions to that prohibition and to limit at any time,
> during the course of the trial, the extent of the questioning.[27]

The balancing aims of the Scottish reform are reflected in the way the legislation is framed. (See Appendix 1 for the precise formulation.) The first part is a general exclusion section stating all the types of evidence that will not ordinarily be admitted, while the second part lays out the exceptions and indicates that, if the defence wishes to elicit evidence on these matters, they must seek permission from the judge or sheriff in the absence of the jury. (This is known as an 'application' and takes place during the trial, usually but not always just before the cross-examination of the complainer.) The Crown is not covered by the exclusions and thus does not need to make an application to introduce such evidence. If the evidence falls under one of the exceptions, then 'the court shall allow such questioning or ... admit such evidence' but may also intervene to 'limit as it thinks fit the extent of that questioning or evidence'.

The 'exclusion' part categorises sexual evidence into three types, ruling out any evidence or questioning that would 'show or tend to show':

1. that the complainer is 'not of good character in relation to sexual matters';

2. 'is a prostitute or associate of prostitutes'

or indeed any discussion of

3. 'sexual behaviour not forming part of the subject matter of the charge'.

By way of 'exceptions' to the prohibition, the Scottish legislation specifies:

1. explaining or rebutting evidence adduced by the Crown

2. evidence concerning behaviour taking place on the same occasion as the behaviour in the charge

3. evidence relevant to a defence of incrimination; and, finally,

4. the 'interests of justice'.

Such is the basic picture of the reform. In Chapter 3 some of the implications and potential shortfalls of the reform will be discussed in more detail as a crucial basis for the ultimate task of assessing whether this legislation is living up to its objectives and principles. Already it is clear that the legislation had at least a symbolic significance in affirming women's worth and status, but whether it was also instrumentally effective, and also whether the 'rape paradigm' can be extended so simply to the range of sexual offence trials, are larger matters.

NOTES

1. Criminal Procedure (Scotland) Act 1975 ss. 141 and 346, as inserted by the Law Reform (Miscellaneous Provisions) (Scotland) Act 1985 s. 36 (see Appendix 1).
2. G. Chambers and A. Millar, *Prosecuting Sexual Assault* (Edinburgh: HMSO, Scottish Office Central Research Unit Study, 1986).
3. Z. Adler, *Rape on Trial* (London and New York: Routledge & Kegan Paul, 1987).
4. DPP v. *Morgan and Others* (1975) Cr. Ap. R. 136; [1976] AC 182.
5. Report of the Advisory Group on the Law of Rape (London: HMSO, 1975) Cmnd. 6532.
6. *Heilbron Report*, para. 131.
7. Sheriff I. D. MacPhail, subsequently published under the title *Evidence: A Revised Version of a Research Paper on the Law of Evidence* (Edinburgh: Law Society of Scotland, 1987).
8. Reform Chronology:

April 1979	'Research Paper on the Law of Evidence' (*MacPhail Report*), published by the Scottish Law Commission.
September 1980	'Consultative Memorandum No. 46', circulated by the SLC (Q 06/proposition 169 and Q 07/proposition 170 concerning sexual evidence).
1982	Lord Advocate invites SLC to make evidence in cases of rape and other sexual assaults a priority.
20 July 1983	*Evidence: Report on Evidence in Cases of Rape and Other Sexual Offences* (Scottish Law Commission No. 78) (*SLC Report*).
July 1984	'Consultation Paper: Evidence in Cases of Rape and Other Sexual Offences', circulated by the Scottish Courts Administration.
5 November 1984	Introduction Bill (Clause 33) Law Reform (Miscellaneous Provisions) (Scotland) Bill 1985.
19 November 1984	Parliamentary Question.
29 November 1984	First Reading.
30 November 1984	Second Reading.
26 March 1985	Committee debate in First Scottish Standing Committee.
2 May 1985	Report Stage.
2 July 1985	House of Lords debate.
30 October 1985	Royal Assent.
December 1985	Commencement Order (SI 1985/2055).
1 January 1986	Legislation comes into force.

9. Conference Resolution No. 73, cited in Chambers and Millar (1986), p. 3.
10. Cited in Chambers and Millar (1986), p. 3.
11. *Meek and Others* v. *HMA* 1982 SCCR 6143 and 1983 SLT 280 (Notes). The reservation is that reasonableness would still be an important test for the jury to apply in deciding whether the accused had really held this belief.
12. H. Kalven and H. Zeisel, *The American Jury* (Boston and Toronto: Little, Brown, 1966), pp. 249–54.
13. *Hansard* col. 423, 21 January 1982 gives the Solicitor General's statement. Discussion here is based on Chambers and Millar (1986), pp. 5 and 129–31.
14. This account is based on R. Harper and A. McWhinnie, *The Glasgow Rape Case* (London: Hutchinson, 1983).
15. G. Chambers and A. Millar, *Investigating Sexual Assault* (Edinburgh: HMSO, Scottish Office Central Research Unit Study, 1983).
16. *SLC Report*, para. 1.2, p. 1.
17. In 1982 Adler published: 'Rape: The Intention of Parliament and the Practice of the Courts' (1982) 45 *Modern Law Review* (cited in *SLC Report*, para. 4.7, p. 12); 'The Reality of Rape Trials' *New Society* (4 February); 'Rape Law The Latest Ruling' *New Law Journal* (5 August), pp. 746–47.
18. See R. Cross and C. Tapper, *Cross on Fact Evidence* (London: Butterworth 1985, 6th edition), pp. 296 and 298, and also J. C. Smith, 'The Heilbron Report' (1976) *Criminal Law Review*, on the surprisingly unprogressive nature of this suggestion.
19. These deeper divisions will not be discussed until the concluding chapter.
20. Law Commissioner's response to the SCA Consultation paper; also *SLC Report*, para. 4.1, p. 10 and para 5.1, p. 13.
21. See for example, *MacPhail Report*,, para. 16.09; First Scottish Standing Committee, col. 946–9.
22. *SLC Report*, para. 5.1, p. 1.
23. *SLC Consultative Memorandum* No. 46; *MacPhail Report*, para. 16.09; *SLC Report*, para. 5.3, p. 14).
24. *MacPhail Report*, para. 16.09; 'SLC Consultative Memorandum No. 46'; *SLC Report*, para. 5.3, p. 14.
25. *SLC Report*, para. 5.19, p. 19. The context was explaining the choice of the phrase 'the interests of justice' as one of the exceptions.
26. *People* v. *Thompson* (1977) 76 Mich. App. 105.
27. SCA Consultation Paper, para. 1.3.

2

The Trial Setting

One of the important lessons from comparing the English and Scots law routes to reform is that sexual evidence can be considered in two different legal contexts. The English way was to consider sexual evidence as part of the overall 'package' of rape offences. This has the advantage of not isolating evidential issues from questions about the definitions of sexual crimes and the possible defences (such as mistaken belief). The Scottish reform, by contrast, placed sexual evidence in a different context – the wider setting of the law of evidence in general, especially in criminal law. The benefit of this approach is a principled understanding of how sexual evidence has functioned in the past and should function in the future in relation to some fundamentals of legal doctrine on evidence.

Neither of these perspectives can be totally separated from the other, even in the abstract modes of legal doctrine. In the courtroom, they cannot help but interact. What is involved there is a process of proving, or contesting, not only that a sexual crime has been committed but that it has been done by the particular person who stands in the dock. The rules of evidence, the definition of the crimes, and the available defences are all involved together. But, even so, this interaction does not fully capture all the ingredients that determine the nature of a sexual offence trial. For this is a trial process with its own structuring principles, in which the key legal and non-legal participants have their roles and places.

Thus, before embarking on any more detailed account of the Scottish reform principles and how they have worked out in practice, this complex setting needs to be described. For, the courtroom is the place at which reforms are directed, and it is the site where their success or failure must ultimately be assessed. Criminal trials are the arena in which sexual evidence is used and its uses cannot be grasped without a preliminary sense of the *structures of evidencing* that are the net resultant of all the different doctrinal and institutional factors at work in the trial setting. (Complainers in sexual crimes are usually women, but it should not be forgotten that the Scottish legislation covers homosexual offences between men.)

One particularly vivid way of perceiving these dynamics is through the debates about sexual offence trials as an ordeal for the complainer. Much feminist and victim-oriented criticism of rape trials has this focus – the use of sexual character and history evidence itself is one of the crucial aspects of the trial ordeal. The shaming process in which a person who presents themselves as the victim of a harm is then questioned in immense detail on their sexual life has many resonances in a culture that is not only highly sexist but that also heavily constrains acceptable modes and sites of sexual life. Even the public speaking of the sexual event that is at the centre of the trial has a quality of 'indecency' since it brings the 'private' area of sexuality into the arena of public visibility.[1] Hence, rape, and by implication, sodomy and incest trials have been characterised as a 'pornographic spectacle' of sex displayed in public in which the woman – or man, boy or girl – who thus speaks is, almost by definition, a person of immense immodesty.[2] Such trials present the highly likely prospect of a 'status degradation ceremony' in which the complainer finds herself or himself transformed into all that is 'other' and alien to the shared values of the community. No less bizarre is the opposite side of the stereotype: the exemplary angel who stands for all that is healthy, respectable, innocent and therefore good.[3]

One of the stated policy aims of the Scottish reform was to minimise 'unnecessary, unacceptable trauma and distress'.[4] But the pain of being subjected to questioning on sexual evidence in the witness box, whether about outside events and relationships, or even the highlighted events of the trial, cannot be viewed in isolation. Such 'evidencing ordeals' are linked to more general background determinants – the terms in which sexual crimes are defined and the general protocols of evidence being two key aspects, combined with the institutional processes by which law's truth is to be discovered. Having to give evidence about sexual matters, already humiliating or embarrassing in itself, thus interacts with a number of other routine aspects of the trial process. By its nature a criminal trial is likely to be a (literally) testing experience for the key witness in which the ability to withstand gruelling questioning is seen as an appropriate mark of truth. The much debated and crucial question is how far a degree of ordeal is necessary.

For the use of sexual evidence in particular, this question will inevitably be judged in legal terms of the distinction between evidence that is 'relevant' and that which is not. Relevant evidence has a right to be heard, even if its extraction is a painful process. The avoidance of an ordeal is a secondary, policy concern, subordinated to the principled concerns of the law of evidence proper. Precisely how these principles of relevance regarding sexual evidence are articulated in past principles, current practice, and the future envisaged by the law reform are matters that will be reserved for the next chapter where they will make better sense after the general introduction provided here.

ORDEAL CONTESTED

For many feminist authors, the rape and sexual assault trials, simply adds a further level of 'secondary victimisation' to the victim's injury.[5] From a woman's perspective, the ordeal of the trial takes its significance from the point of view of the entire experience. The sexual assault is itself the initial ordeal; but the emotional aftermath, the need to decide quickly whether or not to report it to the police, the police questioning and medical examination are all an ordeal. Going to court is but part of a chain that requires reliving the original experience. In all of these situations the woman is at the receiving end of procedures in which she has no say. This replicates aspects of the assault and may exacerbate feelings of powerlessness. Even the key decision of whether or not to prosecute, her perceived means of redress, is taken out of her hands. Throughout she is positioned as a passive victim.

The trial itself is not an occasion for her to tell her story in her own way, rather she can only answer the questions she is asked. She is simply one of the prosecution witnesses, positioned almost as an outside observer, a bystander, of what she in fact has suffered; her suffering itself merely regarded as evidence, her anger unrepresented, and inappropriate. Worse still, through all the buffeting of cross-questioning and, especially if sexual evidence is used to besmirch her character and discredit her, it may seem that it is she, and not the accused who is on trial. So suggested the *Heilbron Report* on English trials[6] and so, too, have many other commentators. For Adler, the rape victim 'occupies a unique position in the legal system which treats her with unequalled suspicion'.[7] And, after all this, her attacker may not even be found guilty. Indeed, in the majority of rape cases the accused is not found guilty and the woman is likely to be left feeling that she has had her character and veracity called into question.

Lees encapsulates all these strands with respect to the situation in England for the rape victim:

> Imagine what it is like to give evidence against a man who has raped you. The case does not come up until over a year later. You have already given evidence at the magistrate's court. You are now obliged to relive the whole life-threatening experience, face-to-face with the man. You face ranks of barristers in wigs, the judge up high, police everywhere, all in the ostentatious surroundings of the Old Bailey. You don't have a legal representative of your own and you are not allowed to meet the prosecuting counsel so you are probably not sure which one is him.
>   You must describe in intimate detail every part of your body that was assaulted in words which are not used by 'respectable' women in

public. You are liable to be mercilessly cross-examined about every aspect of your life style, relationships and (at the judge's discretion) past sexual experience. It is continuously implied that you have lied, invented everything and even really enjoyed it. You have gone to court in the expectation that the accused will be convicted. But you begin to feel that it is you, not him, who is on trial. And finally, as he is three times more likely to be set free than convicted, you may well emerge from the ordeal with your own credibility and reputation undermined by the jury's dismissal of your evidence.[8]

Feminist authors have taken the way law treats women who have suffered sexual assault as evidence of male bias. They suggest that the legal process of rape trials is infused with a male perspective which distorts the possibility of legal justice for women. For some authors this is primarily a problem of a system that is mainly peopled by sexist men. Bias shows up in the anomalies and exceptions of rape law in principle and practice, departures from the legal norms that reflect the outside influence of social bias and sexist attitudes.[9] But for others, the problem is more fundamental and 'normal' to law. Its definitions, procedures and standard rules are thoroughly embedded in a male perspective and hence are inimical to women's interests.[10]

The reply to even the less radical of such arguments from legal quarters is not always sympathetic and is often somewhat dismissive. This is because some of the problems suffered by women complainers in sexual offence trials are a consequence of the routine workings of the court which affect men as well as women, and are the same in all types of criminal trials, not just sexual offence trials. Hence it can be argued that the complainer's lack of power and her status as a mere witness is not a special discrimination against women but due to the way the courts treat *all* victims of crime in a system of public prosecution. In reply to the fact that women in sexual offence trials suffer a particular ordeal with a high acquittal rate, the reply is that there are particular legal reasons why this is so which again are not to do with the fact that the complainer is a woman. Indeed, it would be argued, the problems are the same when the complainer is a man, as in sodomy cases. The legal reasons for the extent of the ordeal concern the special problems in proving sexual offences, which rarely take place in front of, or in the hearing of, witnesses and hence are difficult to substantiate. All complainers giving evidence become the site of a battle between the defence's and the prosecution's version of events.

Thus those intimately acquainted with the court process are impatient with those who criticise aspects of legal-evidential procedure without recognising its 'logic'. To a legal practitioner it seems unfair to focus on the experience of the courtroom without looking at why it works the way it does – the particular determinants and justifications of the institutional structure. What is more, one of the crucial differences between the critics and defenders of the trial system is that the critics tend to start from the point of view of a genuine victim and hence to live through what it is like to experience the trial as one who has been deeply harmed. By contrast, those who point to the 'logic' of the criminal justice system insist that a key part of this logic is not to assume from the start that the complainer is actually presenting the truth but, rather to approach the trial as a process of finding out the truth, which must include the possibility that the accused is innocent.

This chapter does not seek to find a definitive answer to these debates; they are returned to in Chapter 11 after illustrations of what actually happens in trials have been presented. Rather, the rest of this chapter describes the logic of the legal-evidential procedures that occur in trials – the side of the debate that explains all unpleasantness as an inevitable necessity of the system. It is important that the reader has the opportunity to grasp this logic and, hence, to avoid the situation of expecting the impossible from the public prosecution system as it stands at present. In Chapter 11 we return to the more problematic issue of whether complainers continue to suffer an unnecessary ordeal, even accepting the necessarily testing procedures of our adversarial system of prosecution and defence, and its definitions of sexual crimes and protocols of evidence.

FROM EXPERIENCE TO EVIDENCE

The fundamental rationale of the trial is to examine *the evidence*. A trial is a battle between prosecution and defence over the authenticity and meaning of *evidential signs*. It is difficult to convey how this focus on 'evidencing' clashes with general perceptions of what trials are about. The normal, commonsense, understanding is to assume that if some crime has been committed, then all that a witness has to do is to state this publicly in the witness box. On the contrary, the logic of evidence is about *showing* what happened. It is not enough in itself to say you have suffered a cruel attack, for now it must be proved. The focus in the trial is on the signs and traces of past events, and inferences that can thus be made about the events that have occurred. For example, in a rape trial a complainer is often asked many questions about the visible presence or absence of injuries, or the distress after the event, even if these were not significant in terms of how she herself experienced the assault.

What a complainer is asked about and expected to speak about is constrained by a number of factors; these include the way the crimes are legally defined in the first place, the standard rules of evidence, and further conventions concerning what constitutes appropriate evidential signs. Some aspects of what the complainer suffered as part of an assault may not be relevant to the law's conceptions of charges and evidence. The prosecution selects the charges according to their view of what can be proved, although this may not encompass all that the victim experienced as part of the assault or abuse. If under detailed questioning in the witness box the complainer indicates details which are not covered by the actual charges, this, rather than being helpful to the course of justice by revealing a fuller picture of the awful truth, might in fact damage the prosecution case.

Evidential Norms

Corroboration

The standard rules require that the complainer's testimony be cor-roborated, that is, supported and substantiated by some other piece of evidence. In English law, sexual offence trials are exceptional in requiring the jury to be given a special corroboration warning against convicting on the evidence of the complainant alone. This has been much cited as legal sexism, and as a key example of the discriminatory suspicion with which the law regards women.[11] (For even though it is an exception that now covers male complainants too, in sexual offence cases, it affects primarily women who are the overwhelmingly higher proportion of the victims.) In Scots law, however, facts have to be attested by two independent sources in *all* criminal trials, so it is not an exception to demand this in the case of complainers in sexual offence trials.

Thus at least some of the questions put to the complainer are for the purpose of matching the details of her story against other sorts of evidence, especially a medical report or forensic reports. Medical or forensic evidence is often crucially important as corroboration of a complainer's testimony in sexual offences. This is because of the unlike-lihood of other corroboration, since sexual offences usually take place in situations where there are unlikely to be eyewitnesses. Thus, in a rape case a number of standard signs are conventionally looked for to corroborate the complainer's account – injuries as documented by a medical report (as signs of non-consent) and semen as documented by a forensic report (as a sign that sexual intercourse occurred).

Signs of distress after the event, as documented by the police when the complainer reported the crime, or by anyone else to whom the complainer reported the event, is another 'desirable'. In rape and sexual assault cases the complainer is conventionally questioned about whether or not she told anybody about the event, as well as about such details as whom she told and how quickly. The first person in whom the complainer confides is generally called as a 'first report witness', who will in turn be questioned as a potential source of corroboration that an assault occurred. A com-plainer will also be presented with dis-corroborating statements from other witnesses, that is, statements other witnesses will make or have made which contradict the complainer's account. Unpleasant as this will be, it is seen as both a key part of the truth-testing process, and as giving the complainer the important right of refutation.

Hearsay

Sometimes the application of the rules can produce disconcerting instructions. For instance, one of the standard rules of evidence disallows 'hearsay evidence', that is, the reporting by a witness of something that had been told to them about a third party. Hence a witness might suddenly be asked to say nothing more about a particular conversation they are recounting. One exception sometimes allowed to this rule is if the 'first report' was made very soon after the event – the witness may then be allowed to comment not only on the complainer's state but also what she said about what happened to her.

Credibility and Reliability

The legal need to find corroboration and deal with dis-corroboration are important evidential requirements and conventions which mean that a witness's, and particularly a complainer's, account can never simply be telling the story of what happened from beginning to end. Another important legal convention, with this effect, is the testing of the sources of evidence – usually, the witnesses – in relation to reliability and credibility. The general paucity of corroboration places more pressure both on the substance of what the complainer herself or himself has to say, and on their reliability and credibility.

'Reliability' issues concern the witness's capacity to tell the truth – could they really see or hear what was happening at the time? Can they remember it? Are they mentally competent? (Children are often regarded as unreliable witnesses.) An unreliable witness is someone genuinely trying to tell the truth but nonetheless liable to be mistaken. 'Credibility', on the other hand, refers to a witness's sincerity and honesty, their desire to tell the truth. Does a witness have a motive for lying: a grudge, a financial interest, a desire not to lose face? Do they have a 'character for dishonesty'? Internal consistency within a witness's testimony is also regarded as a key test of credibility.

In trials for sexual offences the complainer's reliability and credibility are focused on very strongly, again, it is said, due to the basic corroboration problem. These questions are focused on in a variety of ways ranging from general character evidence to demeanour and consistency in the witness box. For example, in the case of a victim of sexual assault, overcomposure in the witness box can be used to discredit. (The use of sexual evidence as a means of undermining a complainer's credibility as a witness has been widely criticised by a number of commentators on sexual offence trials. It has already been noted that this was one of the key uses of sexual evidence that the legislation was intended to prevent (as will be explained more fully in Chapter 3). But sexual evidence can also be used to suggest mental instability and sexual fantasising, which concern reliability.)

The trial is often regarded as a contest between prosecution and defence over the evidence, for the benefit of the jury and judge. However this suggests too simple a version of the event. Certainly the structure of the trial is that of a two-sided contest. The order of the day is that the prosecution goes first and all the prosecution witnesses are called one after another and then the defence presents their witnesses. Unlike the American system there are no introductory statements by the prosecution and defence, so the jury is plunged straight into the testimony. The case begins simply with the first prosecution witness, usually the complainer but sometimes police witnesses, often scene-of-crime officers. Each prosecution witness is, in turn, cross-examined by the defence. The prosecution may then re-examine. Then the whole process is reversed when the defence brings their witnesses, if any, and they are cross-examined by the prosecution. The defence then has the right to re-examine.

However, the two sides in the contest are not on an equal footing. The prosecution's role is not simply to make out the case against the accused but more generally to present all the relevant facts – even if these facts go against the complainer's account, it is the prosecutor's official duty to present them. Overall, this process can be labelled an 'asymmetrical adversarial system'.

It is adversarial in that the whole truth-finding process is structured in terms of two sides fighting against each other, a system that is sometimes portrayed as a form of trial by combat or ordeal in which the severe rigours of examination and cross-examination are a test of truth. However, the Scottish, like the English, system is not a pure adversarial mode. The criminal justice trial is *asymmetrical* in that it is a system of public prosecution. This means that the burden of proof rests on the Crown, to demonstrate the case against the accused beyond reasonable doubt. The defence on the other hand need not prove anything; rather their task is to cast doubt on the prosecution case. There is no requirement that the accused go into the witness box. Thus, the complainer, as the main prosecution witness, *is* bound to feel on trial in the sense that it is up to the prosecution to do the proving, the defence merely to raise doubts. This is what it means to say that the accused is 'innocent until proven guilty'.

For some commentators – and not only legal practitioners – it is this asymmetric nature of the British adversarial system that largely accounts for the complainer's ordeal. It is the system itself, not those operating it, that is at the root of the problem. Doreen McBarnet has waged a long-standing campaign against the tendency to attribute the problems of legal justice to the gap between the formal rules and actual practice created by factors such as sexist attitudes brought to the courtroom. For her, sexist stereotyping of women in the courtroom is not, in itself, an explanation of the complainer's ordeal. She comments, 'These stereotypes tell us *how* rape victims are degraded in court but [it does] not tell us *why*, nor indeed why degradation in court is an experience not confined to victims of rape alone'.[12] For her the problem stems from the very nature of the public prosecution system, which treats the state, not the victim, as the injured party. In such a system the accused has a legal representative whose job it is to defend the accused's interests. The victim, however, has no legal representative similarly focused on her or him; the role of the public prosecutor is directed towards a more general concern with the public interest rather than the interests of the victim.

EVIDENCE AND DEFINITION OF CRIME

Each sexual offence has its own definition that must be addressed by evidence. In statutory offences defined by reference to the age of the complainer, since the crimes consist in an adult having sex with someone deemed by law as incapable of consenting to sex, then the complainer's age must be proved but non-consent does not. The common law offence of lewd and libidinous practices is usually charged only where the victim is under the age of puberty. Indecent assault may cover any assault accompanied by circumstances of indecency. Some offences, because of their definition are more difficult to prove than others, and the accused are often found guilty of reduced charges. Charges of rape may be reduced to the lesser offences of attempted rape, assault with intent to rape, indecent assault, assault, or even the Sexual Offences Act s. 4 which deals with sexual intercourse with a girl under 16 and removes the issue of consent.

The Definition of Rape

There is no statutory definition of rape in Scots law. Prevailing definitions derive from common law and from institutional writers and criminal law textbooks interpreting this law. The definition establishes two crucial factors which have to be proved: that the sexual act of genital penetration of a woman by a man took place and that it did so against the woman's will – which may or may not be equivalent to 'without consent'. These are the two fundamental requisites of rape.

Rape is limited to acts of heterosexual genital sexual intercourse involving penetration to however slight a degree and not necessarily involving the emission of semen. The definition does not recognise non-consensual oral and anal penetration as rape but as a lesser offence such as indecent assault or attempted rape. Similarly it does not recognise the possibility of homosexual rape. The need to establish that penetration took place inevitably results in questions that complainers find embarrassing and difficult. Complainers are routinely asked such detailed questions as, 'Did you see his private parts? Was he erect? Did he succeed in putting it in? Did he ejaculate? How do you know he tried to put it in if you didn't feel or see it?'

The second, and crucial, factor in rape is non-consent. In the old texts rape was defined as the 'knowledge of a woman's person ... against her will and by force'.[13] There are two closely connected questions here, the emphasis on force and the way the Scots common law definition emphasises the *positive presence* of a will to be overcome, rather than the *negative absence* of consent. This is why, in Scotland, unlike England, sex with a sleeping woman cannot count as rape because her will is in a dormant state; the offence here would be clandestine injury; similarly with a drunken or drugged woman, unless these substances were deliberately administered as a way to have sex. There thus seems to be an important difference between 'overcoming the [active] will' and '[passive] lack of consent', which *might* be taken to explain why there is such an emphasis on force as an evidential requirement in Scottish rape cases. Today, it is true that physical violence is recognised as only one possible means to achieve non-consensual sex, but retaining the old definition in terms of 'overcoming the will' may still lead to privileging the use of physical force as the only 'real' form of rape. Yet as early as the nineteenth century case of William Fraser, Lord Cockburn states:

> Now, I can gather nothing from our books, except that the crime of rape consists of intercourse *without the woman's consent*. It is sometimes said that it must be not only without her consent, but *forcibly*. But this is plainly said loosely; merely because where consent is withheld, force is generally resorted to .... Force is only the evidence and the consequence, of the want of consent. Hence the crime is unquestionably committed wherever consent is impossible ... Moreover, I presume that the prosecutor does not mean to say that there was any *positive* dissent or any *positive* absence of consent, but only intends to set forth that want of consent.[14]

Cockburn emphasises, along with most legal authorities from the mid-19th century onwards, that it is totally erroneous to assume that rape is only rape if there is physical force. Further, the fact that this case is cited in a widely used text means that it should be a currently well-known statement.

A related question concerns the complainer's resistance as required by the notion of a will being 'overcome'. As recently as the 1984 edition, the police handbook on *Scottish Criminal Law, Police Duties and Procedures* included the following:

> Except in the case of a woman who through infirmity is unable to resist, the woman must resist the designs of her assailant to the last. It is not rape if, after offering resistance, she consents to sexual intercourse.[15]

It has now been amended.

TYPICAL AND SPECIAL LINES OF DEFENCE

In any kind of sexual offence trial, it has to be proved that something of an unlawful sexual nature did occur and that it was the accused who was responsible. This immediately points to three possible lines of defence: that nothing sexual occurred, that something sexual occurred but that it was not criminal or that what happened was not committed by the accused.

In the crimes of indecent assault and assault with intent to rape, it is not unusual for the defence to concede the element of assault but to contest the sexual component. For example the defence might argue in an assault with intent to rape case that the accused had not intended sexual intercourse, rather he just chased after and jumped on the complainer, but that landing on top of her had no sexual implications. The most common defence in rape cases is that something sexual occurred but that it was not unlawful, because it happened with the full consent and co-operation of the complainer. A more unusual defence which might occur in any sexual offence trial involves the 'special defences' of alibi or incrimination. An alibi is a defence that the accused could not possible have committed the offence since testimony will demonstrate that the accused was elsewhere at the time. A special defence of incrimination is evidence that another was responsible for the offence, not the accused. If the defence wishes to employ a special defence they must give notice to the court of this intention prior to the trial.

In the case of sexual offences in which the age of the complainer is a defining factor of the offence, then mistaken-belief-in-age is a recognised defence. This defence is only permitted if the male accused is under the age of 24, has not previously been charged with the offence, and had 'reasonable cause to believe' that the 'girl' was 16 years or over (Sexual Offences (Scotland) Act s.4 (2) (*b*)).

CONCLUSION

This chapter has focused on the standard procedures and legal requirements of the criminal trial. It is clear that standard aspects of the trial process in themselves necessarily contribute to what many describe as the ordeal suffered by witnesses and particularly the complainer. The question which is not addressed in this chapter is whether the extent of the ordeal suffered is in fact greater than these procedures require. At this stage the reader is simply invited to understand that the legal-evidential procedures of the trial are necessarily a testing business.

The trial is an ordeal because all criminal trials are ordeals for key witnesses. The trial is necessarily about *evidence* and an investigation of evidence is far removed from simply allowing a witness to tell his or her story. In the adversarial system, the normal rules and conventions of evidence mean that the witness's reliability and credibility is likely to be tested and statements of a key witness must be corroborated and tested by dis-corroborating statements and contradictory evidence.

In sexual offence cases, there may be specific difficulties in proving the offence, due to the typical lack of eye witnesses, which arguably justify particularly rigorous testing of complainers. Hence it can be expected that the ordeal of a complainer in a sexual offence case is even greater. Moreover, the asymmetrical nature of the adversarial system means that the complainer may be more sorely tested than the accused.

In rape cases the actual definition of the crime causes a particular focus on the complainer; that is the requirement to establish that sexual intercourse took place without consent and against the will of the complainer. So it might be expected that complainers in rape trials will suffer the most testing experience. The conventional evidential signs in rape cases have also been referred to. In later chapters, extracts from observed trials are used to demonstrate how this focus on injuries, semen and distress as evidential signs of the crime are translated into questions in the courtroom. By illustrating how evidence unfolds in the courtroom, it becomes possible to comment on whether or not the extent of the complainer's ordeal is justified by necessary legal rules and conventions.

NOTES

1. British legal policy on sexual matters, both in the traditional laws on indecency, and in the Wolfenden-inspired legislation from the late 1960s onwards, has been very much informed by the wish to separate public and private expressions of sexuality. This means not only a condemnation of sex in public places but also of the representation of sex in public. See, notably, the *Williams Report on Obscenity and Film Censorship* (London: HMSO, 1979), Cmnd. 7772.

2. Cf. Carol Smart's summary of these arguments in *Feminism and the Power of Law* (London: Routledge, 1989). She refers to Catherine MacKinnon's account of a rape trial in *Feminism Unmodified: Discourses in Life and Law* (London: Harvard University Press, 1987) and also Anna Clark's analysis of 19th century rape trials in *Men's Violence: Women's Silence* (London: Pandora, 1987). Smart suggests that the 'immodesty' condemnation may not be so true of modern sexual offence trials.

3. Cf. Harold Garfinkel, 'Conditions of Successful Degredation Ceremonies' (1956) 61 *American Journal of Sociology* (March). Where he speaks, incidentally, of 'the rapist' as one exemplar of these solidaristic processes, his arguments can equally be applied to the preferred victim.

4. *SLC Report*, para. 4.1, p. 10 and para. 5.1, p. 13.

5. See, for example, Z. Adler, *Rape on Trial* (London and New York: Routledge and Kegan Paul, 1987), p. 14. The notion is also used in G. Chambers and A. Millar, *Prosecuting Sexual Assault* (Edinburgh: HMSO, Scottish Office Central Research Unit Study, 1983).

6. *Heilbron Report* (Advisory Group on the Law of Rape) (London: HMSO, 1975 Cmnd. 6352), para. 12: ' ... although in a criminal case, it is the accused who is on trial, there is a risk that a rape case may become in effect a trial of the alleged victim ...'

7. Adler (1978), p. 15.

8. Sue Lees, 'Trial by Rape', (1989) *New Statesman and Society* (24 November), p. 10.

9. See Ngaire Naffine, *Law and the Sexes: Explorations in Feminist Jurisprudence* (Sydney, Melbourne, Wellington and London: Allen and Unwin, 1990) for an eloquent summary of the strengths and weaknesses of this approach.

10. See Smart (1989), Chapter 2. On the masculinity of the legal system more generally, see Frances Heidensohn, 'Portia or Persephone' (1986) 14 *International Journal of the Sociology of Law*. See also MacKinnon (1987).

11. Adler (1987), p. 15 and Jennifer Temkin, *Rape and the Legal Process* (London: Sweet & Maxwell, 1987) pp. 133–8.

12. D. McBarnet, 'Victim in the Witness Box – Confronting Victimology's Stereotype' (1983) 7 *Contemporary Crises*, p. 293.

13. Baron Hume, *Commentaries on the Law of Scotland Respecting Crimes* (1844), 4th edition Vol. i, p. 301. English law similarly used to defined rape in terms of 'against her will' – see Temkin (1987), pp. 60–1.

14. William Fraser (1847) Ark. 280, as cited in C. H.W. Gane and C N. Stoddart, *A Casebook on Scottish Criminal Law* (Edinburgh: W. Green & Son, 1980), p. 426.

15. As compiled by Grampian Police for the Scottish Police Service, (Aberdeen: Aberdeen University Press, 1984), p. 17.

3

Changing the Law

Law reforms invariably begin by assaying the existing state of the law. Usually it is found to be out of date and hence in need of updating to keep up with contemporary society. Sometimes it is found to contain appropriate principles that have been undermined in contemporary court practice and need restored. The judgement of the law reformers on the state of the Scots law of evidence in sexual offences was a mixture of the two. The reforms thus set out to restore the classic principles where these were 'enlightened, almost contemporary' and to eliminate those principles and practices that seemed archaic or simply wrong. In the process, they also had to judge what to do about the existing bundle of highly specific rules. Like most modern law reformers they decided to make a fresh start and formulate new rules to express the endorsed principles, and try to ensure that they could be followed in the context of the courtroom. Hence legislation, and hence, in turn, a set of reform discussions stretching from the formal reforms proposal as debated in various rounds of consultation, and continuing right through the entire Parliamentary process.

The principles of reform were stated very broadly in Chapter 1 – a commitment to disallow most 'sexual character' evidence, while retaining 'sexual history' evidence where appropriate; and the broad 'balancing' strategy of the legislative design was also described there. This chapter will look more closely at the reform process in order to get a more precise picture of what was involved both in the principled commitments of law reformers and also of the way the legislation was formulated so as to effect these aims. The two key areas of 'sexual character' and 'sexual history' evidence will each be tracked through from the law reformers' discussions of the pre-existing state of Scots law[1] to the various key debates in the subsequent discussions about the acceptability of the proposed legislative formulations. (A final section will examine some aspects of the legislative design that do not fall neatly under one heading or the other.)

This chapter provides very important groundwork for the ultimate task of assessing the effectiveness of the reform legislation. It provides much needed detail of what exactly the reformers had in mind in terms of the actual issues and contests that were likely to arise in the courtroom, and it shows some of the dilemmas involved in trying to turn abstract principles into effective rules. The specifics of discussion and debate here also give some strong indications of the potential limitations – in terms of means, and also ends – of this reform endeavour. In using the reform discussion to mark the sphere of potential problems, we have concentrated primarily on questions that were actually raised during the reform debates, whether or not these turned out ultimately to be problems according to our research findings. In fact, it was obviously an important finding if some fears proved not to be realised or if they were realised in a rather more complicated way than the prognosis had in mind. However, in this chapter, the opportunity is also taken to indicate some potential problems that were not, in fact, hugely discussed during the reform process, nor even in the immediate reactions to the passing of the legislation.

Necessarily, some of the discussion here is somewhat legalistic, although much of the basics of this were laid down in the last chapter. The following concerns will come up here:

First, what exactly counts as 'sexual character' evidence? This involves two different things. On the one hand, what is legally considered to be 'sexual character' at all, as a category? It is invariably 'bad sexual character' or as the legislation put it, 'not of good character in sexual matters' that is discussed, and what is included in this as a legal category? For example, is only prostitution included in the legal category or 'unchastity' more generally? On the other hand, what kind of evidence can be used to *show* sexual 'bad character', and here a key concern is whether sexual history evidence concerning third parties can be admitted for this purpose. On such, perhaps seemingly obscure points, hang many important consequences for the fate of the complainer in the courtroom and the ultimate justice of sexual offence trials.

Second, what necessarily runs throughout all considerations, past and present, on the admissibility of sexual character or sexual history evidence is how such evidence might properly relate to the key issues in a sexual offence trial. Thus, as outlined in the previous chapter, in a rape trial, attention will focus on the following range of questions: Did the complainer in fact consent to sexual intercourse? Did the accused have intercourse with the complainer, now recognised to be against her will, but at the time, reasonably or at least honestly, believing it to be consensual? Did sexual intercourse with the accused take place at all? If the evidence points to intercourse without consent, could it be that some other person is responsible (i.e., that within the same space of time as to account for injuries, etc., the complainer had sexual relations consensually with the accused and non-consensually with someone else)? If the evidence points to intercourse, and the accused denies it, could some other person's sexual activities account for the evidence of intercourse? Is there any reason to believe that the complainer is deliberately lying either because of some character flaw, or out of some motive, or simply because inconsistencies suggest lack of truth (credibility)? Could the complainer perhaps be not deliberately lying but mistaken in their testimony (reliability)? When statutory age-related sexual offences are included, then another issue is relevant: Did the accused believe that the complainer was older than she/he actually was?

Finally, as also emphasised in Chapter 2, the law reformers' task was not only to formulate clear 'textbook' principles for the sake of legal doctrine in the abstract, but also to relate these to the official rules of the courtroom as defined in an adversarial system. Such rules cannot simply be dismissed by contrast to the reform's 'real' doctrinal principles and commitments, as if they were merely some unofficial 'flim-flam' distorting the true intentions of the law reformers through a 'debased' practice. On the contrary, rules of rebuttal, some highly developed rules on the combat of character, the validation of the idea that the complainer's truth should *properly* be tested by some sort of gruelling 'ordeal' – and also some very important issues about the respective duties of prosecution, defence and judges/sheriffs (although barely touched on here) – are highly important and totally official (if not always clear) elements of the British system of criminal trials. And, while any criminal law reform might implicitly take into consideration the rules and duties of its sphere of application, the Scottish reform on sexual evidence did this very explicitly (by including an exception framed in terms of a defence requirement to 'explain or rebut' prosecution evidence).

SEXUAL CHARACTER

The Law before the Reform

Both the 'enlightened, almost contemporary' aspects of existing law, and its 'archaic' side, concern 'sexual character' evidence. By way of background, a few comments can be made about law's concept of 'character'. The basic point is that 'character' is an accepted legal concept even though it is recognised as carrying many dangerous tendencies for distorting judgment. Hence, there are a number of protections built in for witnesses and especially the accused about when such evidence may be admitted. This includes some rules highly specific to the adversarial system. One that will be important here is the rule that if someone in the witness box makes a claim to having a 'good character', they have 'thrown down their shield' and are thus open to attacks showing 'bad character'. In law, character is primarily defined in the moral terms 'bad' and 'good', which includes some subdivisions, notably a 'character for dishonesty' that may be indicated, for example, by evidence that a person has committed 'crimes of dishonesty' such as theft. Behind the moral categories there is also a kind of psychology according to which people tend to produce patterns of behaviour and repetitions of conduct, as in the idea of a distinctive *modus operandi*. 'Character' thus implies propensities, and tendencies, and predispositions to act in certain predictable ways. This whole apparatus of thinking in terms of 'character' has been subject to some swingeing criticisms.[2]

The Scottish law reform by no means objected to the general legal concept of character. Their concerns were directed solely at the notion of sexual character and specifically sexual 'bad character'. It was noted that, in Scotland, 'bad sexual character' seems to have had a far wider scope than in England where it was limited to prostitution, whereas in Scotland unchastity generally was included. On the other hand, the Scots law tradition allowed a far narrower range of evidence that could be used to show character, plus included some key time-restrictions, and also stipulated the issues that were deemed legitimately relevant to it.

Thus, the most 'enlightened' aspects of past law principles was the position taken on sexual character and consent. In England it was accepted that evidence of 'bad sexual character' was relevant as indicating consent with the accused *and* that such character could be shown through evidence of the complainer's sexual history with specific individuals. By contrast, according to the key Scots law pronouncement as found in the nineteenth century case of *Dickie*:

> ... [Concerning] evidence of individual acts of unchastity with other men at an interval of time. I am not aware that such evidence has ever been allowed, and indeed it could only be allowed upon the footing that a female who yields her person to one man will presumably do so to any man – a proposition which is quite untenable. A woman may not be virtuous, but it would be a most unwarrantable assumption that she could not therefore resist, and resist to the uttermost, an attempt to have connection with her by any man who might endeavour to obtain possession of her person, and to whom she might have no intention to yield. Every woman is entitled to protection from attack upon her person. Even a prostitute may be held to be ravished if the proof establishes a rape, although she may admit that she is a prostitute.[3]

This statement appears to endorse a very wide-sweeping rejection of the idea that a woman who says 'yes' to other men can be presumed to have consented with the accused on the basis of some sort of predisposition to indiscriminate consent. It also specifically rejects introducing sexual history evidence concerning particular third parties on that 'character' basis. The *SLC Report* notes that this judicial pronouncement 'could well, we think, have been written by any of the contemporary critics of the way in which rape trials are conducted in this country ...'[4] On the other hand, and as endorsed in the very same nineteenth-century case, it was seen as legitimate to admit sexual 'bad character' evidence as relevant to the complainer's credibility. Unlike the English rule, such evidence could be admitted only if it concerned behaviour 'at the time of the offence' or, if more remote in time, a continuous link had to be established with the present.

This was always acknowledged to be an exception from the general law of evidence that you cannot raise up a collateral issue, and allow proof of a witness's character and repute – but, in the past it was accepted as a justified exception. The background to this exception is not specific to sexual offence trials at all. In the legal past, including the very recent past, both criminal and civil law of evidence in Scotland accepted the exception that a woman's 'bad sexual character and repute' had a bearing on her general credibility, at least if she were a prostitute. This applied across the board, whether she were a victim or a witness pure and simple. Thus, as recently as 1986 the then standard textbook on the law of evidence stated: 'Since the evidence of a prostitute ... is suspect, it must be competent to ask a witness if she or he holds that character.'[5] A prostitute's word was simply held to be untrustworthy. This general bias is not explicitly discussed by the *SLC Report* as part of the background to the exception in rape cases, although it was noted elsewhere as a matter for reform.[6]

Certainly though, it was strongly suggested by the *SLC Report*, that 'in more modern times' character evidence was being allowed in the courtroom in sexual offence trials simply as relevant to the complainer's general credibility. Hence, what concerned the law reformers was whether *Dickie* had actually affirmed such a very wide principle of admissibility. As against this, they argued that such evidence was, properly, only to be admitted where consent was at issue.[7] Even so, from the 'contemporary' point of view, this does not seem particularly 'enlightened' and would also seem to undermine the strongly negative principle on the irrelevancy of third-party sexual character evidence to the matter of consent.

Some further light may be thrown on the matter by looking at what is said in Dickson's *Treatise on the Law of Evidence in Scotland*, written in 1887, ten years before the case of *Dickie*. He too firmly announces that the admissibility of sexual character evidence is an exception to the general protections offered around character evidence:

> ... it is firmly established in this country (except in one class of cases) the party against whom a witness is adduced may not assail his character by alleging or proving generally that he is a dissolute and base person who cannot be believed on oath. The only exception to this rule are prosecutions for rape and assault with intent to ravish.[8]

This is how he presents the justification for this exception:

> ... proof of unchastity is *circumstantial* evidence to rebut the charge: while so much depends on the truth of her statements, and there is so great a risk of her story having been concocted in a fit of jealousy or with the view to extorting money or covering her shame when discovered in a voluntary connection that a full enquiry into her character is requisite to the jury to estimate her credibility.[9]

Dickson's comments refer only to rape and assault with intent to ravish – crimes defined as committed by men against women. His account relates strongly to some of the points made in the last chapter where credibility was discussed. First, there is the emphasis on the lack of corroboration and hence the reliance on the complainer's word. Second, other established aspects of credibility evidence are being discussed as relevant to general credibility – the notions of some sort of interest or motive for lying. Third, with lack of corroboration and possible motive for lying in mind, it is suggested that sexual 'character' evidence should be allowed as a backcloth for assessing the specific credibility issues. While this may seem a rather convoluted logic, law's reasons in linking sexual character, credibility and consent are laid out – and in a way that arguably does not depend upon a straightforward 'propensity' characterisation. Envisaging possible situations in which women will consent and lie, and therefore seeing the need for evidential procedures to test whether this is the case, is not necessarily the same as assuming that women have a propensity to consent and lie. It is usual for the legal mind to consider the extraordinary as well as the typical possibilities, although the 'so great a risk' of Dickson's formulation suggests he did not regard motives for lying as exceptional. While there is much to quarrel with in the reasoning presented by Dickson from a 'contemporary' point of view, it is a useful presentation of how law thinks (especially from the point of view of considering what sort of exclusionary rule might be appropriate and effective in relation to such roundabout, but highly everyday, legal constructions). It is also interesting to note that Dickson adds, after citing the restrictions on sexual character evidence: 'It is understood however that such evidence is frequently led in practice.'[10] The process of erosion of principles seems to have begun even as the rules were being formulated.

The Reform Principles on Sexual Character

The *SLC Report* proposed a general prohibition of 'sexual character' evidence on the grounds that:

> The phrase 'bad character' is itself very uncertain and unspecifying and in our view opens the door to much that is irrelevant. We can, in general, see no evidence for the view that evidence of bad character,

however defined, is bound to be relevant to a proper determination of
a trial for rape or other sexual offences. To admit such evidence is, in
our view, inconsistent with contemporary sexual attitudes; it may
cause unnecessary distress to a complainer, and it may divert a jury
from the proper issue in a case ... [it is] unlikely to be relevant to
credibility or to a proper determination of the issues in a case[11]

The prior *MacPhail Report* which was primarily concerned with 'sexual
character' and credibility, had posed the principles of excluding sexual
character evidence in terms of the unacceptability of any general link
between sexual immorality and truthfulness:

1. It is wrong to assume a witness is likely to tell the truth because he
   or she is sexually immoral.
2. Evidence of sexual immorality is rightly not generally admitted on
   the grounds of its relevance to credibility in any other class of
   crime.
3. Although the evidence is admitted because of its assumed relevance to credibility, there is a danger that the jury will regard it as
   having a bearing on the issue of consent.
4. It may be that the present admissibility of evidence of bad reputation has the result that victims of sexual offences who are of bad
   character are reluctant to report the offence to the police.[12]

So far as these can be taken together, they articulate an important
statement of intent and give a number of separate reasons for the general
'sexual character' exclusion. The 'policy' concern to protect the complainer is strongly stated by the *SLC Report* and similarly MacPhail
mentions a reluctance to report crimes. The bias involved in the anomaly
of sexual character evidence is emphasised by *MacPhail*. But what they
have in common is an emphasis on the two fundamentals of the law of
evidence – the relevance of evidence and the potential for prejudice.

The *relevance of evidence* is determined by its relevance to the issues in
a sexual offence trial. Under the heading 'sexual behaviour with other
men', the *SLC Report* strongly endorses the exclusion of evidence introduced on the basis that because a woman has had consensual sex with A
and B in the past, she can be presumed to have consented with C, the
accused – in other words evidence introduced on the basis of a sexual
character construction of a predisposition to indiscriminate consent.
Indeed, they add that there is no reason to limit this exclusion of evidence
concerning 'sexual behaviour with other men' to behaviour prior to the
offence, nor even full intercourse, nor even only to cases involving the
crime of rape.

However neither report is entirely clear on the nature of the exclusion
on credibility. On the one hand, MacPhail comments only on general
credibility, the broad equation of sexual immorality and untruthfulness as
such – the idea that 'unchaste' women are liars. This leaves unaddressed

the other aspects of credibility – concerning motive and interest – that Dickson highlights so clearly. On the other hand, when the SLC affirms the principles of excluding sexual bad character in *Dickie*, they do not make clear whether they also accept the exception noted in *Dickie*. That is they endorse the principle that lack of chastity cannot be used as evidence of a general propensity to consent, without commenting on the *Dickie* affirmation of the relevance of sexual behaviour between the complainer and men other than the accused, to credibility when consent is at issue. Hence the *SLC Report* leaves some matters ambiguous with respect to sexual history evidence and credibility.

Relevance is not only a principle of exclusion, but also a principle of inclusion and, accordingly the *SLC Report* also envisaged certain instances, perhaps rare in sexual character evidence, which would justifiably be introduced as relevant:

If the defence were 'mistaken-belief-in-consent' then, if the complainer had a 'bad reputation' in sexual matters (whether or not this was justified) and the accused knew of it, then such evidence should be admitted. However, it was emphasised that 'the introduction of such evidence would not necessarily have any bearing on the complainer's credibility'.[13] In relation to prostitution: if the defence were that the complainer had consented to sex for money, she being a prostitute, then it should be possible for this to be said in the trial. (This possible situation was mentioned specifically as one of the sorts of situations that required the 'interests of justice' exception.) (Not mentioned in the Scottish documents is the commonly associated idea of a 'grudge complaint' of rape by a prostitute when a client refuses to pay.)[14]

The second fundamental principle raised by these statements is 'prejudice'. In law, this has two meanings. One is that 'character' evidence may simply produce an adverse 'gut reaction' so that any consideration of the legal issues in a case are simply ignored. But it is the second meaning that seems to be particularly meant here and this is that evidence introduced as relevant to one issue may be wrongly applied to another, more central, issue. This is clearly what MacPhail's third proposition is about – evidence relating to credibility might be mistakenly applied to consent. In his book, he backs this up with a quotation from Professor J. C. Smith, commenting on the *Heilbron Report*, which says in part:

> ... the jury might be excused if they thought that the prosecutrix's promiscuity had substantially more bearing on whether she had consented than whether she was a liar.[15]

Thus, although in a more muted form, the *SLC Report* comments on the problem that 'sexual character' evidence 'may divert a jury from the proper issues in a case'.

Principle into Practice

In the ensuing process of reform, the questions of character evidence proved a continuing, if understated, source of anxiety. The 'SLC Consultative Memorandum No. 46' formulated MacPhail's concerns as follows:

> In cases of rape or similar assaults evidence that the complainer was of bad moral character or that she associated with prostitutes should no longer be admitted as being relevant to credibility.[16]

The subsequent *SLC Report*, while rejecting any 'axiomatic' relevance of evidence of sexual character or sexual reputation to credibility as 'outdated', nonetheless suggested that in some of the older cases, there might be credibility issues more intimately connected with consent than broad character attacks.[17] While this is not elaborated upon, the thinking here may be along the lines suggested above in connection with Dickson's account, that is, credibility questions based upon motive or interest.

At the next stage of consultation, the question was put whether 'the statutory definition of the type of character of the complainer in respect of which questioning is prohibited, be specifically related to sexual character',[18] with the SLC expressing the view that no distinction could reasonably be made in the context of sexual offence trials between 'sexual' character and 'bad' character more generally. They noted that there was an important grey area, as potentially exemplified in:

> a line of questioning directed to eliciting that a complainer regularly went to bars or dances on her own [that] might not of itself be construed as questioning which shows, or tends to show, she is not of good character. Nevertheless, the intention behind such questioning might be to implant just such a suggestion in the mind of the jury.[19]

For that reason the draft Bill suggested by the SLC simply prohibited 'questioning or evidence which shows or tends to show that the complainer' is not of 'good character' *simpliciter*, without any specific reference to character 'in relation to sexual matters' as the clause ultimately became. The SLC reasoning was that, while normal questioning on nonsexual bad character, such as dishonesty, should, of course be allowed, it should not simply be admitted as a right. The potential confusion with sexual character implications meant that it should be excluded in the first instance in order to be readmitted only under careful judicial control.

However, this proposal was deemed not acceptable by the majority of responding groups who, whatever its ultimate intended effects, did not like the *prima facie* statutory exclusion of character evidence that would normally be admissible in relation to credibility. Fears were expressed that the accused would be placed in an anomalous position in sexual offence trials and that where the defence might wish to argue that an allegation was false or malicious, the prohibition would rule out the admission of evidence of previous dishonesty or perjury or past false allegations of rape. One response particularly emphasised the vulnerability of members of the medical, dental, and police professions to false allegations made by the 'less reputable' women who they might encounter in the course of their duties. Only a small minority favoured the SLC approach, noting, in the words of one response, that 'objectionable questioning of the complainer did not just relate to "sex" narrowly defined.'

In the Introduction Bill, these same problems erupted again because the SLC had adapted its original proposal to compromise with the objections to character exclusions on credibility, while still maintaining some judicial control of what could be introduced. Thus the Bill still excluded character evidence in the first part but now had added the provision that 'Subsection (1) (*a*) [the character exclusion] does not apply to questioning or evidence which the court is satisfied relates wholly or mainly to the question of the truthfulness of the complainer's evidence, or any statement or representation of the complainer to be put in evidence.' At Committee Stage, the SLC proposal to start off on the footing of a general exclusion was defended by Peter Fraser, then Solicitor General for Scotland, who once again reiterated the potential for the blurring of non-sexual and sexual character innuendo and hence the possibly misleading prejudicial effect of such evidence, to use the words of the *SLC Report,* 'to divert a jury from the proper issue in a case':

> In cities such as Glasgow, Dundee or Edinburgh, it is not difficult to envisage situations where the use of evidence may be, 'Were you at such-and such a public house? Were you there on your own? Were you there at 11.30 at night? My honourable and learned friend the Member for Perth and Kinross [Nicholas Fairbairn, Q. C.] could doubtless continue a skillful line of questioning without mentioning the word 'sex' for a considerable time, but his questions would clearly hint that the girl had loose morals and went out late at night into dives of low character. The implication to the jury might be that if someone carried on in such a way she might be prepared to engage in sexual intercourse. The chain of reasoning might establish that there had been consent on her part.[20]

However, Fraser was not only underlining the problems of character innuendo. He was specifically responding to Mr Donald Dewar's criticism of the credibility exception which, he stated, had 'given rise to genuine suspicion among a number of groups in the women's movement about the effectiveness of the provision as whole'.[21] Dewar argued for a compromise, which ultimately won the day, which was to add a sexual specification to the general character prohibition. Hence, the legislation now excluded evidence that 'shows or tends to show' that the complainer 'is not of good character in relation to sexual matters'.

In the process of forging the compromise, something was lost – the specific commitment to do something about the problem of prejudicing a jury through evidence with a very strong tendency to mislead. As noted, this concern was expressed both by the *MacPhail Report* (evidence of a complainer's sexual life if introduced as relevant to credibility might wrongly be seen as bearing on consent) and the *SLC Report* (evidence that might divert a jury from the proper issues in a case). Some jurisdictions have tried to deal with this problem in their legislation by laying down that judges should consider not just whether evidence might be relevant in some general way but also how strong the evidence is and how relevant. So the Michigan legislation says that sexual evidence shall be admitted only if its 'inflammatory or prejudicial nature does not outweigh its probative value.'[22] The New South Wales legislation stipulates that sexual evidence may be admitted only if the 'probative value outweighs any distress, humiliation or embarrassment that the complainant might suffer as a result of its admission.'[23] Yet in Scotland, this principle, clearly important to the law reformers – and one that the more open 'bad character' phrasing seems to have been intended to deal with – ultimately failed to find a legislative formulation.

This neglect of the issue of prejudice was ironic because the legislators remained aware of an aspect of the problem, the tendency to blacken complainers' characters through innuendo and subtle character attacks. The wording of the legislation prohibits not only evidence which shows that a complainer is 'not of good character in sexual matters' but also evidence which *tends to show* that a complainer is 'not of good character in sexual matters'. However, the focus on lack of good character in sexual matters rather than simply 'bad character' left open the door to innuendo which was not sexual but nevertheless cumulatively suggested a person of 'ill repute'.

Finally a word on sexual 'good character'. The category of such 'good character' was obviously not seen as being problematic by the legislators. Yet this assumption was challenged in one of the immediate responses to the reform, Chambers and Millar's *Prosecuting Sexual Assault*, where they commented on the 'dubious' equation of lack of sexual experience with virtue as the converse of equating wide experience with 'loose morals' – a form of stereotyping that is also widely criticised by feminist commentators.

> It could be argued that the justification for equating virtue with lack of sexual experience and loose morals with sexual promiscuity is itself questionable.[24]

In fact in some jurisdictions, presentations of lack of sexual experience is also excluded.[25]

Chambers and Millar's query in fact signals a general danger warning to feminists who might assume that the law-reform principles (in either Scotland or England) do coincide with feminist principles. At first sight it is easy to believe that they do because the problems of sexual character recognised in law reforms echo feminist critiques of stereotypes. Yet what the law recognises as problematic should not be assumed to be as wide as feminist concerns. For example, when MacPhail comments that women of 'bad sexual character' might be afraid to report sexual assault, he still accepts that it makes sense to categorise women in a way which feminists challenge, even in the process of seeking to protect such women. This may be sexism or it may spring from a transposition of the law's way of thinking about those accused who have past convictions, in which case the aim of the restrictions on bad character evidence is that even those with a record – a 'bad character' – deserve a fair trial or a 'sexual bad character' record and the protection of the law.

SEXUAL HISTORY

The Past

The examination of past cases also produced guidance on when sexual history as such was admissible. Thus, again referring to *Dickie*, the *SLC Report* notes that 'proof of unchastity' might be allowed if 'just before and practically on the same occasion' it might be competent as 'proof of all matters bearing on the *res gestae* ... [for example, in relation to] the appearance of the private parts when examined.' In other words, evidence of sexual relations with others would be admitted, by way of exception to the general prohibition, if it might be that someone other than the accused was the source of evidence indicating intercourse (e.g. semen) or non-consensual intercourse (e.g. bruising). To make sense, this would clearly have to be within appropriate time-restrictions. The term *res gestae*, the *SLC Report* notes, is not quite right here where the term means events that form a single sequence linked in time, place and circumstances. However, it could be that the relevant events might be closely linked in time, but not all be part of the same set of circumstances or place.[26]

The second concern is evidence about past relations between the complainer and the accused. Again *Dickie* provides the existing rule. As with evidence concerning third parties, it is notable for its very strict time-restrictions. Such evidence was competent if it showed that 'the witness voluntarily yielded to his embraces a short time before the alleged criminal attack ... it is plainly a relevant matter of enquiry on what terms the parties were immediately before the time of the alleged crime.'[27] The impression of the SLC was, however, that in recent court practice any evidence of past relations was admitted without any concern about closeness in time, or continuity of relationship.[28]

The Reform Principles on Sexual History

Third Parties

Clearly, there is a very strong potential for misconstruing any evidence about sexual behaviour, in terms of character and hence consent or credibility. The *SLC Report* very strongly endorsed the view in *Dickie* that evidence of specific consensual incidents with others should never be admitted as showing consent in relation to the accused, commenting that the reasons 'remain as valid today as they were then'.[29] Here the position is clearly to reject the validity of any general characterological propensity-to-consent constructions, even if based on past intercourse, and certainly any past behaviour with others short of intercourse.

However, the *SLC Report* also notes various instances in which third-party evidence might be relevant:[30]

1. as an alternative source of evidence that would otherwise indicate that intercourse with the accused had taken place (presence of semen, pregnancy, disease), ('explain or rebut'). Such alleged behaviour with others would have to be appropriately restricted to the relevant time period.

2. as an alternative source of evidence that would otherwise indicate that non-consensual sexual intercourse had taken place (evidence of injury or weapons, and so on), ('explain or rebut', incrimination).

3. 'group rapes' or 'some kind of group orgy'. Here the discussion in the *SLC Report* is unclear. The stated relevance is to consent yet the cited case is *Morgan* where the issue was mistaken belief; the implication seems to be both.

4. where the complainer's sexual behaviour after the claimed crime was deemed inappropriate to a recent victim (as in the case of *Viola*).[31]

Complainer and Accused

In the first round of consultation, most respondents had expressed the view that evidence concerning a complainer's previous relations with the accused was likely to be relevant to consent, but the SLC underlines that this would not be so if the evidence 'relates to a chance encounter ... many years before the alleged offence.' It was for that reason that they recommended that such evidence should be ruled out in the first instance, but they made it clear that they believed it would 'normally be relevant' and ought to be admitted, indeed, would normally be led by the Crown.[32]

Principle into Practice

In debate on the legislation, most attention focused on the specific way the legislation was framed – the broad exclusion, coupled with the specific exceptions.

The Exceptions

The exception clauses received the most attention during debate. These determine how otherwise excluded sexual character and conduct evidence will be allowed, on application by defence. While no comments were offered on the general design strategy of these clauses, comparison with other jurisdictions provided some points of contrast. Many versions use what could be called 'issue-based' formulations, since the ultimate rationale for admitting such evidence is its relevance to particular issues (consent, credibility, identity, etc.) and the legislation is directly framed in those terms. For example, relevant evidence concerning identity includes, 'evidence of specific sexual activity showing the source of semen, pregnancy or disease' (Michigan); or 'evidence relevant to whether the presence of semen, pregnancy or disease, or injury is attributable to the sexual intercourse alleged to have been had with the accused person' (New South Wales), or 'evidence of specific instances of the complainant's activity tending to establish the identity of the person who had sexual contact with the complainant on the occasion set out in the charge' (Canada).[33] Similar examples could be given of evidence relevant to mistaken-belief-in-consent.[34]

The design of the Scottish legislation is, it appears, to find common elements that cut across the different potential issues and take account of the trial context. The first, 'explain or rebut', exception could obviously refer to any matter on which defence sought to elaborate or refute evidence introduced by the Crown; the exception referring to evidence about sexual behaviour 'on the same occasion' as the offence covers 'identity' evidence about alternative sources of evidence showing either the fact of intercourse or the absence of consent (injuries), and also some but not all types of mistaken belief defence (e.g., where the accused's alleged belief came from some sort of group sexual event). The 'defence of incrimination' is specific, but also overlaps with 'the same occasion' where a crime is admitted but identity is at stake. Finally, the 'interests of justice' could be seen as a kind of 'mopping up' exception, the need for which perhaps stems from the very way of designing the legislation. Thus, one important overall question must be raised about this design strategy as such: was it a mistake not to specify the admissibility of evidence in terms of its relevance? While generally springing from considerations of relevance whose importance was emphasised in the reform documents there is no statutory requirement that any such relevance be shown by the defence in making an application.

A related point concerns time-restrictions, which are often specified in other versions of such legislation and indeed were indisputably part of the old Scots law rules which required any alleged sexual character and conduct to be current, including evidence concerning a complainer's relations with the accused. Other jurisdictions specify, for example, that such a relationship 'was existing or recent at the time of the commission and the alleged prescribed sexual offence' (Missouri), or refer to the 'sexual conduct of the complaining witness with the defendant where this is reasonably contemporaneous with the date of the alleged crime' (New South Wales).[35] No such restrictions are included in the Scottish legislation although the *SLC Report* made it clear that the intention of the restriction concerning the accused was to rule out evidence being introduced of long past encounters.[36]

Interests of Justice

The 'interests of justice' clause received most comment in debate. The *SLC Report* stated that such a general clause was necessary because of the need for flexibility and the unforseeability of types of circumstances that might arise.[37] In the subsequent consultation this clause was widely criticised but nevertheless the majority of respondents supported it and were not in favour of stipulating any more specific criteria as these would only be either too general or too specific, thus over-limiting flexibility.

Opponents of the exception expressed very strong reservations about both the leeway it would give to defence arguments and the amount of discretion left to judges, pointing to the fact that the *SLC Report* itself stated, '… we do not consider that the interests of justice can best be served by leaving the judges a wholly unfettered discretion… '[38] Attention was drawn to the experience of other jurisdictions, notably south of the Border, where, as some of the respondents put it, such 'catch-all' exceptions had been introduced with the effect of sabotaging the whole point of the legislation. Not only was the English legislation cited but also the fact that in Canada such initial discretionary legislation had now been replaced with a more specified version, while similar recommendations had been made by the Tasmanian Law Commission after disappointment with the performance of the initial open-ended legislation in that Australian state. Some concern was also expressed about this clause during Parliamentary debates, requiring the introduction of such evidence to be specifically justified by specifying prejudice to the accused's case. Donald Dewar at one point suggested an amendment:

> That it would be contrary to the interests of justice to exclude the questioning or evidence referred to in section 141A (1) above and might materially prejudice a defence which, if believed, could lead to the acquittal of the accused.[39]

Dr Norman Godman objected very strongly to the discretionary nature of the clause, citing Adler's research on the English legislation and also Jenifer Temkin's arguments that the old Scots Law rules were in many ways tighter and offered more protection to the complainer than the proposed new legislation.[40] He proposed an alternative, based on one of the unsuccessful recommendations in the *Heilbron Report*, that evidence concerning third parties be admitted only if it were 'strikingly similar' to the evidence about the complainer and accused on the occasion of the incident in the charge. This possibility had been considered and rejected by MacPhail and the *SLC Report* as 'unduly restrictive', but it has also been criticised as being too wide (see Chapter 1). Temkin herself discussed this proposal in negative terms.[41]

Other commentators outside the reform process have been equally sceptical about the 'interests of justice' clause. Chambers and Millar, also drawing on Adler's and Temkin's work, felt this clause meant that the legislation would bring little change because of the scope it gave to 'entrenched attitudes', or at least that it would result in wide variations in interpretation and an excessive success rate for defence applications.[42] In the same vein, a recently published textbook on the Scots Law of evidence by David Field describes this clause as 'a potentially enormous loophole which subverts the primary aim of the entire legislation'.[43]

Temkin also draws attention to a related point, not concerning judicial discretion but its opposite. The legislation states that if the proposed evidence falls under one of the clauses, then 'the court *shall* allow [it].' If this 'shall' is mandatory, then it would seem that a judge has no choice but to let it in. Ironically, it seems that here the legislation does not give a judge *enough* discretion to consider criteria of relevance or sufficiently of evidence.[44]

Ambiguity of Explain or Rebut

Another potentially important issue of interpretation not raised during the reform debates was a possible ambiguity in the meaning of 'explain or rebut' which allows the defence to apply for a return to subjects introduced ('adduced') by the Crown. Does it mean that the defence need not make an application at all, given that the normal rules of evidence allow the defence to return to any subject already introduced? This question is raised by Chambers and Millar and indeed this is how the legislation is interpreted by senior legal figures. But in this case, there seems little point in including this as an exception indicating application is necessary. The general design strategy suggests that the intention was to allow the normal rules on cross-examination to apply but under control of judicial scrutiny, especially concerning sexual 'bad-character' aspects. A further area of uncertainty of interpretation concerns the wording 'show or tends to show': does this mean specifically 'show for the first time', hence allowing defence to question freely on any prosecution evidence that touches on otherwise prohibited areas?[45]

Crown Exemption

The Crown is exempt from the prohibitions. For the *SLC Report* this was part of the logic of the heavy restrictions, which would thus not apply to the sorts of relevant evidence the prosecution would necessarily introduce in their role of laying out all the necessary information. The commissioners expressed the view that this did not conflict with the intention of protecting complainers from 'unnecessary distress caused by wide-ranging examination of their character of past sexual behaviour' since, in their view, such problems did not arise in prosecution questioning and, in any case, such evidence would very rarely be relevant for Crown purposes. They reported that none of the responses to the previous consultation had felt that any restrictions should be imposed on the Crown.[46] This was one of the specific points on which the SCA invited further comment in the second round consultation after the *SLC Report* had been published. The commissioners' view was that the Crown might wish to lead 'uncontroversial evidence, for instance to the effect that the complainer is married or had children, and there may be exceptional cases where the Crown, in the interests of fairness, might wish to lead evidence of a more substantial nature about the complainer'.[47] The responses were mixed, although the majority agreed with the exemption primarily on the ground that otherwise the Crown could not properly perform its 'duty to present all the relevant facts to the Court'. Others who agreed, however, gave reasons but these seem contrary to the general principle of the legislation, saying that this would allow the Crown to lead 'relevant' medical or forensic evidence revealing that a complainer was not a virgin or that she or he engaged in regular sexual activity.

Those against felt the exemption would, wrongly, leave the Crown free from control by the court and, also that it was inconsistent with the objective of protecting the complainer from unnecessary embarrassment and questioning about her character. Further, the Rape Crisis Centres stated that the Crown in practice commonly did ask irrelevant and distressing questions. There was no notable debate about the Crown exemption at any stage as the Bill passed through Parliament. However, it was the subject of considerable concern in Chambers and Millar's study of sexual assault trials, completed just as the new legislation was being introduced. Their research findings on the practice of prosecutors conflicted with the views of the SLC. Prosecution questioning on a complainer's sexual experience occurred quite frequently, they had found, and quite often went into detailed discussion of complainers' relationships with particular men other than the accused, although in some cases, they accepted that prosecution was thus presenting a more objective account of this evidence than if it had simply been left to the defence. However, their main focus of concern was the prosecution portrayals of the complainer's 'good' character in sexual matters, especially the emphasis on lack of sexual experience. Commenting on the 'dubious' equation of the lack of sexual experience with virtue (and, conversely, wide sexual experience with 'loose morals') – a form of stereotyping that is also widely criticised by feminist commentators – they were particularly worried about the practical implications in the courtroom. For, if 'the prosecutor's aim ... was to build up a case against the accused by highlighting the complainer's virtuous character',[48] then the natural consequence would be for the defence to counterattack (under the 'explain or rebut' clause) by focusing on any evidence casting doubt on this virtue, hence leading to the very situation the legislation was designed to avoid, prolonged and distressing cross-examination on character.

The Court's Power to Limit Questioning

In order to control the potential open-endedness of the 'interests of justice' clause as a basis for defence evidence, the *SLC Report* therefore suggested that the court be given further powers to limit any subsequent line of questioning by the defence on evidence allowed on applications.[49] and in the sca consultation paper this was put as a possible recommendation with a query as to whether any specific criteria for such limitations should be laid down which, on the one hand might 'relieve the burden on the Court' but, on the other hand might upset 'the balance between a defined course of action and a necessary flexibility to take account of the circumstances of each particular case'.[50] While the overall response was in favour of such a power, 'flexibility' won the day for the majority of the respondents, although one of those in favour of more specific criteria suggested a restriction in terms of what was 'necessary to enable the accused fairly to establishing his defence.'

This matter did not arise during the Parliamentary debates.

Application Procedure/Advance Notice

Another question raised in the second round of consultation was whether there should be more specific procedure laid down for defence applications and especially whether advance notice should be given (presumably because such notice should normally be given if character attacks are to be made).

Most of the responses favoured the application within the trial procedure recommended by the Scottish Law Commission. Only the Rape Crisis Centres were in favour of some sort of pre-trial notice in order to minimise stress on the complainer. They also suggested that advance notice would give the Crown a chance to prepare arguments against the leading of such evidence. There was a body of opinion that the application should be accompanied by witness statements detailing the evidence that the defence proposed to lead, and it was suggested at one point that the complainer should be entitled to be represented at the application by her own counsel.

Those against advance notice argued that this would maintain flexibility and allow the defence to deal with matters that might arise in cross-examination and which they could not have foreseen. Others expressed concern that such applications might 'seriously interrupt the flow of evidence as it unfolds before a jury' and suggested therefore that 'there should be a clearly defined point during the trial at which such applications can be made', in particular 'not before the conclusion of the examination-in-chief of the complainer and at any time thereafter'.

NOTES

1. Discussion here is based primarily on the *SLC Report* and Jennifer Temkin, 'Evidence in Sexual Assault Cases: The Scottish Proposal and the Alternative' (1984) *Modern Law Review*, Vol. 47, No. 6.
2. See, notably, Rosemary Pattenden, 'The Character of Victims and Third Parties in Criminal Proceedings Other than Rape Trials' (1986) *Criminal Law Review* (June) pp. 367–78.
3. Lord Justice Clerk MacDonald in *Dicke* v. *HMA* (1897) 2 Adam 331 at p. 337, cited in the *SLC Report*, para. 3.5, p. 7. However 'enlightened' this text may be on the question of sexual evidence, the doctrine of 'resistance to the last' is not.
4. *SLC Report*, para. 3.6, pp. 7–8.
5. A. G. Walker, and N. M. L. Walker, *The Law of Evidence in Scotland* (Glasgow: Bell and Bain, 1964/1986), p. 336 citing the civil law case of *Tennant* v. *Tennant* (1883) 10R 1187.
6. 'SLC Consultative Memorandum No. 46', Q 08.
7. *SLC Report*, para. 3.3 p. 7.
8. W. G. Dickson, *Treatise on the Law of Evidence in Scotland* (as updated by S. J. Hamilton Grierson) (T. T. Clark: Edinburgh, 1887), para. 1622, p. 890.
9. Ibid.
10. Ibid. para. 14, p. 891.
11. *SLC Report*, para. 5.3, p. 14.
12. *MacPhail Report*, para. 16.09.
13. *SLC Report*, para. 5.14, p. 18.
14. Ibid.
15. J. C. Smith, 'The Heilbron Report (1976) *Criminal Law Review*, p. 102.
16. *SLC Report*, para. 14, p. 8.
17. *SLC Report*, para. 3.3, p. 7. See also discussion above pp. 32–3.
18. Scottish Courts Administration Consultation Paper, para. 2.3
19. SLC response to SCA Consultation Paper.

20. First Scottish Standing Committee, col. 878.
21. Ibid., col. 880.
22. Michigan Criminal Sexual Conduct Act s. 520j (Mich. Comp. Laws Ann s. 750).
23. New South Wales: The Crimes Act 1900, s. 409B(3)(f).
24. Chambers and Millar, *Prosecuting Sexual Assault* (Edinburgh: HMSO Scottish Office Central Research Unit Study, 1986), p. 139.
25. New South Wales: The Crimes Act 1900, s. 409B(3)(c)(i).
26. *SLC Report* para. 3.7, p. 8.
27. MacDonald in *Dickie* v. *HMA* (1897, quoted in *SLC Report* para 3.9, p. 9.
28. *SLC Report*, para. 3.9, p. 9.
29. *SLC Report*, para. 5.4, p. 14.
30. *SLC Report*, paras. 5.10–5.15, pp. 17–19.
31. *R.* v. *Viola* [1982] 1 W. L. R. 1138. This was a case where the fact that a naked man had been seen in a complainer's flat the morning after her claimed rape was held to cast doubt on her complaint.
32. *SLC Report*, para. 3.9, pp. 8–9 and para. 5.16, p. 19.
33. Michigan: s. 520j (1) (*b*); New South Wales: Crimes Act, s. 409B (3) (c) (ii); Canada: Criminal Code, s. 246.6 (1) (c).
34. Canada: 'is evidence of sexual activity that took place on the same occasion as the sexual activity that forms the subject matter of the charge where that evidence relates to the consent that the accused alleges he believed was given by the complainant'. Criminal Code s. 246.6 (1) (c).
35. Missouri: Mo. Rev. Stat. s. 491.015. New South Wales: The Crimes Act 1900, s. 409B (3) (*b*).
36. *SLC Report*, para. 5.5, p. 15.
37. *SLC Report*, paras. 5.14–5.19, pp. 18–19.
38. Ibid., para. 5.2, p. 13.
39. First Scottish Standing Committee, col. 893–4.
40. J. Temkin (1984) and also 'Regulating Sexual History Evidence – The Limits of Discretionary Legislation' 33 *International and Comparative Law Quarterly*; see also Adler (1982).
41. Temkin (1984), pp. 643–4.
42. Chambers and Millar (1986), p. 139.
43. D. Field, *The Law of Evidence in Scotland* (Edinburgh: W. Green & Sons, 1988), p. 218.
44. Temkin (1984), pp. 635–6.
45. As argued to us by John Willis, Senior Lecturer in Legal Studies at Latrobe University, Melbourne, and Visitor to the Scottish Office in Summer 1991, on the basis of *Leggatt* but also the literal wording of the statute.
46. *SLC Report*, para. 5.7, pp. 15–16.
47. Scottish Courts Administration Consultation Paper, para. 3.4.
48. Chambers and Millar (1986), pp. 137–41.
49. *SLC Report* para. 5.21, p. 20.
50. Scottish Courts Administration Consultation Paper, para. 6.4.

4

Overview of the Research

This is essentially a court-based study, which was designed to produce as full a picture as possible of the use of sexual history and sexual character evidence in Scottish courts over a three and a half year period. This chapter describes the research design, our method of study and the type of data collected.

Information regarding the use of the legislation and the use of sexual evidence was gathered from three principal sources:

1. a large-scale monitoring exercise based on information from clerks of court;

2. observation of sexual offence trials; and,

3. a series of interviews with legal practitioners who were familiar with sexual offence cases.

A retrospective trawl of court records of sexual offence cases heard in Edinburgh and Glasgow Sheriff Courts during the period 1987–89 provided an additional source of information about contested Sheriff Court trials.

Throughout the book, reference is made to three sets of data. Two of these, the data from the monitoring exercise and the data from the court observation, overlap but are qualitatively distinct; for every trial observed, there is corresponding information from the monitoring exercise. The interview sample comprises the third set of data. This material is drawn on throughout the text and used extensively in Chapters 8 and 10. Comments and views given by interviewees are used to illustrate points, provide examples and to convey similarities and differences of opinion between practitioners. Each method of data collection is described in more detail below.

MONITORING

The Clerk Forms

The aim of the monitoring exercise was to provide maximum coverage of all trials where the legislation could apply.[1] The legislation is potentially applicable in a wide range of offences, falling under different types of procedure, solemn and summary, in the High Court and Sheriff Court. Because of the widespread coverage required, a nation-wide system of monitoring was developed whereby clerks of court at High and Sheriff Court level recorded information on all contested trials involving charges covered by the legislation. This information was returned to the authors for analysis.[2]

Two types of clerk-return forms, for Sheriff Courts and High Courts respectively, were used. Both forms recorded basic trial details such as the court in which the trial occurred, the charge(s) involved in the case, the verdict and the sentence, as well as details about the use of the legislation. All forms were coded and analysed using the Statistical Package for the Social Sciences (SPSS-X).

Overall, the monitoring system provided a broad base of information about numbers and outcomes of trials, the distribution of particular offences going to trial and contested, the reasons for and outcomes of applications to have the prohibitions lifted, and the use of sexual history and sexual character evidence. The monitoring exercise also provided a national context for the more detailed court observation work.

Monitoring in the High Court

Monitoring commenced in January 1987 and continued for a period of three and a half years to May 1990. In July 1987, a more elaborate clerk-return form which documented the use of sexual history evidence in the absence of an application to use the legislation, was introduced for High Court trials only, thereby substituting the original High Court form. Although information on 339 High Court contested trials was received from High Court clerks during the monitoring period, the analysis here is based on only the 305 trials which were monitored by means of the updated and elaborated High Court form.

There were facilities on the form for recording evidence concerning sexual relations between the complainer and the accused, sexual relations between the complainer and someone other than the accused, and any evidence of prostitution, virginity, masturbation or pregnancy relating to the complainer that was heard *in the absence of an application.* (There were 207 trials which did not involve an application.) A number of estimates of the level of breach of the legislation were constructed from these items and these are discussed below. It should be noted that each item is an indicator of sexual behaviour. Clerks were not asked to record sexual character evidence in addition to these items. Hence, the estimates are of sexual history evidence introduced without regard to the legislation, rather than sexual history and sexual character evidence.

If there was no application in a case, the clerk was asked to indicate whether the items listed above were mentioned with respect to the complainer and to indicate whether this was by the prosecution or the defence or both. Sexual relations with the accused was further subdivided into 'in the past', 'on occasion of the offence' and 'since the offence', as was sexual relations with others. More or less inclusive estimates of evidence, introduced in breach of the legislation, were constructed using these indicators. In the most conservative measure, sexual relations with the accused on the occasion of the offence was excluded, as was masturbation and pregnancy. The former was excluded because of the possibility that it was simply the subject matter of the charge that was being recorded rather than sexual behaviour around the time of the charge, but outwith the actual subject matter of the charge. Comparison of clerks' returns and court observation suggests that this was an occasional problem. Masturbation was initially omitted because it had not featured in any of the pre-legislation discussion but there are no real grounds for its exclusion. Pregnancy was excluded because it is possible to envisage circumstances in which pregnancy is introduced without reference to sexual conduct. However, because reference was made to sexual conduct in all of the observed cases in which pregnancy was at issue, there is a powerful argument for its inclusion. In the construction of each of these estimates, cases were counted as being in breach of the legislation if the clerk indicated that the defence (either alone or in conjunction with the prosecution) had introduced one or more of the relevant indicators of sexual behaviour. The measure used extensively in this book includes all indicators except sexual relations with the accused on the occasion of the offence.

Monitoring in the Sheriff Court

This took place for a two year period from January 1987 to December 1988, and resulted in 74 Sheriff Court clerk returns, which can be broken down to 29 trials heard under solemn procedure and 45 trials heard under summary procedure.[3]

Information from Court Records

In early 1990, a retrospective trawl was undertaken of Sheriff Court records in Edinburgh and Glasgow to establish numbers of *contested trials* involving sexual offences, heard under both solemn and summary procedure. This was done to check the completeness of the monitoring system which had resulted in clerks returning forms for 74 Sheriff Court trials conducted across Scotland between January 1987 and December 1988. The trawl showed that there were 84 Sheriff Court trials involving sexual offences in Edinburgh alone, in the same period. Inspection of summary cases in Glasgow Sheriff Court was not possible but solemn cases outnumbered those heard in Edinburgh several fold. It is clear from these figures of Glasgow and Edinburgh alone, that all the Sheriff Court trials in Scotland have not been successfully monitored and this must be kept in mind when reading the figures derived from the monitoring exercise. Table 4.1 shows the numbers of cases, by year, in each court.

TABLE 4.1: Number of cases, by year, involving sexual offences in Edinburgh and Glasgow's Sheriff Courts.[4]

	1987		1988		1989	
	Solemn	Summary	Solemn	Summary	Solemn	Summary
EDINBURGH	3 (8)	18 (25)	5 (10)	25 (58)	3 (12)	28 (58)
GLASGOW	15 (25)	–	16 (34)	–	15 (30)	–

Note: Numbers in brackets denote those cases called for trial. The discrepancies between those called and those resulting in contested trials are due to cases pleading guilty, either before any evidence is heard, or after some evidence has been heard.

COURT OBSERVATION

Court observation provided the means of obtaining more detailed information to supplement the evidence recorded by the clerks. Permission was obtained to remain in court during the complainer's evidence – a part of the trial normally closed to the public. Hence, it was possible to observe the entire trial. In this exercise of observing trials, the authors were greatly assisted by a team of carefully briefed researchers.[5] This assistance facilitated observation in a number of trials held at different locations simultaneously.

Court observation entailed attending court for the duration of the trial. Trials varied in length from one day to five or six days (although one case took three weeks for all the evidence to be heard). Detailed notes of the proceedings were taken throughout each trial (as far as possible researchers recorded the proceedings verbatim), and a set of preliminary analysis forms were completed. These forms shared similarities with the clerk-return forms, although allowed scope for more detailed information to be given about the types of evidence introduced, and how that evidence was used during the trials.[6]

The observation notes and forms were read independently by each of the authors to ensure a measure of reliability and consistency in interpretation. The observation notes and preliminary analysis form of each trial were matched with the corresponding clerk-return form (see Matching Data from the Monitoring Exercise with Court Observation Data, p. 53). The trial notes were coded and sorted using the Ethnograph, a computer software package designed to accommodate large amounts of qualitative data. Observed trials were numbered in chronological order, and are referred to throughout the text by this number, e.g., case 014, case 027. Appendix 3 lists details of all observed trials by High Court and Sheriff Court, solemn and summary procedure.

Court Observation Periods

Fieldwork commenced in February 1987 in both Sheriff and High Courts and continued on an intensive level for 14 months until the end of March 1988. Thereafter, a more selective attendance was maintained at some High and Sheriff Courts from April 1988 to November 1988 inclusive. Court observation for High Court trials only re-commenced for a further period from June to August 1989.

Sites of Court Observation

Observation in the High Court

It was not feasible, despite the relatively small numbers of sexual offence trials throughout Scotland, to attend all such trials. Within the practical limits of research resources, attendance was attempted at all trials in Edinburgh and Glasgow High Courts during the 14 month intensive attendance period (January 1987 – March 1988). From August 1987, observation was extended to cover the High Court sittings at Airdrie, Dundee, Dunfermline, Jedburgh, Kilmarnock, Paisley and Stirling.

Observation in the Sheriff Court

During the 14 month intensive observation period, thorough coverage was aimed for in the Edinburgh and Glasgow Sheriff Courts, and three other Sheriff Courts in central Scotland. An early pilot study conducted in Dunfermline, Kirkcaldy, and Stirling revealed that relevant cases involving charges covered by the legislation rarely appeared in these Courts, confirming what was said by court officials in those Courts about the infrequency of sexual offence trials. However, notification was given whenever a relevant case was due to appear.[7]

Observation in the District Court

Court observation was attempted from July 1987 to October 1987 in Edinburgh, and during April 1988 and May 1988 in Glasgow. For both periods, attendance proved difficult to sustain due to the extra demands placed on the District Court personnel to identify the relevant cases. In all, researchers attended the District Court on 16 occasions, although none of the cases observed on those occasions involved charges covered by the legislation.[8] Hence, these cases are not included as part of the research data.

Notification Procedure

In order to find out when the relevant trials were to take place, a notification procedure was developed whereby the Justiciary Office and the Sheriff Clerk's Office in Edinburgh, Glasgow and Stirling provided a list of court sittings, forthcoming trial diets, relevant charges and indictments – although this system was not foolproof because scheduled trials are often subject to shifts and uncertainties in time-tabling. A continuous dialogue was maintained with advocates, fiscals, clerks, court police and other court officials who gave, whenever possible, advance warning of guilty pleas, and up-to-date information about changes in scheduling. Without such assistance, such widespread coverage would not have been possible.

Courts were notified in advance of intended trial attendance by researchers. Wherever possible, before the day of the trial, the prosecution would be informed and a request made that he or she seek permission from the complainer(s) for a researcher to attend the trial (no complainer ever refused). On the day of the trial, researchers liaised with the Clerks of court who informed the individual judge or sheriff of the research presence and sought permission to remain.

Matching Data from the Monitoring Exercise with Court Observation Data

It was possible to crosscheck the data from the monitoring of 38 of the 207 trials in which no applications were made, by matching with the detailed notes from the court observation of those trials. This was done to cross-check recorded instances of sexual history or sexual character evidence used without an application. Court observation provided more detailed information than that gained from monitoring clerk returns, and not surprisingly indicated a higher incidence of such evidence. Nine omissions and two wrongly counted cases were found using the observation as a check on the clerk forms. This suggests that the clerk forms provide a reasonable, albeit possibly conservative estimate of sexual history evidence in violation of the legislation.

Coverage of Cases Achieved by Observation

Researchers attended 179 sexual offence cases scheduled for trial, 115 of which resulted in a full trial.[9] Court observation data is drawn from attendance at 79 High Court contested trials (which can be matched with corresponding data from the High Court monitoring exercise) and 36 (14 solemn and 22 summary procedure) Sheriff Court contested trials (not all of which have corresponding Sheriff Court clerk forms).

Comparing researchers' attendance at trials with data from the monitoring exercise, it appears that, during the intensive period of court observation, (February 1987 to March 1988) researchers observed 60 per cent of contested High Court trials heard throughout Scotland. In this period, researchers observed 15 of the 19 High Court trials which involved applications to use the legislation. In Edinburgh and Glasgow during the same period, attendance was achieved at 88 per cent and 73 per cent respectively of contested trials tried at those courts, and at all trials with applications in those two courts. In the two subsequent periods of more selective court attendance (from April to November 1988 and from June to August 1989) researchers attended another five trials where applications were made, thereby attending a total of 20 trials which involved applications to use the legislation.

THE INTERVIEWS

From September 1989 to July 1990, when the court observation was almost complete, interviews were conducted with members of the legal profession who had experience of sexual offence trials. In all, 33 individual interviews were conducted with judges, sheriffs, advocate deputes, defence counsel, fiscals, and defence lawyers. Interviewees were selected primarily on the basis that they had participated in the largest numbers of sexual offence trials per occupational subgroup during the period(s) of the court observation. It must be made clear, however, that not all of those interviewed had direct experience of the use of the legislation.

The purpose of the interviews was to ascertain practitioners' views on the legislation, their general views on the use and relevance of sexual history evidence, and to discuss with them various issues which had arisen from the court observation and clerk returns.

The interviews were semi-structured by means of a fairly detailed questionnaire which had slight modifications for each occupational subgroup of practitioners, that is, judges, sheriffs, fiscals, etc. Information gleaned from the interviews included both subjective views and factual data relating to each individual's experience of sexual offence trials and the use of the legislation. Each interview took roughly an hour to complete, although some took over two hours. Approximately two-thirds of the interviews were tape recorded, although all participants have been anonymised. Interviewees are referred to throughout the text by number, for example, judge 2, sheriff 6.

A simple content analysis was carried out on the interviews, which were transcribed using the Ethnograph software package.

NOTES

1. A decision was taken by the authors at the commencement of the research to broaden the investigation to include the charges of incest, clandestine injury, and shameless and indecent conduct. There were two reasons for this: a) the possible similarities in the type of evidence that may be introduced and b) rape and some offences under the Sexual Offences (Scotland) Act 1976 are often charged as alternative charges to incest.

2. High Court forms were forwarded by clerks to the Justiciary Office where they were checked for completeness by the Depute Principal Clerk of Justiciary. The forms were then collected by the researchers and underwent a second check for accuracy, followed by a content analysis. The Sheriff Court forms were forwarded to the Scottish Courts Administration before being sent on to the authors for checking and analysis.

3. There is an imbalance of information obtained from the High Court and Sheriff Court clerk returns. The Sheriff Court coverage was less thorough than the High Court coverage. This was due to the considerable existing workload of Sheriff Court clerks and to the fact that they perform a number of diverse duties during the course of the trial. The authors are conscious that research such as this is often criticised for over-focusing on the High Court, and to a lesser extent on the lower courts. However, greater difficulties were found in conducting research in some of the Sheriff Courts.

4. The research obtained only scant information relating to the cases dealt with under summary procedure in Glasgow Sheriff Courts. This is because, first, the authors were acting on information obtained from preliminary consultations with Glasgow Sheriff Court officials to the effect that no cases relevant to the research were dealt with in the summary courts. Second, because of the sheer numbers of cases of all types of offences dealt with in the summary courts in Glasgow, trawling to find those involving sexual offences would be too mammoth an undertaking given the time and resources available. Third, such an exercise would require a lot of assistance from already hard-pressed Sheriff Court staff. We decided it would be too much of an imposition on their time and good humour.

5. Researchers were selected on the basis of their familiarity with relevant aspects of the Scottish legal system and their interest in law reform in the area of sexual offences. Most were engaged in postgraduate work in the areas of law, criminology, social policy and forensic medicine, and three were second degree undergraduate law students. All researchers were women. Each researcher was inducted, briefed and issued with a set of comprehensive guidelines drawn up by the authors to assist in their note-taking.

6. The authors checked all the observation notes of trial proceedings and the corresponding preliminary analysis forms, and discussed each trial with the individual researcher involved.

7. As a result, researchers attended two cases, both in Stirling, one each under solemn and summary procedure. Only the summary case went to full trial.
8. Charges in these cases were either assault, breach of the peace, or disorderly conduct with elements of indecency. Rarely did a case go to trial. In those where the accused was present when the case was called, by far the most common result was a plea of guilty.
9. Of the 64 cases which did not result in a full trial – due to either a guilty plea, desertion by the prosecution or because they were scheduled under s. 102 of the Criminal Procedure (S) Act – 48 were in the High Court and 16 were in the Sheriff Court.

5

Characteristics of Sexual Offence Trials

There were 379 full trials monitored by clerks of court at 74 Sheriff Court and 305 High Court trials. This data provides a general picture of sexual offence trials in Scotland and the context for the more detailed study of the trials observed by researchers. Where appropriate, the equivalent findings from court observation are also presented by way of comparison.

THE HIGH COURT TRIALS

Although a total of 339 High Court trials were recorded by clerks over the High Court monitoring period of January 1987 to May 1990, analysis is based on 305 trials that were recorded using the elaborated clerk return form which was introduced in July 1987. Table 5.1 specifies the number of High Court contested trials by year.

TABLE 5.1: Number of High Court trials for sexual offences.

Year	Number
1987*	47
1988	115
1989	107
1990†	36
TOTAL	305

* From 1 July 1987.
† Up to and including May only.

The Justiciary Office confirmed that a High Court clerk form was forwarded for every contested trial that took place during the monitoring period. Table 1 in Appendix 2 shows High Court trials by location.

The Charges in the High Court

There were 132 High Court trials which involved a single charge, and 173 which involved multiple charges of a sexual nature.[1]

Rape was by far the most common charge in all trials whether single or multiple charges were involved. Overall, 74 per cent of all trials involved rape and 21 per cent involved rape-related charges, that is, attempted rape and assault with intent to rape. 16 per cent involved offences under the Sexual Offences (Scotland) Act 1976. 6 per cent involved homosexual offences (sodomy, attempted sodomy and s.80(7) of the Criminal Justice (Scotland) Act 1980). 6 per cent involved incest and incest-related offences (s.2A, s.2B and s.2C of the Incest and Related Offences Act 1986).

Table 2 in Appendix 2 shows High Court trials involving single charges. Of single charge trials, 77 per cent were for rape. In those single charge cases involving rape, 80 per cent retained rape as the final charge, whereas in 20 per cent rape was reduced to a lesser charge during the course of the trial. Of those single charge cases where the final charge remained rape, 22 per cent were found guilty, 47 per cent were found not guilty and 31 per cent were found not proven. A high acquittal rate (78 per cent) was found in cases involving a single charge of rape.

Complainers and Accused in the High Court

In all, there was a total of 458 complainers in the 305 cases, 90 per cent of which were female and 10 per cent male. The age of 342 complainers was recorded. At the time of the trial, 50 per cent of the complainers were aged less than 20 years old. A large proportion (23 per cent·(80)) were aged between 13 and 16 years old, 11 per cent (37) were aged between 10 and 12 years old and 9 per cent (29) were aged between 6 and 9 years old. A further 3 per cent (11) were 5 years old or younger, 3 per cent were aged between 17 and 19 years old. On the other hand only a small percentage of the complainers were elderly – 1 per cent (4) were aged over 60 years old.

All of the accused were male. In 152 cases (just over half of all the cases recorded by the clerks), the relationship between the complainer and the accused was given. The data confirmed that in the vast majority of cases (78 per cent), the accused was known to the complainer; 25 per cent were close relatives, 47 per cent were long-term acquaintances, 2 per cent were members of the same household (but not related), and 4 per cent were ex-partners. The accused was a stranger to the complainer in 22 per cent of cases.

Applications in the High Court

There were 98 High Court trials involving applications to lift the prohibitions during the monitoring period of January 1987 to May 1990. Researchers attended 20 of these. In 1987, 17 per cent of all High Court trials with charges covered by the legislation contained applications. In 1988 this rose to 31 per cent. In 1989, there was a slight drop to 28 per cent. In the first five months of 1990, 41 per cent of trials contained applications.

Out of the 98 trials, 89 (90 per cent) involved a single application. Four trials involved two applications; two trials involved three applications; two trials involved four applications; and one trial (which had seven accused and two complainers) involved 10 applications. In all, then, a total of 121 applications were made, details of which were recorded on the clerk forms.

The vast majority (91) of the 98 application trials in the High Court involved a single accused. There were three which involved two accused, three which involved three accused, and one case which involved seven accused.

There were 51 out of the 98 trials (52 per cent) containing applications which involved a single charge, 43 of these were single charges of rape. In those trials involving multiple charges, rape was again the most common charge – 15 of the 20 observed application trials involved the charge(s) of rape. The other five application trials involved multiple charges. In three the most serious charge was attempted rape; sodomy was the most serious charge in another; incest, indecent assault, and offences under the Sexual Offences (S) Act 1979 were the charges in the other trial.

Point in Trial at which Application(s) Made

The number of applications made to lift the prohibitions just prior to the cross-examination of the complainer totalled 70 per cent and 22 per cent were made during the complainer's cross-examination. (In 8 per cent of applications, the clerks did not record when the application was made.) Out of all the applications made, 83 per cent were on the independent initiative of the defence in the trial, that is, without any intervention by the presiding judge or objection by the prosecution precipitating the application. A further 11 per cent of applications arose due to a judicial intervention, and 5 per cent due to an objection by the prosecution.

The Exceptions Cited in High Court Applications

In virtually all cases one or more exception clauses were cited by the defence as part of the application. Exception clause 141B (1) (c) ('the interests of justice') was cited in 72 per cent of application cases, making it the most frequently cited clause. The least common clause used was 141B (1) (b) (ii) ('the defence of incrimination') which was referred to in only 2 per cent of cases. A number of clauses in conjunction with each other were more frequently cited that an application involving a single exception clause.

Court observation data showed that the 'interests of justice' clause was cited in 17 of the 20 trials involving an application which were observed by researchers. The 'interests of justice' was cited on its own in seven trials; in conjunction with 'explain or rebut' in five trials; once in conjunction with 'the same occasion' clause; once with both 'explain and rebut' and 'the same occasion'; once with 'defence of incrimination'; and in two trials with 'explain or rebut', 'the same occasion' and 'defence of incrimination'. Two of the observed trials cited 'the same occasion' solely. In one application trial no exception clause was cited. (See diagram, Chapter 6.)

Issues Raised in High Court Applications

Applications on the whole sought to introduce past sexual relations between the accused and/or someone other than the accused. In 54 per cent of cases the defence raised the question of sexual relations between the complainer and the accused, whereas 56 per cent of cases involved defence references to sexual relations between the complainer and someone other than the accused. In about a third of cases, both were raised. Indeed, the introduction of several sexual matters occurred in a number of cases. In 13 per cent of application cases there were references to the complainer's virginity (or lack of virginity), 7 per cent contained references to prostitution, 1 per cent to masturbatory practices by the complainer, and 1 per cent to the complainer's pregnancy history.

In most cases, more than one issue or justificatory argument was raised per application. In 16 of the 20 observed application trials, the issue of consent was the crux of the defence case, although this was not always directly referred to in the application. The issue of credibility was, however, commonly raised during an application. For example, it was explicitly raised in 9 out of the 20 observed applications, where the defence wished to question on the sexual relations between the complainer and someone other than the accused. However, the ways in which sexual history evidence was used to question the credibility of the complainer, almost always introduced some implication of consent.

The Outcome of High Court Applications

In 37 per cent of applications, the prosecution mounted an argument disputing the admissibility and/or relevance of the proposed line of questioning by the defence. Overall, 85 per cent of applications were granted. The success rate, or percentage of applications granted by the presiding judge, has however, increased since 1987. In 1987, 65 per cent of all applications made were granted. In 1988, this rose to 89 per cent. In 1989, 85 per cent of applications were granted. A full 100 per cent of applications made in 1990 (for the first five months of the year) were granted. In 12 of the 20 observed application trials, the application was granted; in three cases, it was partially successful, in four cases the applications were refused outright. The other case was withdrawn by the defence in the face of doubts expressed by the judge and the prosecution's stated intention of leading some of the evidence which the defence sought to introduce. In observed cases, applications were always successful when they had the support of the prosecution, although the converse did not necessarily follow. The observation data showed that when an application was successful, it was not always the case that the defence had complete freedom to pursue all of the evidence outlined in the application. In five of the 12 observed successful applications, the judge imposed limits on the defence questioning. This could take the form of specific instructions to the defence regarding the boundary points of questioning or more general cautionary remarks.

Sexual History Evidence Without an Application

The most, and arguably over-conservative, estimate of the introduction of prohibited evidence indicated that 46 High Court trials involved such evidence. The inclusion of masturbation added two cases and pregnancy added one, bringing the total to 49. This figure is a very 'safe' estimate of prohibited sexual history evidence introduced without application and it is the figure used throughout the text. These 49 cases amounted to 16 per cent of all High Court cases monitored by clerks and 24 per cent of cases without an application. By including the cases involving 'sexual relations with the accused on occasion of the offence', a further 15 cases were added, giving a figure of 21 per cent of all High Court cases and 31 per cent of cases without application.

The incidence of these categories of evidence heard without application is slightly higher in cases where the charge was rape, that is 28 per cent of all rape cases that did not involve applications (see Table A2.3) using the 'safe' measure. (The inclusion of 'sexual relations with the accused on the occasion of offence' makes a more significant difference in the case of rape than in other charges, see Table A2.3.)

In 23 per cent of cases without an application, sexual history evidence was introduced by the prosecution. This is not in breach of the legislation due to the Crown exemption. But in 29 per cent of these cases the defence picked up on this evidence. (In some cases the defence also independently introduced additional prohibited evidence.)

Cases could involve combinations of sexual history evidence, some of which were introduced only by the prosecution, some picked up on by the defence, and some introduced independently by the defence. In 28 per cent of breaches of the legislation, the evidence was introduced by the prosecution and subsequently used by the defence without an application to do so; 75 per cent of the estimated breaches involved the defence independently introducing sexual history evidence.

When the incidence of sexual history evidence heard without an application is tabulated by year, there has been little change from 14 per cent of all cases, without an application, in 1987 to 16 per cent in 1989, the last full year recorded. The figures for 1990 (up to and including May) suggest that there may be a slight further increase. Since the rate of applications is increasing this means that there is an increase overall in the amount of sexual history evidence that is being heard in the High Court.

THE SHERIFF COURT TRIALS

Of the 74 Sheriff Court trials monitored over the two-year period from January 1987 to December 1988, 29 were jury trials – four were heard in Edinburgh and 18 in Glasgow; 45 were summary trials (non-jury), 22 of which were heard in Edinburgh and four in Glasgow. (NB The lower number in Glasgow reflects different rates of monitoring not a lower incidence, since as noted previously, there are more trials in Glasgow.)

In the jury trials, 34 per cent (10) of trials involved the charge of assault with intent to rape, 24 per cent (7) involved the statutory offences s. 4 and s. 5 of the Sexual Offences (Scotland) Act 1976, or s. 80 (7) of the Criminal Justice (Scotland) Act 1980, and 17 per cent (5) involved the charge of lewd and libidinous practices. Other charges were sodomy, attempted sodomy, indecent assault, and shameless and indecent conduct.

In the non-jury (summary) trials, statutory offences under the Sexual Offences (Scotland) Act 1976 were involved in one third of trials (15). A further 28 per cent of trials (13) involved the charge of lewd and libidinous practices, and 17 per cent (8) involved indecent exposure. Other charges were indecent assault and breach of the peace with elements of indecency.

Applications in the Sheriff Court

The clerks recorded that five of the 74 Sheriff Court trials involved applications to have the prohibitions lifted. Three applications were made under solemn procedure (jury trials) and two were made under summary procedure (non-jury trials).

In the jury trials, the charges concerned were assault with intent to rape (Edinburgh), indecent assault (Stranraer), and assault (Glasgow). Assault is not one of the charges covered by the legislation, so this case was double-checked. The two accused in the case were charged with assault, although the indictment revealed the substance of the charges as having sexual intercourse with the complainer whilst she was 'in a state of unconsciousness and bereft of the power of resistance.'

The charges in the two non-jury trials were unlawful sexual intercourse with a girl under 16 years old, and indecent behaviour towards a girl aged between 12 and 16 years old (Dunoon and Perth Sheriff Courts respectively).[2]

The clerks recorded that all of these applications in the Sheriff Court were granted.

The Exceptions Cited in Sheriff Court Applications

In three cases, where the charges were assault with intent to rape, indecent assault, and unlawful sexual intercourse with a girl under 16 years old respectively, (141B/346B (1(c)), 'the interests of justice' was the exception cited by the defence in order to introduce evidence of past sexual relations with the accused and/or with others. Two of these cases resulted in an acquittal, and in the third case the accused was found guilty of a lesser (and a non-sexual) charge.

The assault trial had two separate applications, involving sexual intercourse with a complainer who was unconscious, one for each of the accused involved, the exception cited in both applications was 141B (1) (a) ('explain or rebut'). In both applications, the defence sought to introduce evidence of past sexual relations with others. The outcome was that one accused was acquitted, whilst the other was found guilty and fined £250.

In the fifth application case, which involved two counts of indecent behaviour towards a girl aged between 12 and 16 years old, two exceptions were cited, that is 346B (1) (a) ('explain or rebut') and (1) (b) (ii) ('the defence of incrimination'). The accused was the biological father of the complainer and medical evidence was at issue. The defence wished to question on the sexual relations between the complainer and someone other than the accused, on the same occasion as the offence. The accused, who had previous analogous convictions, was found guilty and sentenced to 240 hours' community service.

Researchers were unfortunately not in attendance at any of the Sheriff Court trials where applications were made to use the legislation. The data from court observation reveals, however, that in two summary trials, prosecution objections were made on the grounds that questioning by the defence contravened the legislation, but no application ensued.

Sexual History Evidence Without Application

Sheriff Court clerks were not asked to record information about evidence introduced without application. The following information is based on observation data only.

Although only the most cautious reckoning has been applied here, observation documented some defence questioning on sexual matters in nine of the 14 solemn trials and four of the 22 summary trials. In five solemn cases and three summary cases, defence questions pertained to whether the complainer had had sex with anybody other than the accused. In fact the special defence of incrimination was lodged in two of these cases. In six of the solemn trials and in one summary trial, questions were asked by the defence about sexual relations between the complainer and the accused (on an occasion other than that of the alleged incident). These cases are discussed more fully in Chapter 8.

The numbers of observed cases are too small for a precise percentage figure to be given for the rate of prohibited sexual history evidence heard without application, although the data tends to suggest that the incidence of sexual history evidence in Sheriff Court trials is considerably higher than the rate of applications. The evidence also indicates a higher incidence of sexual history evidence in jury trials heard under solemn procedure. Indeed it is possible that solemn Sheriff Court trials may involve levels of sexual history evidence not dissimilar to that in the High Court.

NOTES

1. Some of these cases also involved charges of a non-sexual nature.
2. Sexual Offences (Scotland) Act 1976, s. 4(1) and s. 5.

6

Observed Trials Containing Applications

This chapter and the following one are based on the observation of sexual offence trials in which the defence made an application to introduce sexual history or character evidence. The detailed notes taken of these trials include the dialogue which took place between the defence advocate, the judge and the prosecution during an application. When a particular trial is referred to in the text, the case number allocated to it in the study is cited. (This allows the reader to look up further details of the case in Appendix 3. Cases are also identified by case number in Figure 6.1, p. 67). Applications to introduce the prohibited evidence are crucial to understanding the new legislation's effectiveness. This chapter describes how the balance of exclusions and exceptions works out in practice, what type of evidence is ultimately regarded as allowable and why, and what type of questions are ultimately put to complainers as a consequence.

In the discussion that ensues when an application is made, first the defence states their case and then the judge, and sometimes the prosecution, responds. This can be a very brief affair with no questions asked because the matter is regarded as straight forward, but sometimes a lengthy exchange follows. When judges chose to ask questions beyond clarifying the precise nature of the evidence, it was to seek justification of the proposed use of the prohibited sexual evidence. Two types of questions were asked. What exclusions and exceptions does it fall under? How is it relevant to the issues in the case? In the application, a simple citing of the subsections by the defence was not generally regarded as adequate, rather the relevance of proposed evidence to crucial issues in the case – consent, the credibility of the complainer, the identity of the accused – were as, if not more, important, although there were a number of cases where relevance was not mentioned. In practice, the defence response was sometimes to slide between issue-based and provision-based justification, emphasising whichever seemed best suited to their purposes. This could involve trying to focus discussion on the letter of the law rather than the precise relevance of the evidence to the issue of the trial. (As noted in Chapter 3, the legislation as such does not require any reference to relevance).

The prosecution did not always play an active role in the 'application dialogue'. However, when they did it was an important one. In cases where they stated that they had no objection (007, 134, 158) or were actively supportive of the defence case (165, 118) then the application was quickly brought to a successful conclusion. The converse was not always true in that the prosecution could mount a series of objections and the application could still succeed (089). However, it was generally true that the evidence refused in cases matched prosecution objections (002, 049, 052, 077, 092). The prosecution were sometimes in the position of actively supporting some evidence and objecting to other aspects of the defence case (003, 052). Evidence which they spoke of supportively was always admitted. This was affirmed very directly by one of the advocate deputes interviewed who made the following observation on the likely success of an application: 'Well, I think if I didn't object to it then the judge would let it go. I think that's probably the case. Most judges would do ... But the mere fact that I do object doesn't necessarily mean that it won't.' (advocate depute 2)

While not objecting, the prosecution might seek limits to be placed on the line of questioning. For example, in case 156 when the prosecution stated that they had no objection (to further questions to the complainer about her sexual behaviour) if the questioning was limited to the source of the pubic hair (part of the forensic evidence) and one week prior to the incident. Or in case 007 when the prosecution stated that they had no objection (to questioning the complainer about sexual behaviour in search of an alternative explanation to vaginal swelling) provided questioning was limited to between the time of the incident and the medical examination.

A successful application did not always mean that the defence had complete freedom to pursue their declared line of questioning. In five cases the judge indicated limits. This could take the form of specific instructions like 'limited to the time of the incident and medical examination' (007) or more general cautionary remarks.

In what follows, two different aspects of the 20 observed application cases are described and discussed. There is necessarily some repetition in this and the subsequent chapter, since the same trials are discussed from different perspectives. Readers who are less interested in the way the specific subsections of the Act are being used, may wish to concentrate on Chapter 7 dealing with the issues that the defence sought to address by introducing sexual history and character evidence. This chapter describes the frequency with which exclusion and exception sections of the legislation were cited, and the types of evidence regarded as pertaining to these

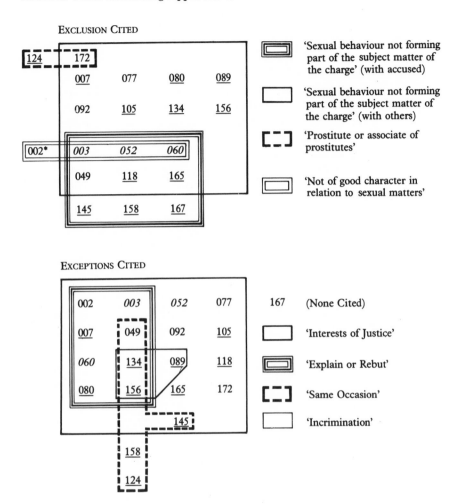

FIGURE 6.1: OBSERVED CASES WITH APPLICATIONS.

Notes:

Each observed trial was allocated a case number, e.g. 007
Underlined numbers denote successful application
Italic numbers denote partially successful application
* There were two applications in case 002 but only the first is shown

exclusion and exception sections of the legislation. The first part of the chapter summarises the types of prohibited evidence in question, according to the exclusions section of the legislation. In the application, sections are usually explicitly named by the defence, but not always, and when this is not the case, categorisation is difficult. Most imaginable questions about sexual character and sexual history, other than, of course, asking details about the incident, would fall under the exclusion of 'sexual behaviour not forming part of the subject matter of the charge'. The exclusion concerning prostitution refers to a specific sort of sexual behaviour, while the exclusion referring to showing a complainer is 'not of good character in relation to sexual matters' mops up questioning which is not about specific behaviour but a more general character attack. However, the most common way of attacking sexual character is to suggest promiscuity which again involves reference to behaviour.

The 20 applications that we observed in detail are categorised by the exclusion provisions in Figure 6.1 (see p. 67). As the figure illustrates, while 'sexual behaviour not forming part of the subject matter of the charge' was the exclusion most often invoked, evidence in this category was more often sexual behaviour with someone other than the accused than with the accused, although quite often the two sorts of evidence were raised in the same case.

In the second part of the chapter, attention turns to the exceptions under which sexual evidence may be admitted. Again use is made of the diagram to illustrate at a glance, the frequency with which particular exceptions were used and with what success.

EVIDENCE BY EXCLUSIONS

Sexual Behaviour Not Forming Part of the Subject Matter of the Charge
[s. 141A (1) (c)]

In some sense all applications attempt to introduce this type of evidence since the cases in which another exception and not this one was named, concerned 'entertaining black men in her room' (case 002) and prostitution (case 124). This type of evidence may be sexual relations with the accused or with others (or even masturbation). It may concern actual sexual intercourse or other sorts of sexual behaviour. It may have occurred in the distant past or closer in time to the incident in question.

Bearing in mind the differences between the English/Welsh and Scottish legislation, it may be reasonable to expect to find more applications in Scotland, simply because the evidence concerning the accused is not excluded in the southern legislation. In fact, in the observed cases *most* applications in relation to this exclusion included sexual behaviour with third parties (15/20). The clerk returns, however, suggest that the bigger picture is of greater symmetry between applications involving sexual relations with the accused and sexual relations with others. (Of those indicating sexual relations not forming part of the subject matter of the charge, about a third referred to accused only, about a third referred to others only, and about a third referred to both). Nevertheless, two thirds of applications involved third parties.

Sexual Behaviour with the Accused

Nine of the applications specifically referring to 'sexual behaviour not forming part of the subject matter of the charge' concerned the accused (003, 049, 052, 060, 118, 145, 158, 165, 167). All these cases involved rape or attempted rape. Six of these applications referred to (alleged) sexual intercourse, while one referred to a 'sexual romp' (003), and one to 'kissing or flirting' (049). With the exception of the last case, all of these applications were successful. As is discussed in Chapter 7, it seemed to be taken for granted that if the complainer and accused had sexual contact in the past, that was relevant.

In three of these cases the accused was the husband of the complainer (167) or her ex-husband (145) or ex-lover (118) and the defence wished to investigate the history of their relationship. In case 118 for example, the defence state his aims as follows: ' I wish to ascertain the extent of sexual relations, when it commenced, its regularity, and when it ceased' and, in case 145, as a desire to cross-examine the complainer regarding her 'long period of sexual relations with the accused'. The defence advocates in these cases did not put forward any additional arguments as to why this evidence was relevant, presumably feeling that none was needed, and there was no objection from prosecution or judge. No time restrictions were placed on the scope of questioning. The absence of time restrictions is surprising given the intentions of the legislation

Indeed, in case 167 in which the complainer and accused were currently husband and wife the defence advocate referred to the exclusion, 'sexual behaviour not forming part of the subject matter of the charge' and commented, 'I don't believe the Act envisaged being applied to husband and wife.' The judge intervened and asked 'Are you seeking to introduce questions to show the complainer indulged in sexual behaviour with the accused at another time?' To which the defence replied, 'Yes My Lord, both before and after.' The following completed the exchange:

JUDGE:	Is that all?
DEFENCE ADVOCATE:	Before and after.
JUDGE:	Does the prosecution have any objection to this?
ADVOCATE DEPUTE:	No, My Lord. Not at all.
JUDGE:	Carry on then.

In the other six cases there was no suggestion of a long standing relationship between the complainer and the accused. In only one of these other cases was the alleged sexual behaviour close enough in time to be part of the charge or on the 'same occasion' as the subject matter of the charge. This was case 158 in which the defence advocate referred to the accused's statement to the police, claiming that consensual intercourse took place not only on the occasion that was the subject of the charge, but two times earlier that day. The rest involve alleged incidents earlier in the same day (003, 052, 158) but not immediately preceding the incident, while the other cases were more remote in time: one week before (060); an unspecified occasion in the previous three weeks (052); an unspecified occasion (165), and the application that failed – kissing and flirting with the accused five to six weeks before (049).

In practically none of these cases was this a matter of bringing any independent evidence but rather 'putting such questions to' the complainer, on the basis of what the accused had presumably said to his counsel or, in two cases (158, 165), also in a statement to the police. There is no requirement that the defence provides evidence or that the accused goes into the witness box to make these statements and be cross-examined by the prosecution. In cross-examination of the complainer the defence sometimes puts very detailed step-by-step (this happened and then this happened) questions concerning the accused's version of the sexual act. (This provides a considerable ordeal for the complainer.) In fact, most accused did enter the witness box but were not routinely questioned in matching detail. Indeed, in one case (052) the accused was asked nothing about his previous sexual relations with the complainer while she had been asked about this at length. In this sense, it is *not* 'his word' against hers.

Sexual Behaviour with Someone Other than the Accused

In six applications (003, 049, 052, 060, 118, 165), the defence wished to introduce questioning about sexual behaviour not forming the subject matter of the charge, with reference to the accused *and* with reference to others. In most of these cases, this involved quite *separate* events in time and place. Only in case 003 did this involve an alleged incident including both the accused and others (the only case involving multiple accused). Thus, a substantial proportion of the applications were seeking to ask the complainer about sexual behaviour with third parties, which occurred without the accused's involvement.

Of the 20 applications, 15 were seeking permission to question complainers about sexual conduct that did not directly involve the accused. To this can be added two other cases which made reference to alternative exclusions: (002) which contained a more generalised attack on sexual character (although it did refer to the specific behaviour of the complainer frequently entertaining black men in her room), and (124) which referred to prostitution. Ten of these applications were successful. None of these involved the defence that the accused, as a result of this sexual conduct, had a mistaken belief that the complainer consented. Permission was generally sought to introduce the evidence on the grounds that it was a test of the credibility of the complainer, or sometimes it was argued that the evidence indicated some predisposition to consent. In three cases (049, 052, 060), it was suggested that the sexual behaviour with another demonstrated a 'flirtatious' nature but in only one of these cases was it suggested that the accused knew this (case 060). This application sought permission for four areas of questioning including reference to the complainer's pregnancy as a result of sex with a third party, but also to the 'not of good character' evidence that she allegedly boasted of her sexual conquests.

Nine applications referred to specific incidents or relationships with particular people: alleged sexual intercourse (089, 105, 118, 134, 165) and/or sexual behaviour (003, 049, 052, 172). With the exception of the unsuccessful 049 which referred to kissing, all these involved alleged genital activity. In some cases this was alleged to have occurred in the days immediately preceding the incident and in others in the unspecified past. In one case, 118, this turned out to be seven years previously. Of these nine applications, in addition to case 049, case 052 was also unsuccessful.

Two of the 15 cases sought to introduce questions around a later pregnancy (060, 092). One succeeded (060) and one did not (092). Four cases (007, 077, 080, 156) involved less specific allegations of sexual activity. In three of these cases (007, 077, 080) the defence argued that the medical report's findings concerning the complainer's vagina provided a basis for asking the complainer about her past sexual experience. Two were successful (007 and 080). In case 156, forensic evidence was similarly the basis for the defence successfully seeking to ask the complainer about other sexual activity at the time of the incident.

Prostitute or Associate of Prostitutes [s. 141A (1) (b)]

In only two cases did the defence seek to introduce evidence which clearly fell under the subsection prohibiting evidence that the complainer was a prostitute or associate of prostitutes. In one case (124) the defence advocate wished to put to one of the complainers that sex was offered for money. This was a case involving a number of complainers and charges including sodomy, but the relevant charge was s.80 (7) (c) of the Criminal Justice (Scotland) Act which refers to homosexual offences with a male under 21. The judge suggested that the legislation was not necessary as the allegation formed part of the subject matter of the charge and the application was granted without further discussion.

In fact suggestions of prostitution preceded the application in the following exchange (with a 16 year old male complainer) (124).

DEFENCE:	The advocate depute asked you if you frequented the bus station?
COMPLAINER:	Yes.
DEFENCE:	You said, [to the advocate depute] 'Not really'
DEFENCE:	Did you or did you not hang around the bus station?
COMPLAINER:	Not really.

[later]

DEFENCE:	If evidence is led suggesting you hang around the bus station, that would be correct?
COMPLAINER:	Yes.
DEFENCE:	What kind of place did [the accused] say he'd take you to?
COMPLAINER:	I can't remember, discos and that.
DEFENCE:	Any kind of discos?
COMPLAINER:	Don't know.
DEFENCE:	On the first occasion he promised to take you places and offered you so many things it was too good to be true?
COMPLAINER:	Yes.
DEFENCE:	Do you know people in Edinburgh who are members of the homosexual community?
COMPLAINER:	Yes.
DEFENCE:	Were you not aware that [the accused] was a wealthy man?

Other complainers in this case were asked similar questions about the bus station and the homosexual community, although there was no further application to suggest that they were prostitutes. This is perhaps because the matter had been settled by the first application. However, the fact that such questioning took place *without intervention prior to the application* also suggests that the legal practitioners concerned did not believe an application was necessary and no intervention would have occurred even if no application had been made.

In the other case (172), the defence sought to introduce evidence that one of the two complainers had worked as a prostitute in London hotels and had provided customers with 'sexual favours' when working as a hairdresser. The accused was the father of both complainers in the case and the alleged prostitution was some considerable time after the alleged sexual abuse. The defence claimed that this was relevant to credibility and particularly so since the 'prostitution' preceded the reporting of the alleged sexual abuse. The prosecution challenged the relevance and the judge also raised doubts and decided on an adjournment to consider the matter. On recommencing, the defence advocate stated that he had spoken to the advocate depute and it appeared that 'certain matters I am concerned with will be raised by the advocate depute and certain others [the issue of prostitution] are not strictly proper' and so he withdrew his application. The issue of prostitution did not re-emerge in the trial.

In summary, then, applications to introduce evidence of the complainer's prostitution were very rare but the suggestion that the complainer was a 'rent boy' or, as noted in the previous section, a 'loose woman', was a feature of a number of cases.

Not of Good Character in Relation to Sexual Matters [s. 141A (1) (a)]

Four applications explicitly sought to develop lines of questions designed to show that the complainer was not of good character in relation to sexual matters. All of these were rape cases (002, 003, 052, 060). Such evidence could generally be categorised as allegations of promiscuity. In case 003 the evidence concerned the number of men the complainer 'entertained in her room', and the defence also wished to use medical notes showing that the complainer attended a gynaecological clinic for cervical cancer (presumably on the basis that multiple sexual partners is a contributory factor in cervical cancer). In case 052, the defence wished to put to the complainer, among other things, that she 'engaged in casual sex', was 'of loose moral virtue', and 'flirtatious nature'. In case 060 the defence sought to introduce, again among other things: 'evidence of the complainer's repeated casual sexual intercourse with a large number of youths in the area over the period of the past three years and the fact that she boasted of sexual conquests'. This aspect of these applications was not successful in any of the cases.

Case 002 was more complicated in that the evidence which the defence advocate wished to introduce was that the 'complainer regularly entertained men in her room. In the main, these men were black ... [The accused in this case was black.] ... I am not seeking to prove promiscuity ... ' This line of questioning was also disallowed by the judge. The judge commented that the evidence was liable to be extremely prejudicial and he was satisfied that to admit it would be contrary to the interests of justice. However, the defence subsequently did all he could to get round this ruling. He tried repeatedly to establish the colour of the men with whom she was acquainted and asked questions about the colour of the pop stars in the posters pinned up in her room. (Of the four applications refused outright, this was the most flagrant example of the defence virtually ignoring the ruling.) The judge persistently intervened and finally demanded that a second application be made. This was as a result of a question put to a friend of the complainer, 'Did many black boys come round?' by the defence. When asked the relevance and reminded that the judge had already ruled against such questions, the defence replied that it was a different position. He tried to argue that he was testing the consistency of the complainer's claims about her visitors and was allowed to pursue this question without reference to black men. However, the defence probably succeeded in making the point.

Sometimes character evidence was more indirect – the application in case 052 included, in a long list of items, some of which were very directly about character, 'loose moral virtue' and 'flirtatious nature', and some more indirect, the fact that the complainer kept 'exotic underwear in her bedroom'. She was, in fact, a sales representative for a company that sold underwear and sex aids. The prosecution objected to some questions and not others. Underwear was not objected to, but the more blatant character material was, and subsequently disallowed by the judge. The judge's ruling did not expressly forbid or allow questioning on underwear. Subsequent questions included the following:

DEFENCE: Did you have kinky underwear?
COMPLAINER: Yes. Ann Summers stock.
DEFENCE: Did you have two vibrators?
COMPLAINER: Yes.
DEFENCE: What did you have them for?

In addition to these four cases, in case 080 the judge was concerned that proposed evidence had character connotations and therefore fell under the exclusion. The defence wished to ask the complainer if she had ever had sexual intercourse prior to the incident. The judge asked if this matter was excluded by s. 141A (1) (*a*) 'not of good character in relation to sexual matters', and the defence then invoked 141A (1),(*c*) 'has at any time engaged with any person in sexual behaviour not forming part of the subject matter of the charge.' Although the judge seemed to have initial reservations the application was granted. The observation notes record the beginning of the exchange between the judge and the defence as follows:

JUDGE: ... can you take me back to s. 141A (1) (*a*), are you interested in that?
DEFENCE: Probably a mixture of (*a*) and (*c*), but I'm not putting character at issue. It is just a question regarding the medical report.
JUDGE: But you will be referring to her character?
DEFENCE: I think it probably falls under (*c*).
JUDGE: The girl may use an instrument to engage in masturbation.
DEFENCE: Well, maybe she has an explanation. The accused is not in a position to say, just to challenge the assumption ...
JUDGE: What I really need to know is what line of questioning you intend to engage in.
DEFENCE: To put the findings of the medical report that she does not have a hymen and that that is indicative of sexual interference.

The defence advocate's purpose was not further clarified but the response was that the evidence was being introduced for some purpose other than establishing 'not of good character'. This serves as a reminder that character evidence is often introduced, whether coincidentally or by design, in another guise. Although there were few instances of applications in which the defence explicitly sought to introduce 'not of good character in relation to sexual matters', the subject matter of other applications often had connotations of bad character and character evidence was often introduced when not mentioned in the application. Thus, although applications explicitly seeking to put to a female complainer that she was a 'loose woman' were rare, this suggestion was a feature of the defence in a larger number of cases.

EVIDENCE BY EXCEPTIONS

The overwhelming majority of observed applications referred to the 'interests of justice' (as confirmed more widely by the clerk returns which record that 72 per cent of application cases use this exception). However, it was rarely used alone.

Explain or Rebut

This provision makes room for the defence to ask questions or bring evidence in relation to matters introduced by the Crown (including prosecution evidence not yet led at the time of the application). In all cases of its use it was ultimately also cited with the 'interests of justice' but this, rather than the 'interests of justice' was often the first preference as the relevant exception in applications. At the same time it should be noted that essentially similar arguments were sometimes used under different exceptions. Occasionally, arguments which could have been made with reference to 'explain or rebut' used only 'the interests of justice', and in one case 'the same occasion' was used where 'explain or rebut' would have been more usual.

Obviously the 'explain or rebut' exception is dependent on what the Crown does, since that is what is to be rebutted or re-explained. A number of cases involved skirmishes about what the Crown had, to use the word of the statute, 'adduced', intended to adduce or, even, should adduce. Where the Crown case was non-consent, did that license defence to bring in under 'explain or rebut' anything they could construe as showing non-consent? If the testimony of the complainer (or even her appearance or manner) indirectly suggested certain inferences, or implications or assumptions, about her sexual life then could defence seek to 'rebut' these implications?

One important argument that emerged in several cases was the status of some of the material in Crown productions which, although lodged, was not going to be used in court by the Crown. The problem was whether or not this material counted as having been adduced by the Crown and hence whether it was open to questioning by the defence. Ultimately, these were arguments not simply about technicalities – whether the evidence was adduced or not – but also about the relevance of evidence, given that the Crown has an obligation to lead *all* relevant facts.

In case 002, a rape case, the defence was wishing to raise issues in the precognitions given by Crown witnesses, which the Crown did not intend to put before the court. This evidence suggested that the complainer regularly entertained black men in her room, and, as noted above, it is likely that the intention was to suggest that the complainer had a predisposition to consent to sexual intercourse with black men. The judge commented, 'I do not understand the application ... Are you saying that the Crown is going to lead evidence that the complainer frequently entertained men in her room? What effect does this have on evidence you lead or on your cross-examination? ... Are the Crown proposing to do this? Parliament has indicated its disapproval of such questioning.' When the advocate-depute indicated that he would not lead such evidence, the defence advocate declared in protest, 'The Crown has a duty to place all evidence before them to the jury.' However, the judge quashed the application.

In another rape case, the advocate depute objected that he had no intention of leading the evidence of the complainer kissing or flirting five or six weeks previously with the accused, which the defence seemed to think they could 'explain or rebut' (case 049). The advocate depute said of the defence, 'He points to the evidence adduced, the further adducing of evidence. This cannot be used by an accused person. The evidence that is to be explained or rebutted must be adduced by the Crown in these cases. With respect to [the defence counsel], I have not heard anything that rebuts incidents prior to the times given at the trial. Every casual cuddle at a party would give licence to rape at a future date.' The defence tried to justify the use of 'explain or rebut' and to defend the relevance of kissing and cuddling to consent. He argued that lack of consent was being rebutted and then threw in the 'interests of justice':

> [The prosecutor's comments] indicate that my approach is too broad. If your Lordship considers the proposition, because there was kissing and cuddling and evidence of sexual attraction five weeks earlier, 'designed to explain or rebut' in my submission to rebut the complainer's evidence – quite simply that sexual intercourse took place fully with her consent. ... Perhaps I can also put the matter this way. 141B (*c*) is 'contrary to the interests of justice'. If my application [under 'explain or rebut'] is refused, having heard the accused giving evidence, 'No it did not start on the day in question, it started at a party five or six weeks before, where she was kissing and cuddling me'. There is a background.

The judge responded that there were insufficient grounds and refused the application.

In case 060, also a rape case, there was a tussle concerning what had been adduced by the Crown but in this case permission to proceed was given. The defence wished to question the complainer about her medical record which revealed that, in her dealings with a gynaecologist, she had initially falsely attributed a pregnancy to the alleged rape. The defence argued that this put the credibility of the complainer at issue. In this case, this exchange between judge and prosecution took place :

JUDGE: Surely it is difficult to object if the defence case rests on a Crown production?

PROSECUTION: It is there simply as part of the medical records and the fact that it is lodged as a production does not mean that it will be or should be referred to. It is there as a matter of administrative convenience.

This raises an important issue concerning the status of Crown productions: is everything they contain open to being introduced by the defence even if only present as a matter of 'administrative convenience'? The judge allowed the line of questioning to be pursued. It is unclear whether the judge was responding to the force of the argument about the relevance of the evidence to credibility, rather than rejecting the prosecution's case that a Crown production, which was there as an administrative convenience was not automatically open to rebuttal. Significantly, the judge referred to the 'interests of justice', not 'explain or rebut', in his judgment. The potential use by the defence of medical records or details of reports which are there for administrative convenience – including details recorded for routine medical reasons rather than for forensic reasons to do with the crime – is a matter of concern because they can contain much confidential information such as contraceptive and pregnancy history.

In only one case (134), an attempted rape case, was the defence attempting to give an alternative explanation of the forensic evidence of semen linking the accused to the crime, by asking the complainer when intercourse took place with her boyfriend – the medical report stating the time of last sexual intercourse with her boyfriend as being close to the incident. In this case the defence also suggested that the complainer had consented to sexual intercourse and changed her mind at the last minute, a defence which weakened the requirement of an alternative source. As in many cases the defence tried alternative and somewhat contradictory arguments in parallel. In one rape case (007) the defence wished to rebut medical evidence of sexual assault, that is, swelling round the vagina, but had no specific evidence with which to contradict this. He successfully sought leave to ask the teenage complainer if she had ever masturbated or engaged in any other sexual activity, despite medical evidence of virginity.

In addition to case 060, there were three other rape cases, in which the defence sought to rebut the credibility of the complainer and sometimes also aspects of the evidence which would suggest the absence of consent. For example, in one case what was being rebutted, was the complainer's assertion that she did not know the accused. Case 003 involved successfully applying to rebut the complainer's account by putting to her the version of the accused and others concerning an earlier 'sexual romp'.

In two cases this involved rebutting statements which the complainer had made about herself (080 and 156). Judges, sheriffs, prosecution and defence interviewed mentioned 'the complainer who sets herself up' as a virgin or a virtuous woman. Indeed this was one of the circumstances which most frequently came to mind when interviewees were asked to envisage how and when past sexual relations between the complainer and someone other than the accused would be relevant evidence. In two observed cases in which 'explain or rebut' was cited for this purpose, the complainer was more 'set up' than 'setting herself up'. In one case, rather than being 'set up' as a 'good character', it was the prosecution who started to establish her 'bad sexual character'. In case 156, the complainer was asked by the prosecution, with at least a hint of scepticism, whether she had had sexual intercourse with anyone other than her husband and the accused around the time of the alleged rape. This was followed by asking for her explanation of the fact that a pubic hair, which did not match those of her husband or the accused (citing evidence in the Crown's forensic report) had been found by the police surgeon. Not surprisingly, it was followed up by a successful application from the defence to question her further on her sexual history. Every exception was cited during the ensuing discussion – 'incrimination', 'the same occasion', 'the interests of justice', as well as 'rebut and explain'.

Case 080 was a successful application to follow up 'good character' evidence led by the Crown concerning the complainer's history. This involved 'rebutting' the complainer's affirmative answer to, 'Was this the first time anything like this had happened to you?' This ambiguous and rather puzzling question paved the way for defence questions about alleged sexual intercourse with another on the grounds that the medical report showed the absence of a hymen. A very similar set of circumstances resulted in an application seeking to contradict a complainer's statement about her sexual history in another rape case (105). But in this application, which was again successful, only the 'interests of justice' exception was cited. In these cases the defence was attributing good character constructions to the prosecution. It is as if the actual questions asked by the prosecution are construed by the defence as 'good-character' evidence in order to provide a 'straw man' to be knocked down, a 'phantom' claim to be attacked. This is analogous to the prosecution construing defence evidence as showing 'innocent association' (a form of good character evidence) in order to attack the accused by introducing 'similar fact evidence' (damaging evidence that the accused was responsible for similar acts on another occasion). This practice has been condemned when indulged in by the prosecution as 'a specious manner of outflanking the exclusionary rule'.[1] Clearly similar 'specious outflanking' by the defence of exclusionary rules which prohibit attacks on sexual character, deserves equal condemnation.

Commonly the questions which the defence was seeking to ask by reference to 'explain or rebut' involved suggestions about the complainer's conduct which could undoubtedly have wider character innuendo: entertains men in room (002), took part in a sexual romp (003), masturbated (007), kissing and flirting (049), got pregnant at a party and lied to a doctor about her pregnancy (060), was not a virgin at 14 years old (080), had sex with someone other than her husband and is lying about it (156). Only two of these applications (002, 049) were unsuccessful.

The versatility of the phrase 'explain or rebut' was exploited to the full. There is clearly a thin line here between legitimate questioning and pure speculative questioning. In one successful application (060) the defence advocate asked merely to 'explore or rebut what the young lady may say in cross-examination'. It must be remembered that what are being allowed here are 'questions' as well as 'evidence' and there is no need for the defence to do more than 'put to' the complainer challenges or alternatives. The defence does not have to produce evidence from other witnesses or the accused to prove the alternative scenarios suggested by these questions. But, at the same time, the various professionals interviewed, generally agreed that the defence should have some evidential basis for their questions. One defence counsel, defence counsel 3, stated, for example, that it was not legitimate to ask a complainer about masturbation as an alternative cause of swelling round the vagina (as in case 007) without medical testimony to the effect that it was a plausible alternative. Such medical evidence had not been obtained by the defence counsel who successfully made an application to pursue this line of questioning. Although all interviewed agreed that purely speculative questions were not legitimate, some of the defence acknowledged that they would pursue such questions on occasions. One application was obviously rejected because it was speculative questioning. This was case 077 in which only the 'interests of justice' was cited.

The Same Occasion

Evidence may also be admitted if it occurred on the same occasion as the incident in the charge. The phrase 'the same occasion' has something of the elasticity of 'explain or rebut'.

In case 049, the defence wished to put to the complainer that she had been kissing with someone other than the accused earlier in the same evening, invoking the 'same occasion' exception. (This is the case involving kissing and flirting with the accused five or six weeks previously which was forced towards 'the same occasion' exception by prosecution arguments against 'explain or rebut'). The prosecution objected:

> That is not said to be sexual behaviour that goes to any sexual act ... If one considers a sequence of events in chronological order, one can have a group of people indulging in sexual behaviour and one person taking a girl from the room to indulge in unacceptable behaviour. There is nothing the accused knew about between [named witness and the complainer]. The Act provides no help other than to impress it is 'the same occasion'. There is only one reference [point] provided by Parliament and that is 'the subject matter of the charge'.

The application was refused outright.

Two cases fulfilled the *res gestae* definition of 'the same occasion'; that is they were part of a set of events clearly connected to the incident which was the subject matter of the charge. One was the rape case (158) in which the accused claimed he had consensual intercourse three times with the complainer on the day in question, with only the third being the subject matter of the charge. The other was case 124, a sodomy case, in which the defence argued that the complainer was offering sex for money.

There were also two cases which used the other possible logic for 'the same occasion' that is by referring to the timespan of the traces left by medical or forensic evidence. The application in both these cases also referred to 'explain or rebut'.

Case 134 (as described above) was constructed around the written report of the police surgeon. The doctor had recorded the complainer's last occasion of sexual intercourse as being with her boyfriend on the same date as that of the indicted incident. The defence wished to question the complainer on this matter in order to establish whether the semen reported in forensic evidence could have come from her boyfriend. The prosecution gave some support to this application and it was successful. In case 156 which involved an unidentified pubic hair, the 'same occasion' exception was cited (as well as incrimination). Although this was making an appeal to the logic of the same period of time as medical or forensic evidence, the judge, following the suggestion of the prosecution, allowed questions restricted to the previous week. In this case no specific other event could be cited as the alternative source. Rather the defence sought permission to try to establish what else might have been going on, on the same occasion.

One application (145) which cited 'the same occasion' fitted neither a *res gestae* nor a medically, or forensically relevant definition of 'the same occasion as the subject matter of the charge'. This was one of the cases in which the complainer and the accused were ex-partners. The defence made no claim that their sexual relationship had a current status but rather sought leave to investigate its history. This was granted without question under the 'same occasion'.

Incrimination

Incrimination was referred to in three cases. In none of these had a relevant special defence of incrimination been lodged in advance.

In case 156 involving an unidentified pubic hair, the issue of incrimination was raised. The prosecution asked the complainer a number of questions about her sexual history and for her explanation of this pubic hair. The defence then wished to make an application to cross-examine on this point and on the length of time she had been on the pill, as revealed by the medical report. Since there was strong forensic evidence of sexual intercourse between the accused and the complainer, and since the defence case was that consensual intercourse had taken place between the accused and the complainer, there was no straightforward possibility of suggesting some other person was responsible. It was as if the unidentified pubic hair was too 'good' an opportunity to miss and the defence was casting around for rationales for questioning on it. Incrimination was an alternative rationale to the issue of credibility. Despite also objecting, questioning on the grounds of credibility was given some support by the prosecution, not surprisingly since it was prosecution questions which opened up the issue of the pubic hair. The prosecution suggested restricting questions to establishing with which other person the complainer had sexual intercourse with in the previous week.

PROSECUTION: I have a slight difficulty here as I don't know what the position of the defence is. There is no intimation of special defence of incrimination having been lodged. If it be the case that it is to be suggested that intercourse took place with consent then one only can go into this matter regarding the question of credibility … If the defence position is that intercourse did take place consensually, then there is a question of credibility, but if the defence position is it did not take place there's no note of incrimination. I would not object if your lordship sets limits on questioning that she had intercourse with someone other than accused in the week prior, limited to ascertaining the source of the pubic hair.

DEFENCE: If it could be established that complainer had intercourse within 48 hours it is not so much a question of credibility but also incrimination.

The defence was allowed to pursue this line of questioning.

The Interests of Justice

The 'interests of justice' exception was more often cited together with other exceptions (and then often not as the leading exception) than on its own. When cited with other provisions, it was used as a fallback for evidence that could not be fitted in under the other two, or when debate produced awkward legal issues (such as the status of Crown productions). It was also used simply to assert the rightness of whatever argument was being made.

The applications that cited *only* 'the interests of justice' were not typically seeking to introduce evidence essentially different from other cases. With the exception of case 165, all of these applications had their counterpart in cases which also cited an alternative exception. For example, among the cases in which the complainer was an ex-partner of the accused (118, 145, 167), 'the same occasion' is cited in one and not in the others (all were successful). Case 105 is very similar to case 060, in that the complainer seems to have been 'set up' by the prosecution to make, in both cases, some rather ambiguous statement about her sexual history. The latter was described under 'explain or rebut' but in the former application only 'the interests of justice' was referred to. In this case the prosecution asked the complainer, 'Did you ever have sex with [the man with whom she stayed]?' To which she replied, 'Once, never again, too sore'. The defence wished to challenge this on the grounds that another prosecution witness (a relative of the man with whom she shared a flat, who had arrived on the night of the incident with the accused) claimed 'full intimate knowledge' of the complainer. Although the 'explain or rebut' exception was not cited, clearly it could have been used in the same way as in case 060.

Or, compare case 077 and case 080 which both seek to question young complainers about their virginity, on the grounds that the medical report shows the absence of an intact hymen; the latter also invokes 'explain or rebut' (and was successful), the former does not (and was refused). The telling difference could have been one of a number of factors. With respect to the persuasiveness of the arguments made in each case, which exceptions were cited probably made very little difference. Two other factors seem more important. One difference which probably was important concerned the fact that the evidential basis for suggesting the complainer was sexually experienced never became an issue in case 080 (the defence referred to information from an 'other source') but was flatly admitted as a problem in case 077. And the different prior questions of the prosecution were probably also significant. In cases 080 the prosecution had asked whether anything like this had ever happened before, which the defence construed as 'good character'. In case 077 the prosecution asked the complainer if and when her periods had started and what form of sanitary protection she used. The defence put their case as follows:

DEFENCE: The doctor narrates that the hymen is not intact and the vagina could only hold one finger. It could be consistent with use of a tampon. I want to put to the doctor that it could also be consistent with prior sexual intercourse. I want to inquire of the complainer if she has had sexual intercourse. I have no contrary evidence to lead if she replies in the negative.

JUDGE: Is this not therefore speculative questioning?

DEFENCE: No. I want to raise questions about the medical report. The answer to the questions may bear on credibility. I want to question the complainer about her knowledge of sexual matters. The defence is not going to be based on consent.

In case 080 the main plea was as follows:

The advocate depute has chosen to take from the complainer as part of her evidence that this was the first time it had happened to her. So she is being presented to the jury as a person who had never had sex before. But if my Lord looks at the medical report ... there is a conclusion, no hymen identified, no internal damage. Well, according to information from other sources, unless she falls within 5 per cent of females where the hymen is normally absent, her evidence of being a virgin is not borne out by the medical exam.

The judge expressed concern that the intention was to put the character of the girl at issue but allowed the application. The resulting questions were similar to case 007 in which there was medical evidence of virginity (hymen intact) and of injury to the vagina (swelling), and yet the defence similarly wished to ask about sexual experience or masturbation, seeking an alternative explanation to injuries.

In conclusion, it seems that in fact, and unexpectedly, the 'interests of justice' is being used interchangeably with the other exceptions. All of the exceptions have a certain elasticity which makes this possible, although, as expected, 'interests of justice' remains the most elastic of all. It seems also that, when used in combination with another exception, the chance of success may be slightly enhanced. In particular, the 'interests of justice' provides important backup when the defence seeks to embark on questioning relevant to the issue of *credibility*. The following example is taken from case 089 in which the leading exception cited was 'incrimination' backed by 'the interests of justice'. In this case the defence wished to ask the complainer whether she told her father (the accused) about an incident involving 'a boy in the park'. The advocate depute tried to turn reference to 'the interests of justice' against the defence argument but without success.

PROSECUTION: The defence seeks to found on the 'interests of jus-
                 tice'. The absence of clear notice [lodging a defence
                 of incrimination] from defence, and age of child,
                 must be taken into account in the interests of justice.
                 Section 141A [excluding sexual history and sexual
                 character evidence] does not allow questioning for
                 the sake of credibility unless covered by the excep-
                 tions.
DEFENCE: Credibility is extremely important in this case. The
                 complainer admitted that she was trying to cover up
                 for her grandfather.
JUDGE: It is a matter of considerable difficulty but of I am of
                 the view that the main thrust of objection ... must be
                 sustained but ... it is in the interests of justice that the
                 question is allowed that she said something different
                 to the father [accused] on another occasion. I am
                 upholding the substance of the objection but allowing
                 questioning on the basis of credibility, and allowing a
                 limited line of questioning.

CONCLUSION

Most applications contained requests for permission either to question
the complainer about sexual behaviour with the accused or with a specific
third party, or both. Explicit requests to attack the sexual character of the
complainer were rare and heard unfavourably by judges; applications
overtly seeking to show the complainer as 'not of good character in sexual
matters' always failed. In one case the judge explicitly referred to balancing the relevance of this evidence against its prejudicial effect. However,
evidence impugning the sexual character of the complainer was much
more common than this would suggest. This is because sexual history
evidence brought for other reasons, such as a test of credibility, had this
effect and because this was often done subtly through innuendo and
attacks on moral character.

The prosecution played an important role in the admission of sexual
history and sexual character evidence. In a number of cases it was
evidence that was led by the prosecution that became the starting point
for an application by the defence. Support from the prosecution helped
applications to introduce prohibited evidence to succeed. Prosecution
objections to applications were the exception rather than the rule. The
prosecution often did not play an active role in the application dialogue.

In terms of the use made of particular exceptions, the 'interests of
justice', which at the time when the new legislation was being discussed,
received so much adverse comment on the problems of discretion, was
cited most frequently. However it was usually cited in conjunction with
other exceptions. It was acting as a backup to the more specific exceptions, particularly when the evidence did not fit easily into any specific

subsection. Sometimes the defence advocate being short of justifications cited the 'interests of justice' because all else failed. Yet to a degree all exceptions were being used interchangeably. 'Explain or rebut', an exception not subject to any great criticism, in fact turned out to be almost equally 'discretionary'. The defence called for the right to rebut anything which could be interpreted as suggesting virginity, chastity or monogomy by the complainer. The defence even claimed the right to rebut aspects of Crown productions which were not put before the jury. Hence, the defence might seek to 'rebut' a medical report which contains details of pregancy or contraceptive history for medical reasons rather than because of relevance to the issues of the trial.

In applications to introduce evidence of sexual relations between the complainer and others (not the accused), the types of evidential issues that sexual history evidence was used to address were very rarely the sorts of situations which the pre-reform discussion expected to be relevant. There were only two examples of sexual history evidence introduced to contest the sources of evidence either establishing the accused's link to the alleged incident or establishing the incident had occurred. There was one application in which the sexual history evidence seemed to be essential to the narrative of events. Among the successful applications to query the complainer about sexual behaviour which did not involve the accused, these three cases were the only ones which fitted the envisaged examples discussed in the Scottish Law Commission Report.

In the next chapter, the application cases are re-analysed from the point of view of the issues involved – the various grounds of relevance.

NOTES

1. Lord Wilberforce in *Boardmann* [1975] AC at 443, speaking of rebuttals of 'innocent association', quoted by D. W. Elliott, 'The Young Person's Guide to Similar Fact Evidence' (1983) *Criminal Law Review*, p. 293.

7

Applications: Justifying Issues and Resulting Cross-Examination

This chapter describes the issues which the defence sought to address by introducing the prohibited evidence and on which the evidence was ultimately judged as relevant or irrelevant. Finally, some examples of extracts from cross-examinations are used to illustrate the outcome in terms of the questions which were put to the complainer.

ISSUE-BASED JUSTIFICATIONS

During the course of making an application, as well as citing the relevant exceptions, the defence may indicate the relevance of the evidence they are seeking to introduce to the issues in the trial. If this is not done spontaneously by the defence, this information may be requested by the judge or the prosecution. The exceptions are cases in which discussion remains focused on whether the wording of the subsection applies and cases in which the proposed questioning is regarded as self-evidently relevant (for example, when the defence seeks to investigate the past sexual history of a complainer who is an ex-partner of the accused). The following section summarises the issues cited as the rationale for introducing the prohibited evidence and compares these to the exceptions envisaged by the reformers when drafting the legislation. This completes the picture of the arguments given during the application for introducing sexual history and sexual character evidence. This section also moves beyond the application dialogue to its consequences in terms of questions actually put to the complainer in cross-examination.

Contested Sources/Identity

One circumstance envisaged by law reformers as necessitating the admission of sexual history evidence was if it provided an alternative explanation of evidence which otherwise linked the accused to the crime. If sexual history evidence could provide an alternative source of such evidence – injuries, semen, pregnancy, sexual disease, for example – then it is legitimate and should be allowed (see Chapter 3). Only two of the 20 applications were for this purpose, and even these are problematic in some respects. A number of other applications did focus on medical or forensic evidence but were trying to cast doubt on or redeploy this evidence for some other purpose.

In the most 'straight forward' case (134), an attempted rape case, the defence sought to question the complainer about the time of last intercourse with her boyfriend in order to provide an alternative explanation for the forensic evidence of semen. However, for much of the trial the defence story was one of consent followed by a late change of mind. A defence of consent makes finding an alternative source of sperm a less central issue. The defence advocate appeared to be keeping a number of contradictory lines of defence in play. In the witness box, however, the accused did deny trying to have sexual intercourse with the complainer despite eyewitness evidence to the contrary.

In the other 'straight forward' case of disputing prosecution evidence (007), the defence wished to seek an alternative source to the medical finding of swelling round the vagina. He had no alternative to point to, but wished to question the complainer about other forms of genital activity, despite medical evidence of virginity. In this case (007), the complainer was 15 and the defence advocate portrayed her as a semi-delinquent 'bad girl' beyond the control of her mother. The questions consequent on the application were fitted into this general approach.

DEFENCE: Were you involved with any boy apart from [the accused]?
COMPLAINER: No.
DEFENCE: Did you insert anything into your private parts?
COMPLAINER: No.

[And later]

DEFENCE: Do you know what masturbation is?
COMPLAINER: Yes.
DEFENCE: Were you in the habit of masturbating last year in July?
COMPLAINER: No.

In itself this exchange may not seem particularly prejudicial to the outcome of the case. However, a great many non-sexual bad character questions were asked and cumulatively they created an impression of the 'bad girl' liable to be engaged in sexual experimentation. 'Were you injecting drugs?' 'Do you have a tattoo?' 'Did you tell your mother?' 'Was she happy for you to be tattooed?' 'Have you been glue sniffing?' 'Was there a time when you ran away from home?' The prosecution objected to the first question in this series about injecting drugs. This resulted in the judge telling the complainer that she could decline to answer. The defence asked the rest of the questions uninterrupted. It should be noted that questions about sexual behaviour with others often have 'bad character' connotations.

Situation-Relevance

Sexual history is sometimes introduced as being essential simply to understand the basic narrative of events. This only came up in one of the observed applications (165) (introduced under 'in the interests of justice'); the defence wished to ask the complainer about her history as an incest victim. The defence story was that the accused claimed he and she had become intimate when she told him about the incest, and she took off her clothing to show him the scars (the nature of the scars never became clear). There was no objection and the application was successful.

Consent

The Scottish Law Commission envisaged that sexual behaviour between the complainer and the accused would 'normally be relevant' unless it was an event in the distant past. Although not stating this explicitly, they apparently viewed recent sexual relations with the accused as relevant to consent. The reformers also envisaged sexual relations with someone other than the accused as sometimes being relevant to a defence of mistaken-belief-in-consent, and a 'sexual orgy' was specifically mentioned as such a circumstance. Otherwise their aim was to outlaw any suggestion that because a complainer had had sex with A or B she consented to C.

For 16 of the 20 application cases, consent was the crux of the defence case. (The exceptions were case 089 which involved a defence of incrimination, case 077 in which the defence was that no attempt at sexual intercourse had taken place, and case 172 which involved incest and the defence was that the complainers had fabricated the incidents. Case 124 was also technically an exception since the charges were sodomy and homosexual offences involving complainers under 21, but consent was nevertheless suggested by the defence.) This did not mean that the issue of consent necessarily dominated the application dialogue; it was often left implicit and other issues were to the fore. But relevance to consent – rather than the words of the statute – was a key test in a number of cases. As one judge stated 'this goes right to the root of the matter, whether [it is an] act of rape or consensual' (060).

In general, practically any sexual conduct with the accused was regarded in the application dialogue as being relevant to consent. The only exception was alleged 'kissing and flirting' six weeks previously (049). Here the prosecution argued that this must be rejected, else 'every casual cuddle at a party would give licence to rape at a future date' and the judge appeared to accept this as he refused the application. Cases where the accused was a husband (167), an ex-lover or ex-husband (118, 145), apparently created a totally unproblematic presumption of consent (or at least an obvious counter to a presumption of non-consent). In the latter two cases the fact of a previous sexual relationship was led by the advocate depute and there was no objection from the prosecution or the judge to further questioning by the defence.

Most frequently, questions about prior sexual activity with the accused were used to suggest that the complainer had, in effect, indicated her consent to the accused at some point before the incident. This is a crucial presumption. In the course of the cross-examination following an application, the allegation of past sexual intercourse between the complainer and the accused often took its place as the culmination of many other ways of trying to establish a friendly and, by presumption, therefore, a likely-to-be-consenting relationship between the complainer and accused. In case 060, for example, the defence having early on underlined the fact that the complainer had known the accused for some time, and had borrowed his bike and his gloves on the evening in question, asked the following:

DEFENCE:	How did your pants come down?
COMPLAINER:	They came down with my trousers.
DEFENCE :	Did you try and pull his clothes?
COMPLAINER:	No.
DEFENCE:	Did you try and pull him off you?
COMPLAINER:	Aye.
DEFENCE:	Was it not a situation where you were kissing and cuddling?
COMPLAINER:	No.
DEFENCE:	And that he then wanted to go further and you didn't.
COMPLAINER:	No.
DEFENCE:	So everything of a sexual nature was against your will?
COMPLAINER:	Yes.
DEFENCE:	And hateful to you?
COMPLAINER:	Yes.
DEFENCE:	Was it not a situation where you were happy to go to a certain point?
COMPLAINER:	I don't understand. I already told you [no].
DEFENCE:	Was it not true that when you saw the lady [a passerby] you said, 'Here's my ma's pal', and told him to get up?
COMPLAINER:	No.
DEFENCE:	Were you worried that this friend of your mother would tell your mother.
COMPLAINER:	No.
DEFENCE:	You were further distressed about going home … with very obvious signs of having had sex with a boy?
COMPLAINER:	Not my fault, he came all over my clothes.
DEFENCE:	You've told us sperm was all over your clothes. That you had love bites. That you had lost money. And that [accused] was not pleasant on the way home on bike.
COMPLAINER:	Yes.
DEFENCE:	One further matter. Had [accused] ever been to your house?

COMPLAINER: Before? No.
DEFENCE: Is it not true that he came to your house and had
              sexual intercourse with you with your consent as on
              the current occasion?
COMPLAINER: Not on either occasion.

The questions about the alleged consensual intercourse prior to the incident do not overstep the permission to investigate this area. Also, none of the above questions would be regarded as irrelevant by many of the interviewees. But, in combination with many other questions designed to impugn the complainer's character, the potential for suggesting consent and a motive for false allegation is heightened. In combination, also, they provide a considerable ordeal for the complainer. (In this case a motive for false allegation was also suggested by noting that the complainer had tried to attribute a subsequent pregnancy to the alleged rape when seeking an abortion. Again questioning in this area was legitimate as it was part of the successful application. No dates were specified or requested in order to support the implied temporal connection between making the rape allegation to the police and pursuing the abortion. If scrutinised, the temporal connection might have been difficult to sustain since the complainer was seeking an abortion two and a half months after the incident that was the subject matter of the charge.)

In some cases the defence put even more detailed step-by-step questions regarding the defence version of events to the complainer, simultaneously providing an ordeal for the complainer and unfolding a version of the defence story to the jury which may be convincing by its very detail (see also Chapter 11).

Examples of questioning designed to show that the complainer was interested in the accused and encouraged him to have sex with her are not confined to successful applications. Questions were asked about 'sexually interested' behaviour *without an application*. This is discussed in Chapter 9 but, among the 20 cases under consideration in this chapter, it was most extreme in a case in which the application had been refused. In case 049 the application to introduce past sexual history evidence – kissing and flirting with the accused five or six weeks before and kissing another man the night before – was refused. The defence nevertheless did manage to construct other indicators of consent and, through questions about sexually provocative behaviour, to play up the presumption of a likely-to-be-consenting relationship.

DEFENCE: Do you remember admiring the jacket [the accused]
              was wearing and dancing around the room in it, trying
              it on? Had you said to [the accused and his wife] 'Why
              don't I go out with you [the accused] and leave [ac-
              cused's wife] here.'

[And in the same vein]

DEFENCE: Even before the others had gone you were making sexual overtures to [the accused]. And thereafter you and [the accused] had sexual intercourse throughout the night, and you felt guilty thereafter. '

As noted earlier, it was perhaps surprising to find how questions concerning sexual behaviour between the complainer and someone other than the accused were also allowed. In the majority of these cases credibility is the explicit issue, but, in some, the alleged sexual behaviour with someone other than the accused is sought to show some disposition to consent *on the occasion* of the offence. One of these (003) involved multiple accused. The others involved allegations which seemed to be designed to suggest that the complainer was 'that kind of woman': casual sex with an acquaintance of the accused's the night before (052), and the kissing with a named other the night before (049). Neither of these was successful.

So far as evidence concerning prior sexual relations between the complainer and accused were concerned, the successful appeals to consent were largely of the sort anticipated by the reformers, except that neither prosecution nor judge routinely tried to establish how long had lapsed since a past relationship between the accused and the complainer. Hence there was no real safeguard against 'a chance encounter many years before' which the Scottish Law Commission cited as an inappropriate use of such evidence. However, in the two cases where the defence tried to argue that consent with A or B indicated consent with C, this was not successful (although it should be noted that the defence succeeded in suggesting such a predisposition to consent in other ways). No application was made on the grounds that the evidence was relevant to belief-in-consent.

Mistaken-Belief-in-Consent

It is important to reiterate the negative finding that mistaken-belief-in-consent was never an issue argued by defence. In none of the cases introducing or seeking to introduce sexual behaviour between the complainer and someone other than the accused, was it being suggested that because the accused knew about this he mistakenly believed the woman consented. Rather it was simply being argued that the woman did in fact consent. As was noted in the previous chapter, in only one case (003) was it alleged that the accused knew about a specific previous sexual incident, but he was not questioned on any belief formed on this basis. The defence did seek to introduce evidence of 'boasting of sexual conquests' in case 060 but this was to show consent rather than belief-in-consent and it was unsuccessful. In interviews with the defence, they were generally of the opinion that consent was more straightforward to argue than mistaken-belief-in-consent and this was explained in detail by one interviewee (see Chapter 8). However, in case 060 and in one other case 167 the *judge* raised the possibility of a defence of belief-in-consent in his summing up at the end.

> JUDGE: Had she had intercourse with the accused the week before? This must put things in a different light. The accused maintains she was leading him on, having had sex the week before. Did the accused force himself upon the complainer or did she consent? You are here to consider if the accused could honestly hold that belief. (060)
>
> JUDGE: There is no reason why a husband should assume his wife is not consenting to intercourse unless she makes it abundantly clear to him that she is refusing consent. Rape must be committed with intent. The accused must know he is doing wrong. If an accused has an honest and genuine belief that a woman is consenting then no crime is committed. (167)

The judicial view expressed in these cases and accepted generally where permission was granted to investigate past relations between the complainer and the accused is that consent in the past means a man can subsequently take consent for granted subsequently unless he meets with what he recognises as resistance. Clearly this is a view which is highly contentious.

Credibility

The issue of credibility was raised explicitly in the application dialogue even more often than consent. It was the most explicit issue in the majority of applications to introduce sexual behaviour with others (060, 077, 080, 089, 092, 105, 118, 156, 172). However, the ways in which sexual history evidence was used to question the credibility of the complainer almost always introduced some implication of consent. Apart from the issue of 'character', the use of sexual evidence in relation to credibility was not discussed by the Scottish Law Commission Report. Credibility was also the substance of an unsuccessful amendment when the legislation passed through Parliament (see Chapter 3). It appears that credibility was used by the defence in ways largely unanticipated – or at least not discussed – by the reformers to introduce the type of evidence they aimed to exclude.

Three applications which referred to credibility were unsuccessful. In case 092, the defence wished to raise the complainer's history of depression and particularly wished to put to her that she had deliberately gone out and got pregnant after the rape. He claimed that this was relevant to her credibility (more properly, reliability) as it demonstrated general instability at the time. The prosecution objected strongly, pointing out that the pregnancy was three months subsequent to the alleged rape, and the application was quashed. Case 077 involved seeking to use the absence of a hymen revealed in the medical report to ask the complainer about past sexual experience (the defence in this case was not one of consent). In case 172 the defence wished to demonstrate that one complainer was sexually experienced both as a child and in later years as part of an attempt to establish that she was capable of fabricating the charges of incest. These applications were not granted but appeals to credibility which seemed no more or less plausible were often successful.

One common use of credibility was to test the consistency of the complainer's statements about her sexual experience. It should be noted that in the following examples this was not always the first argument of relevance introduced by the defence during the application but it was the one finally settled on as the basis for admitting the evidence. These examples discussed below were cases in which the defence successfully applied to introduce questions along these lines. One example is in case 156 when the defence wished to use the unidentified pubic hair which was found in forensic analysis to challenge the complainer's account of monogamy as a claim to 'good character'.

In case 089, the defence asked the complainer 'Apart from your father and grandfather, has anyone else ever touched you in a sexual way? ... Have you ever told your father that someone else has?' Forced into an application by the prosecution's objections, as noted above, the defence said that he wished to question the complainer about whether she had told her father (the accused) that she had also been molested by someone else, claiming (among other things) that if she gave a different answer in court (from the earlier statement the accused would say she made to him) it would be relevant to credibility. The judge seemed supportive of the credibility argument, responding that he could see that 'might be relevant to the credibility of the witness if shown that [she] gives a different answer now'. Thus, even though the judge in fact rejected the other claims to relevance, this was nonetheless allowed. The judge stated: '... not clear what difference yet another person would make. Could only go to credibility.' This is credibility in relation to consistency. The justification was to see if the complainer contradicted herself. This case also illustrates quite clearly a lack of concern to weigh the probative value of the proposed defence questioning in deciding its admissibility. The questioning may have had some relevance to credibility but its probative value is surely slight.

Another example is in case 105; the defence wished to ask the complainer about past sexual relations with a particular defence witness because it would counter her suggestion that she was celibate which was taken as a claim to 'good character'. Here it was doubtful whether the complainer had even made such a suggestion. The entire defence argument rested on interpreting the following exchange:

PROSECUTION: Did you ever have sex with [the man with whom she shared a house]?
COMPLAINER: Once. Never again. Too sore.

This illustrates the eagerness of the defence to attribute good character constructions to the prosecution as a 'specious manner of outflanking the exclusionary rule' (see earlier discussion under 'explain or rebut' on pp. 77–9).

Testing consistency-credibility has nothing to do with consent as such. Yet it seemed more than fortuitous that consistency should be challenged in relation to sexual matters. The dangers of conflation are obvious. A jury might think that sexual matters are being allowed as evidence because of their relevance to the issue of consent. Yet the question of prejudicing the outcome of the trial in this way was not discussed during the dialogue about the admissibility of this type of credibility evidence. Thus, even in case 080 cited earlier, to show judicial concern with evidence that a complainer was 'not of good character in sexual matters', relevance to credibility ultimately wins out. A fuller extract of the exchange is given from our notes here:

JUDGE: ... can you take me back to s. 141A (1) (*a*), are you interested in that?
DEFENCE: Probably a mixture of (*a*) and (*c*), but I'm not putting character at issue. It is just a question regarding the medical report.
JUDGE: But you will be referring to her character?
DEFENCE: I think it probably falls under (*c*).
JUDGE: The girl may use an instrument to engage in masturbation.
DEFENCE: Well, maybe she has an explanation. The accused is not in a position to say, just to challenge assumption ...
JUDGE: What I really need to know is what line of questioning you intend to engage in.
DEFENCE: To put the findings of the medical report that she does not have a hymen and that that is indicative of sexual interference.

[After inaudible deliberations]

JUDGE: I shall allow the question in because, as put to me by counsel, as necessary or proper to clarify the witness's answer in examination-in-chief insofar as she said, 'This is the first time anything like this ever happened to me.' And also to explore matters in relation to production 7, the medical report.

The judge allowed the questioning about the absence of hymen as a test of the complainer's credibility. The defence had argued that they were not introducing the evidence to attack her character and reiterated that the complainer's evidence was not borne out by the medical evidence. This is how it came out.

DEFENCE: You said to the advocate depute that this was the first time anything like this had happened to you. What does this mean?

COMPLAINER: It means I never had sexual intercourse before.

DEFENCE: In biology classes you were told about the hymen?

COMPLAINER: Yes.

DEFENCE: Would it surprise you to know there are no signs of a hymen in you?

COMPLAINER: What do you mean? What's 'hymen'?

DEFENCE: It means you were not a virgin at the time.

The judge intervened saying that this was not the question.

DEFENCE: What do you say to that?

COMPLAINER: It's a lie.

DEFENCE: So you say until then you never had a penis inside you?

COMPLAINER: No.

DEFENCE: Or anything else?

COMPLAINER: No.

DEFENCE: And you say that on your oath?

COMPLAINER: Yes.

[The defence goes on to ask if she may have had a vaginal discharge and then if she has ever seen 'that sort of thing on films or videos ... Or have you heard talk?']

DEFENCE: You are just making this up from those things.

COMPLAINER: No.

DEFENCE: To provide an explanation of why you were not a virgin at the time.

COMPLAINER: No.

Clearly some of this questioning is putting evidence to the complainer which apparently contradicts her statement and hence is testing her consistency. But the defence is also developing a *motive* for false allegation. Arguably some of the questioning also strays into matters of bad character. These lines of questioning could not have been anticipated by what the defence advocate said in the application dialogue.

The danger of conflation between credibility and consent is associated particularly with the use of 'bad sexual character' evidence. Explicit use of 'bad sexual character' evidence to attack the complainer's credibility was not common. The defence in case 052 made the link between credibility and consent during the application. He wished to introduce a number of items of sexual history and character evidence and said 'I have enumerated the line I would propose on the basis that defence is one of consent. The question of credibility is important. From the complainer's evidence, she will deny consent and the question of her credibility in relation to the denial is for the jury.' What the defence sought to introduce was a battery of evidence, much of it was to show that the complainer was 'not of good character in sexual matters' including indulging in casual sex, possessing exotic underwear, wearing a mini-skirt, wearing suspenders and being of flirtatious nature. Some of these items were also linked to a defence of consent through alleged sexually provocative behaviour towards the accused – allegedly showing him her suspender marks, trying on clothes in front of him and asking his opinion and enjoying his obscene phone calls. In addition, the defence also wished to question the complainer about alleged previous sexual intercourse with the accused and sexual relations with another witness, and it was the former which the judge allowed. However, as noted earlier, the prosecution did not object to some of the character evidence. Much of it was in fact introduced.

In case 002, the judge referred to the danger of the conflation of credibility and consent when disallowing questions designed to show that the complainer frequently entertained black men in her room. This is the only case in which this issue of prejudicial effect was explicitly addressed. Yet the defence ultimately was allowed to put questions about entertaining men, in order to test the complainer's consistency, by contradicting a specific statement she made about whom she signed into her building. However, the tack ultimately adopted in the first application was that it showed she was 'not of good character' which was supposedly relevant to credibility. The defence explicitly denied trying to show promiscuity. The judge asked if the intention was to suggest that 'engaging in this kind of conduct makes it more likely that she is lying?' To which the defence answered, 'yes'.

> JUDGE: This must be for the purpose of demonstrating that the witness is a liar, not that she consented to the act in question. You have to satisfy me that it is in the interests of justice to attack the person's credibility. It is likely to be extremely prejudicial. The jury might think it demonstrates that she consented on this question. (002)

The other main credibility issue was whether there was any motive for false allegation. Here credibility and consent are necessarily bound up. In case 060, medical notes of a hospital gynaecologist revealed that the complainer had initially attributed a later pregnancy to the alleged rape, but then had said it was the result of a later incident which had occurred when she got drunk at a party. The defence claimed that this was relevant to credibility as it showed a motive for sticking to a false allegation although it is not clear that the dates involved supported this claim (and also inconsistency in her statements to the doctor). The defence was allowed to pursue this line of questioning. In this case, the defence intention of putting to the complainer a possible motive for false allegation was made clear during the application, when questions about the absence of a hymen led into the suggestion that the complainer made allegations of rape in order to explain the lack of virginity. However, a motive for false allegation was more often developed through defence questioning without being prefigured in the actual application, as in case 080.

In a number of other cases, issues of credibility were raised in a variety of overlapping ways. Sometimes this occurred in the application itself but more commonly complexities emerged during the actual cross-examination – perhaps with the defence advocate referring in the first instance to the need to test the consistency of the complainer, but then in the actual cross-examination developing a motive for false allegation and also casting doubt on the character of the complainer.

In case 118, the defence wished to bring a witness to say that the complainer had had a sexual relationship with him. The defence partly justified this by arguing that she had 'behaved in a similar manner' with this man. The claimed similarity was an alleged pattern of feigning pregnancy when the man broke off the relationship. It became clear that the defence was trying to characterise the complainer as a woman who became desperate and was liable to tell lies when a relationship ended. No questions were asked by the judge or prosecution about how distant in time this previous sexual relationship was, and, while the complainer was questioned about her relationship with this defence witness, he was not subsequently called to give evidence. This was also a case in which sexual history evidence was introduced following appeals to credibility. The defence claimed an understanding that the complainer would maintain that the accused was the first person with whom she had had sexual relations, and hence this was an issue of consistency (although at the time of application no such claim had been made by the complainer nor was such a claim made by her). Implicitly the defence was also establishing a tendency on the part of the complainer to make false allegations against ex-lovers. There was no objection to these lines of argument from the prosecution, and the judge appeared to accept both lines of reasoning in granting the application. The questioning developed as follows:

DEFENCE: About your relationship with [the accused] ... When did you start going out with him?
COMPLAINER: Beginning of August.
DEFENCE: When did you first have sexual relations with him?
COMPLAINER: About two or three weeks after I first met him.
DEFENCE: Not sooner than that?

COMPLAINER: No.
DEFENCE: Did you have sex on a regular basis?
COMPLAINER: About four or five times.
DEFENCE: Was he the first person with whom you had sex?

[At this stage the prosecution objected saying that, the defence should name the specific person being alluded to.]

DEFENCE: Do you know [a defence witness]?
COMPLAINER: Yes.
DEFENCE: Did you have a sexual relationship with him?
COMPLAINER: Yes.
DEFENCE: When was this relationship?
COMPLAINER: About seven years ago.
DEFENCE: Who terminated it?
COMPLAINER: We just stopped going out together.
DEFENCE: Did you tell him at the end of relationship that you were pregnant?
COMPLAINER: No.
DEFENCE: Are you quite sure?
COMPLAINER: Yes.
DEFENCE: Were you not upset and told him you were pregnant to hang on to him?
COMPLAINER: No.
DEFENCE: Is he lying if he says you did?
COMPLAINER: Yes.
DEFENCE: When was the last time you had sexual relations with him before the relationship terminated?

None of the actual questioning was investigating the complainer's consistency. As in a number of other cases the defence wished to establish how soon after knowing somebody the complainer had sexual intercourse with them. This could well be classified as questioning about her character. Most of the questioning however was directed towards the defence story of motive for false allegation and suggesting a pattern of conduct which explained the current allegation. The next day the defence continued with a longer line of questions about pestering both the accused and this witness when the complainer's relationship with them terminated. The defence also introduced questions about her state and actions when her relationship finished with her ex-fiancé suggesting she took an overdose because this relationship ended.

Attacks on the complainer's consistency blur in practice into attacks on the complainer's character, often also suggesting a predisposition to consent. A number of the cases involved examples of this in cross-examination which could not have been anticipated by what was specified in the application. Usually, this went unchecked by either the prosecution or the judge.

These combinations and something of the unexpected can be illustrated conveniently by an example which is already familiar to the reader. In case 156 the defence sought permission not only to cross-examine the complainer about the unidentified pubic hair itemised in the forensic report (neither her husband's nor the accused's), but also about the fact that she was on the pill, which had been stated in the medical report. In the case of both pieces of evidence, the defence, having first tried a few alternatives, argued that the complainer 'sets herself up' as only having sex with her husband but that this picture of herself was inconsistent with these pieces of evidence. Because the defence successfully attributed a 'good character' construction to the prosecution, claim was laid for the right to attack the character of the complainer through introducing questions regarding the pubic hair and the fact that she was on the pill. However, again, the actual questioning took a number of yet additional lines, introducing a motive for false allegation. For the sake of brevity in this instance only the questions are presented.

The defence began with a set of questions about the complainer's relationship with her boyfriend , now her husband, at the time of the incident. These had not been intimated in the application.

DEFENCE: When did you meet your husband?
          When start going out with him?
          Had you been out with him before?
          And you had intercourse with him then?
          And he was not your fiancé?

[This line of questioning was repeated more dramatically after dealing with other issues.]

DEFENCE: Were you attracted to the man who later became your
          husband?
          Instantly?
          Is that why you had intercourse with him the first night
          you went out with him?

As well as general questions about sex, the defence advocate asked if she had had sex with a male friend with whom she spent some time on the evening of the incident. Again permission for this specific line of questioning was not sought in the application. Finally he suggested a motive for false allegation. Again only the sequence of questions is presented.

DEFENCE: Did you have intercourse with anyone else within a week
          or two of this incident?
          You went with this friend; did you have intercourse with
          him?
          Are you sure?

[He went on to ask about the pill and returns to this theme with this sequence:]

DEFENCE: Is it not the case that when you told the police you'd had sex with another man that was the truth?
You'd seen [the friend], had you not, the previous evening?
Had you had sex with anyone the previous evening?
Why go on the pill?
Your evidence to the jury is that your sexual experience before this occasion was only with [husband]
And even if pubic hair was found, you had not had sex with anyone else?
Is that what you told your husband?
Isn't that what you told your husband, so you can't tell him anything else?
It wouldn't do for it to be anything else would it?

CONCLUSION

The permitted use of sexual history evidence is noteworthy in a number of respects. As anticipated in the pre-reform discussion by the Scottish Law Commission, sexual behaviour between the complainer and the accused was normally regarded as relevant. But the taken-for-granted way in which this happened is problematic. Agreement in this area meant that the precise nature of the relevance was often left implicit and no limits were placed on questioning. For example there was no routine attempt to place restictions on how far back in time questioning could go.

Questions concerning sexual behaviour between the complainer and a third party were more debated in application and were often successfully presented by the defence as relevant to credibility. The defence typically used lines of argument that had not been discussed at the time of the reform. The defence took every opportunity to present questions to the complainer, concerning her sexual history, as a test of her consistency or truthfulness as a witness and this strategy was often successful. It is worth reiterating that the types of evidential issues that sexual history evidence was used to address were very rarely the sorts of situations which the pre-reform discussion expected to be relevant. Among the successful applications to query the complainer about sexual behaviour which did not involve the accused, there were only three cases which fitted the envisaged examples discussed in the Scottish Law Commission Report.

Issues of credibility were raised under all the exceptions but particularly through 'explain or rebut' and the 'interests of justice'. They came up under 'explain or rebut' in cases where this was used to bring evidence and to contradict the complainer's testimony concerning her relationship with the accused or her sexual experience, and more loosely, as a licence to rebut the complainer's credibility by any fact or allegation that could be gleaned from the prosecution for this purpose, even when it was in no sense central to the incident at issue. The defence used questions about the complainer's sexual history to develop arguments about the complainer's motive for making a false allegation in ways which were rarely specified in the application.

Mistaken-belief-in-consent, reasonable or merely honest, is *not* a major issue in the Scottish courtroom. This is despite the furore around cases in which this defence was permitted – the case of *Morgan*[1] in England and Wales and *Meek*[2] in Scotland – and the fear that the legal recognition of honest belief was a 'rapist's charter'. As noted above, this is regarded as a more difficult defence. The accused must go into the witness box – having already acknowledged that the woman did not consent – and try to convince the jury that he nonetheless misread the signals. It is far easier to claim consent on the part of the woman. It was also suggested during the interviews that the accused man rarely thinks of this defence. The rarity of mistaken-belief defence (there were none in the observed cases) may also be connected to the fact that only one of the application cases observed was a group event. However, Scottish judges do sometimes put the possibility of this defence before the jury and this was done in the judicial summing up in two application cases. This is surprising in that this defence is usually understood to require some testing of what the accused's belief *actually* was, which requires questioning him on the subject.

The relevance of the proposed evidence to the trial issues was not always revealed by the application dialogue. Sometimes discussion focused exclusively on which was the technically correct subsection to use, thus neglecting to discuss the issues in the case. The 'interests of justice' was sometimes simply asserted and no mapping out of relevance was offered or demanded. This occurred when shared presumptions allowed relevance to be treated as self-evident (as is the case with reference to sexual history evidence when the complainer and accused have been married). Given that exceptions can be used interchangeably, one main implication is that the basis for assessing the admissibility of evidence must be its relevance rather than the skill in manipulating discretionary provisions. However, relevance was not stringently investigated during all applications. Moreover, the next chapter reveals a range of opinions and contradictory views concerning the relevance of sexual history evidence among legal practitioners. So any legal formulation which made general appeal to relevance might result in uneven practice.

As stated in the previous chapter, the prosecution played an important role in the admission of sexual history and sexual character evidence. In Chapter 6 it was noted that in a number of cases it was evidence led by the prosecution that became the starting point for an application and that prosecution objections to applications were the exception rather than the rule. Nor did the prosecution always object to questioning, which could not have been anticipated as flowing from the case put by the defence during the application. Prosecutors who were interviewed were divided on whether they could legitimately challenge defence questions once an application has been allowed and, while some prosecutors were acutely aware of their power to influence the success or failure of an application, others felt that the correct stance during the application dialogue was that of a neutral observer (see Chapter 9).

Comparison with England

How far does the Scottish legislation in practice compare with the English experience? Adler's study[3] of the working of section 2 of the 1976 Sexual Offences (Amendment) Act provides the basis for constructing a comparison. However, given the wider scope of the Scottish legislation, it is necessary to select a 'subsample' involving only cases concerning rape and rape-related offences,[4] and to consider only evidence concerning the complainer and persons other than the accused. This includes evidence about specific individuals or sexual character, allegations of prostitution, or doubts raised about a complainer's previous virginity.

There are some similarities in the typical rape-offence case in the Scottish and English courts. As in Adler's study, the research showed that, in many cases, additional or alternative charges are involved: on the one hand, age-of-consent charges (as alternatives); on the other hand, non-sexual assault charges (as alternatives or additions), and also additional charges such as breach of the peace and malicious damage.

One striking difference from the results of Adler's study is the number of cases with co-accused. She found that 43 per cent of the accused were charged together with others and that the majority of these multiple rapes involved three or more co-accused. For the most part these accused chose to plead 'not guilty' and it was in these trials, too, that applications were most common. In Scotland, cases with co-accused are very rare.

In Adler's study, 18 out of the 45 contested rape-offence trials (40 per cent, on behalf of 29 accuseds) involved applications, three-quarters of which were successful. In the Scottish study 15 of the 72 rape-offence trials (20 per cent) involved applications about sexual conduct of the same sort covered by the English legislation, that is excluding applications to introduce sexual history between the complainer and accused. Of these, 12 were at least partially successful. This gives a success rate of 80 per cent. In other words, while Scottish cases show a slightly higher success rate of applications, they occur in only half as many rape-offence trials as in England. (However it should also be noted that the rate of applications increased over the period of the Scottish research and it may be that this trend will continue.)

A lower rate of applications suggest that the Scottish legislation is having a stronger impact in screening out sexual history and character evidence than its (much criticised) English equivalent. However, within this same comparative 'subsample', 12 additional cases (one sixth of the total) involved similar third-party or sexual character evidence used *without* application. Thus, putting together the (12) cases with officially admitted evidence and those (12) where it was used unofficially, comparable sexual evidence was used in one third (33 per cent) of the Scottish cases. (Adler does not present figures for such non-authorised evidence in the English courts, although she does note its occurrence and also the wide range of judicial response from severe reprimand to total silence. She too comments on the widespread use of innuendo, indirect evidence and suggestion.)

Turning now to the grounds of application, there appears to be one striking difference between English and Scottish patterns. According to Adler, most of these applications involved the defence successfully arguing that the evidence was relevant to consent. This included evidence, for example that a 17-year-old girl was not a virgin and, in other cases, evidence concerning past sexual relations with black men or older men. By contrast, in the Scottish courts such direct linkages with consent were rarely attempted and never succeeded. Indeed, in a comparable case involving a black accused, the judge ruled that to admit such evidence would be highly prejudicial and positively contrary to the interests of justice. However, the contrast looks less strong when put in the context of the high use and success rate of credibility as a ground of relevance, especially given the strong inferences that were often made or implied with consent. In the bulk of successful applications involving third-party evidence, the defence was consent, and in six out of 15, the evidence also admitted evidence of past sexual relations with the accused. (In the English cases, on Adler's account, credibility was correspondingly not a significant ground of application.)

A further difference between the two jurisdictions is that in Scotland, far more frequently than in England, it appears that defence counsel attempt to introduce sexual history evidence to suggest some other source of semen or injury. However, the end picture is much the same, as such attempts usually fail unless represented as issues of complainers' credibility.

Mistaken-belief defences are apparently virtually a non-issue in both jurisdictions, and this is particularly surprising in England and Wales given the very high number of cases with co-accused. (In Adler's study, the 50 cases had a total of 80 accused.)

One final difference is worth noting. Adler noted the very disturbing phenomenon that occasionally judges would be the ones to ask the complainer probing questions about their sexual lives. As mentioned earlier, this finding caused some concern that the Scottish legislation should specifically bar judges from this practice, which it does not do. In fact, though, we found very few instances of judges in the Scottish courts asking such questions.

NOTES

1. This English case was discussed in Chapter 1. *Morgan* validated for the first time the defence that a man had not committed rape if he genuinely believed the woman was consenting at the time, even if it was unreasonable to have believed this.
2. *Meek* was also discussed in Chapter 1. This was the case which in 1982 inscribed the principles of *Morgan* (with some reservations) in Scots law.
3. Z. Adler *Rape on Trial*, (London and New York: Routledge and Kegan Paul, 1987).
4. Rape offences include rape, attempted rape, and assault with intent to rape.

8

Inclusion and Exclusion of Prohibited Evidence: Views of Practitioners

This chapter is based on interviews with judges, sheriffs, advocates, depute, procurators fiscal, defence counsel and defence lawyers. Interviewees were asked for their views on when sexual history and sexual character evidence was relevant and should be allowed. They were asked directly about the relevance of such evidence to the credibility of complainers as witnesses and to their consent in the sexual acts which were the subject matter of the charge – issues commonly invoked as the reason to introduce such evidence. This was done through specific questions, including taking the interviewee through the exclusionary clauses, breaking down sexual history evidence into sexual relations between the complainer and the accused, and sexual relations between the complainer and others. A series of detailed questions were asked about the exception clauses of the legislation and the appropriate gauge of admissibility during applications to introduce prohibited evidence. In doing so, reactions were sought to examples, taken from court observation, of the types of evidence that defence had applied to introduce and the sorts of arguments made in the application.

All interviewees stressed that generally the main test of admissibility of evidence had to be its relevance to the issues of the trial. Clearly the legislation as such does not require relevance to be taken into account, yet, as noted in the last two chapters on applications, judges usually, although not always, ask the defence to explain the putative relevance of the evidence they seek to introduce. What became clear during the course of the interviews was a striking lack of consensus among practitioners, even within their own specific ranks, on when and why evidence was relevant.

Some also said that evidence was sometimes introduced or tolerated for pragmatic reasons unconnected with its relevance. The most frank statement to this effect came from a defence lawyer:

> If I thought it was irrelevant, but that it might influence the jury in considering the case of my client, would I still have a crack at it? Yes I would. (defence lawyer 1)

A number of sheriffs and fiscals pointed out that the procedure under which the evidence is heard – that is, solemn or summary – sometimes affects the inclusion or exclusion of certain evidence. On the subject of excluding certain evidence, discussion suggested that interviewees distinguished between summary and solemn trials, their arguments being that sheriffs (unlike juries) could 'mentally exclude' irrelevant evidence. As Sheriff 6 put it, 'a professional trial judge would daily hear evidence which sometimes you throw out of your mind. It is a normal exercise.' Sheriffs and judges then, the argument goes, do not need protecting from irrelevant or prejudicial evidence to the same extent as juries.

At the same time as stressing relevance as a general criterion, many interviewees appeared to rule out the possibility of very specific exclusionary rules of relevance, by expressing a general reluctance to shelter juries from any details. For example, the same sheriff went on to argue that although juries could not be expected to put irrelevant evidence out of their mind in this way, nevertheless it was always safer to include than exclude.

> There is an American expression called throwing a skunk to the jury and asking them not to smell it. On the other hand, I tend to say let the evidence in and let the Appeal Courts sort it out. If in doubt, allow the evidence in, and then decide at the end.

When asking about the relevance of sexual history evidence, most judges were wary of 'diluting' evidence. They felt that both they and the jury were entitled to hear 'the whole story', to 'see the full picture', that it would be 'artificial for the jury to decide without having the background'.

> I don't like editing. Editing is offensive. I like the jury to have an unedited version of what they are going to hear ... if you can exclude a whole topic, then okay, but I don't like editing out. (judge 4)

These sentiments were not restricted to the High Court. Similar views were held by sheriffs and Sheriff Court lawyers. The most extreme position concerning the relevance of past sexual history was taken by defence lawyer 2, who said:

> I consider before any court at all that any past history of a complainer is relevant.

Finally there was also a diverse range of views on what was actually occurring in the courts in terms of sexual character attacks and the use of sexual history evidence.

THE RELEVANCE OF NOT OF GOOD CHARACTER IN RELATION TO
SEXUAL MATTERS

Sexual Character and Credibility

One of the reasons for excluding evidence designed to show that a complainer is 'not of good character in sexual matters' was to repudiate the previous doctrine that the sexual immorality of a witness has a general relevance in assessing their credibility as a witness. (This repudiation was one of the principles asserted by MacPhail and the Scottish Law Commission and it was one of the intentions of the legislation – see Chapters 1 and 3.) This issue was explored through a variety of routes in the interview with interesting results. While the majority of sheriffs, judges and prosecutors accepted that sexual character evidence could cause harm, many thought there was little problem in this area. They believed that sexual character attacks were and always had been a rare occurrence in Scottish courts. However, among each group of interviewees there was at least one respondent who disagreed with the principle endorsed by MacPhail and the Scottish Law Commission, and presumably now embodied in the new legislation, saying in contrast that the sexual/moral character of a complainer *was* relevant to their credibility as a witness. Some interviewees also made a separation between what they themselves thought and what they believed juries thought. Defence lawyers and counsel argued that such evidence was relevant and should be introduced because some jurors thought it was relevant.

Those who thought that the introduction of sexual character evidence simply did not happen argued that it was not in the interests of the defence to do this.

> Bringing into question the ... character of the victim ... would be putting his own [the accused's] character at issue. And that seems to me to overlay this area, so perhaps it's not really a great problem, simply because the accused would be slow to embark on an attack of this type, and perhaps would prefer to test credibility with some other form of circumstance. (sheriff 1)[1]

> It's always open in any case for the defence to attack the character. It very rarely happens because there are consequences for the defence. (advocate depute 4)

In addition, it was sometimes argued that gratuitous character attacks were never allowed.

> I don't think either the bench or a prosecutor could ever sit back and simply allow evidence to be led that was prejudicial to the victim and had no clear purpose to it, the purpose would have to be explained. (fiscal 3)

The use of character attacks was both acknowledged and defended by some, however.

> An accused must be entitled to put forward some kind of defence, which may very well involve making imputations against the general character of the complainer. (sheriff 4)

And indeed, judge 2, in response to a question concerning whether he saw the legislation as dealing with the dangers of linking sexual character and credibility, emphasised that it is still permitted to attack bad repute in general, suggesting that sexual 'bad character' was simply one form of bad repute that might be properly investigated.

> Common law has recognised that if a person is of bad repute, then there is a possibility that it could relate to credibility, and therefore it is something to be borne in mind by someone assessing that witness's credibility.

With one exception all the defence interviewed acknowledged that in some circumstances they would seek to introduce evidence to show that a complainer was promiscuous or 'of easy virtue' or 'of bad repute' in sexual matters. Most also accepted that they would occasionally use character evidence which was not explicitly sexual – such as staying out late, drinking, swearing, etc. – to help build a picture of sexual immorality and hence impugn sexual character. Such imputations of 'not of good character in sexual matters' were part of the defence strategies for winning the case. Defence lawyer 1 referred to creating a 'smoke screen of immorality around the girl'. Many, although not all, defence lawyers believed that jurors, or at least some jurors, would regard someone of 'bad repute' as an untrustworthy witness. According to defence lawyer 1:

> You try to get away with anything which you think the jury will use in assessing the credibility of the complainer or the credibility of your client. And it may be that by cross-examining the complainer about certain issues which are not in themselves clearly sexual, but which somehow or other cast some kind of slur on her sexual character or whatever. Would I do that sort of thing if it seemed to be a worthwhile tactic in a particular case? Yes, I probably would.

The view taken by judges was that bad character evidence which was building a picture of 'bad sexual character', even if not always by explicitly sexual matters, could have some legitimate bearing on the credibility of the complainer, and if the evidence was irrelevant then it was up to the prosecution to object to such lines of questioning.

Prosecutors often recognised the examples given in the interviews as being consistent with their experience and generally accepted that a picture of a complainer as 'not of good character in sexual matters' could be painted in subtle ways. But they also felt that there were little grounds for objecting at the time. Moreover, opinions were divided throughout this professional group and the other professional groupings as to the effect of such evidence on the jury. For example, fiscal 4 said:

> If all the evidence shows [is] that she likes to go out and have a good time then there's quite a lot of us who are of bad character, so [we] can't afford to be seen to call that bad character. So we can't object to it really.

Lack of objection in a more obviously character blackening case was explained by fiscal 6, using an example from his own experience:

> The cross-examining of the victim, for example, might include questions like 'Are you a junkie?' Now that might tend to show that she is someone who might be 'not of good character in relation to sexual matters', but there might be no evidence at all that the person is a junkie ... but I don't see that that question is *per se* objectionable and I can't think of any ground, unless it comes within the ambit of 141A, which would make it objectionable.

Defence lawyer 4 alluded to some ethical difficulties in tactics which get guilty men acquitted but described it as a 'mistake' not to use such tactics. He explained this through his deliberations on whether or not he should have introduced evidence about a complainer's past abortions in a rape case.

> The complainer in the case, a woman, had had previously three abortions and that was within a period of about 21 months. And that was never brought out in the course of the trial. And I think with hindsight if that had been, we would have won. That's the sort of ... it's a difficult thing to say because he was found guilty. But on that particular occasion it was considered by counsel, and I think wrongly now, that the attack on her character, simply because of these abortions, would not help us establish anything other than the fact that she had had three abortions. Now I think it would have established that she was completely irresponsible in relation to contraception and that she was prepared to take risks, continuously, even in regard to the fact that she had had an abortion. And I think women in particular who were on the jury would form a view about her irresponsibility. Whether or not that would have any direct bearing on whether or not she had been raped again, is a different matter.

In this instance the defence lawyer regretted not introducing evidence to discredit the complainer's character believing in retrospect that it would have sufficiently damaged her general credibility as a witness and resulted in an acquittal. By contrast, that this sort of tactic would be used to discredit a complainer was totally incredible to defence counsel 2:

> We're in the last decade of the twentieth century. Victoria's been dead for coming on 90 years. Perhaps I'm being over cynical but there's just no percentage in a defence attempting to set up that a

woman is non-credible because of her sexual history. Life isn't like that any more.

While only a minority, with the possible exception of the defence, thought that 'bad sexual repute' was always of relevance to the complainer's credibility as a witness, it was a different matter if the complainer was seen to put her own character at issue during the trial. If the complainer had claimed virginity or chastity, or otherwise presented herself as virtuous, and if the defence could bring evidence to contradict this, then it was universally accepted that they should be allowed to do so, since it is part of the normal rules of evidence. Judge 1 summed up this majority position:

> I don't think that the mere fact that a complainer has previously transgressed in a sexual sense from a moral point of view has a bearing on credibility. But if they are holding themselves out as highly moral, and it is demonstrable that they weren't, then that would be highly relevant and clearly has a bearing on credibility.

Although the research did not find instances of complainers making elaborate claims of virtue, judge 4 commented:

> You know, it is a sad thing, but my impression is that complainers do somehow feel obliged – and quite gratuitously – to insist on what good girls they are. They say that they've never ever had a drink, they've never gone out with boys. Well, that is not the kind of world that I live in. And this results in their being hit with riposte-type stuff. It does just leave themselves open.

Sexual Character and Consent

Sexual character evidence of promiscuity was often regarded by defence as primarily relevant to consent. The relevance of sexual character to consent was spelled out by defence lawyer 4, as a relevance in the minds of some accused and jurors rather than his own mind but, nevertheless, a relevance that it was his job to pursue.

> I think a lot of males think a woman of 'easy virtue' is more likely to give her consent than a 15-year-old virgin. I think it's a male attitude, and these male attitudes manifest themselves in cross-examination. But you can't get away from the fact that advocates are in court to win. Now they are there to present the case as best they can on behalf of an accused person. If an accused person says that this lady is of easy virtue, and if you know that it can be established that she is of easy virtue, you know that the people on a jury will take that into consideration, it would be foolish to say that they will not. The commonsense of the situation demands that they will. Then I think there is a sort of societal pressure on the advocate to raise those points. Whether or not he likes to, or wishes to.

It was put to the interviewees that the defence sometimes tried to construct 'that sort of girl', a caricature of the complainer as liable to consent, through non-sexual characteristics, such as dress, and general life style, as well as explicitly sexual matters. The prosecution did not have a consistent line on whether or not to object to such evidence. Advocate depute 2 gave an example of how he would object to character or life-style evidence suggesting consent when he might not object to it in its own right.

> I wouldn't as a matter of course object to evidence that a girl is hitchhiking on her own ... The problem is where you have the mentality that 'Well, if this girl is hitchhiking on her own, she's asking for it' ... if they then started to insinuate that this implied consent, well perhaps that would be the point, in a hypothetical case.

Fiscal 5 would only object if the defence lawyer was not to his liking.

> Ah yes, well, exactly, I know what you mean. There are ten questions and you stop at nine. Now, let's be blunt about this. If I thought that the defence was a decent sort of person, trying to do his best for his client in a case that could perhaps be awkward, I wouldn't object at all.

Advocate depute 3 noted that he dealt with such matters by addressing the jury directly in the summing-up rather than through objection:

> Well ladies and gentleman, it *was* a skimpy blouse, it *was* a short skirt, she *was* wearing make-up ... you have heard evidence to that effect but it takes a pretty depraved mind, ladies and gentlemen, to put all those things together and come to the conclusion that on this particular occasion the woman consented. Your daughters and sisters are entitled to behave in that way and to be protected from that sort of thing.

Nor was there agreement among judges and sheriffs concerning whether this sort of indirect evidence should be covered by the exclusionary section dealing with 'not of good character in relation to sexual matters'. Several of the defence thought that such evidence could not be excluded. Defence lawyer 3 put this particularly graphically: 'No I don't think you could stop questioning, for example, on the basis of, "You were out this Friday night when this happened. What's your normal practice on Friday night? Who looks after your children, you are a single parent?"'

THE RELEVANCE OF PROSTITUTE OR ASSOCIATE OF PROSTITUTES

It was generally accepted that if a woman was working as a prostitute at the time of an alleged rape or sexual assault then this was relevant and could not be excluded. There was uncertainty about whether or not the exclusion also covered male prostitution, although many practitioners believed that it did.

THE RELEVANCE OF SEXUAL BEHAVIOUR NOT FORMING PART OF THE
SUBJECT MATTER OF THE CHARGE

Sexual Behaviour with the Accused

It was generally accepted that when there was a *recent* history of sexual relations between the complainer and the accused that this should be put before the court. For some this was simply a matter of background facts and the inclusion of this information was consistent with the general view held by a number of interviewees, that the jury should have 'the full picture' as far as possible. A common response from the prosecution was that such information would have to be introduced briefly 'for completeness of narrative'. As advocate depute 3 put it, 'if that has a bearing on credibility, which it may do, if there are factors that a jury would not expect to see in a case of two strangers meeting one evening.'

However, another reason given by the prosecution for leading evidence of a past relationship between the complainer and the accused was tactical rather than due to any perceived relevance. This was explained as follows:

> In most cases I would think it would be wise to do so. But that would largely be for tactical reasons because if one allowed – especially the jury – if one allowed the defence to bring out something like that, then in the jury's eyes they might start asking questions as to why we hadn't done so, and maybe draw unfortunate inferences from that for no good reason. (fiscal 1)

> If I gather that that evidence will be led by the defence and the judge will allow it, then I find that the Crown will look stupid if we didn't lead it, so I would lead it. (advocate depute 2)

Sometimes the reasons for leading evidence were a mixture of the above and other reasons. Fiscal 2 gave an example of when a past relationship would be included in evidence led by the prosecution:

> Particularly if the complainer has said it to me beforehand. If she has said that yes they had had a consenting relationship in the past and everything was hunky dory and then suddenly something had gone sour and the incident had occurred, then I would lead the evidence. It seems to me to be relevant to the court to know this. What they do with the evidence, that is, those on the bench, is another matter.

Later in the interview the same fiscal suggested a more specific reason for looking at the history of the relationship between the complainer and the accused – looking for any past 'prejudice' between them, thus suggesting a motive for a false accusation. Other prosecutors also raised the possible relevance of the general quality of past relations and in particular any history of animosity. And, of course, it was emphasised that, as part of the general rules of evidence if the complainer claimed not to know or be intimate with the accused while he claimed otherwise, then this had to be put to the complainer.

Past Relations with the Accused and Consent

In the reform discussions, there was a consensus that such evidence would usually be relevant to consent. Yet there turned out to be quite a wide range of views about whether and when past sexual relations between the complainer and the accused were relevant to the issue of consent. Some respondents believed that such a history either demonstrated that the complainer had a predisposition to consent with this man, or at least that it cast in doubt any presumption against consent. Others argued, that although they did not subscribe to such a view themselves, some jurors probably did. Both points were strenuously denied by others who thought that any jury ought to have the wit to realise that consent in the past did not necessarily mean consent in the present. The most succinct quotes from respondents who saw 'past relations' with the accused as relevant to consent are given below. They include examples from each of the professional groupings interviewed.

> It boils down to the issue of consent. It is relevant to say that they have had sexual intercourse before. If she has consented in the past, then is there any reason she is refusing on this occasion? But if it is the first time, then it is regarded as less likely that she would consent. (judge 5)

> Either the girl consents or she does not consent. I suppose it might have this relevance that, if she had consented in the past, then it might be more likely that she was indicating consent, or not indicating dissent, on that occasion. So it would be less than fair to cut all of that out. (sheriff 5)

> I think it might be relevant to picture that ongoing relationship, to say that she probably did consent because she had consented on all the previous occasions. (sheriff 8)

> Now any normal juror would consider it relevant to know whether or not they had had a relationship in the past, because it's less likely that a woman who is just walking home from a dancehall or gets off a bus – a total stranger – is liable to consent with a man, than if she has lived with him and shared his bed for five years. It seems to me a matter of commonsense that how people are in their total relationship is relevant. I'm not saying that it means she can't be raped. (advocate depute 4)

> If over a period, or even an isolated occasion, the man has had permissible sexual relationship with a woman, and then has sex with her again and the defence is consent, clearly I would have thought that the previous intercourse was relevant. (defence counsel 2)

Most interviewees believed that only *recent* past sexual relationships were relevant and hence judges and sheriffs said they were inclined to limit questioning to the recent past. The research suggests that practice with reference to time constraints is considerably less vigilant than this would suggest. A number of judges interviewed did think of situations in which relationships in the distant past might be of some relevance. For example, judge 1 stated:

> One may have the case where the complainer and the accused had been living as husband and wife, as cohabitees, and then separated. The man may have been away for five to ten years and then comes back and demands that the previous relationship be resumed. In such a case, I would say that the previous relationship would be of doubtful relevance, but I am not sure whether it would be of no relevance at all.

For sheriff 4 no limits based on how far back in time a relationship had been were appropriate:

> if it were relevant as relating to consent, then the whole history has to be relevant. All or none at all.

The notion that consent with the accused in the past shows a predisposition to consent with this particular man was totally unacceptable to other respondents who considered consent as something specific to each occasion of intercourse and quite independent of past consent.

> The mere fact that couples have in fact had sexual relations is, in my mind, neither here nor there. I don't think that's relevant. (advocate depute 2)

Advocate depute 3 was not convinced that juries would put any credence on such a 'predisposition to consent' notion, in any case:

> I am not persuaded that juries tend to approach it in that way and I would hope ... that there would be no misapprehension that simply because there had been a relationship in the past, that goes some way to demonstrating that consent was given.

Fiscal 6 thought that evidence of past consensual relations was more plausible as a defence of mistaken-belief-in-consent than as part of a defence of consent:

> It's more likely to be relevant to the question of whether the accused thought the victim was consenting, albeit that he's genuinely mistaken.

However, observation of trials indicates that appeals to mistaken-belief-in-consent are not typically made in practice. In the following extracts, defence counsel 1 gives an interesting insight into his understanding of likely events and of the appropriate defence, consent or mistaken-belief-in-consent.

> People, both males and females, can misread, misinterpret signals that intelligent people, or sober people, might think are not positive in

any way. But these are interpreted wrongly. Well, it's very important that the jury hear the whole story. Because it is a defence to rape that the man reasonably believed that the girl was consenting.

Later in the interview, defence counsel 1 introduced the much attacked notion that 'women say no when they mean yes' as part of an elaboration of this argument:

> ... at what stage does the girl make up her mind? At what stage does the man know what is going to happen or what is happening, or whether there's a token protest or more than that.

And he then went on to explain that a 'belief-in-consent' defence is more difficult than one simply of consent, to be reserved for cases in which the medical evidence indicating non-consent is going against the accused.

> I think the most common defence, as you know, is consent, but [when it is raised] the belief-in-consent one is virtually always put to the jury by the judge, and it's a lot more difficult. Because the straightforward consent one normally comes in where the girl doesn't have any signs of injury at all. The belief-in-consent one is normally a situation where there's been a bit of a struggle and the man says he thought she was doing a token protest, as very often happens.

Flirting with the Accused and Consent

Interviewees were asked whether they regarded past sexual behaviour which did not include sexual intercourse – in particular, flirting – as relevant in the same way. Again, there were a range of views on this issue. A minority did not accept that 'flirting' counted as sexual behaviour and therefore did not see it as prohibited evidence in the first place. Most regarded it as covered by the legislation but were divided as to its relevance to consent, although 'some relevance' was a more common response than 'none'. 'It could be heavy petting the previous night. Then it would be difficult to exclude as irrelevant if the defence is consent' (judge 3). The desire not to exclude such evidence also stemmed from the view that the jury should have 'the full picture'. Judge 4 noted:

> I think it is relevant. It may not take you very far, but it's difficult for the jury to draw inferences knowing nothing at all about the relationship.[2]

Again the defence were most united in asserting the relevance of such evidence. Defence lawyer 4 and defence counsel 1 raised again the much criticised notion of 'women who say no when they mean yes'.

> I think that what a jury must be made aware of, or a judge, is that the circumstances surrounding the refusal can often really muddy the refusal. If a woman, – to 'lead a man on' – that line may not be the

proper term to use – but if he says that he was led on and it's the classic sort of case out of a joke book of 'a woman who says "no" once really means "yes" and a woman who says "no" twice is frigid'. And the fact of the matter is that there's almost a sort of certain expectation that a woman will say 'no' to some extent but can be persuaded. And I think the jury have simply got to be made aware of the whole circumstances.

Defence counsel 2 stressed its relevance to the accused's belief-in-consent:

> If a client says to me this girl on this occasion was flirting and allowed me to go so far, and I was quite sure that she was consenting to me going further, then I would have thought that, yes indeed, the flirting would be relevant.

Again some of the defence talked about this at the level of the susceptibilities of the jury rather than the relevance of the evidence *per se*. This was explored at length with defence counsel 1 who had strong views on what juries did and did not believe:

> If we were to go before a jury to say any girl who has a few drinks and a wee bit kissing and cuddling is obviously consenting, at least half the jury would laugh at us. Well, we all know from our own experience that doesn't happen.

When asked then why he would bother with such details, he continued, illustrating by a fluent example of a summing-up speech to the jury:

> Well, we are convincing 15, or at least eight out of the 15, non-lawyers who are really there just as people from all different backgrounds, with different views, experiences, there to apply their commonsense, so we've got to say to them, 'Well, this is what happened: x, y, and z in the pub, kissing and cuddling in the bus, back to her house, couple of large vodkas and a wee bit more kissing and cuddling happening there.' And we don't know what happened after that. The accused said she consented. The girl said she didn't. Well, you've got to look at the whole background, what happened that night, and you've got to decide, she had no bruises on her, no scratches or anything like that, her clothes weren't torn, did she consent, did she get out of these skin tight jeans single-handed, being pulled off her with no bruises or anything like that? Even if you don't accept that it was total literal consent, if you're left with a reasonable doubt, then that's the end of the story.

Defence lawyer 1 clearly also believed that juries were swayed by such evidence and illustrated with a real rather than hypothetical case. Although he acknowledged that irrelevance and 'dirty tactics' were involved, the rest of his interview suggests that he would continue to introduce such evidence in the interests of his client.

> This was years ago before the legislation was introduced. We led

evidence that the girl was kissing and fondling with the guy in a bar, that she had a lot to drink with him and we led evidence to that effect. And it shouldn't really have been of any significance, I don't know what I was doing, but you do all kinds of things. In that particular case I even went so far as to employ a female junior to act in the case, because I didn't want the jury to think it was a male conspiracy ... I wanted the best looking female junior at the bar. And they got me this girl and she was used as a junior, and it was specifically so that the sort of male conspiracy theory would not hold. That's a pretty dirty thing to do. He got off as well. ... He had a previous conviction for rape.

Finally, it was also argued by many practitioners that consent was often necessarily entailed by certain challenges to credibility. For instance:

The issue of credibility which can sometimes arise, is the issue of whether she is credible when she says she doesn't consent. So to my mind the issues of credibility and consent are inevitably bound up. (defence lawyer 1)

Sexual Behaviour with Someone Other than the Accused

Interviewees regarded this information about the complainer as a more problematic form of evidence than sexual relations with the accused. The initial reaction of some of the prosecution was that they could see no reason for its relevance. For example:

It's neither here nor there [past relations between the complainer and a third party]. I would object to that in any circumstances. (advocate depute 2)

I find it very difficult to envisage a situation where a relationship between the complainer and a third party, from the Crown's point of view, would be of significance. (advocate depute 3)

However, judges raised the other type of circumstance conceived of by the Scottish Law Commission, that of rebutting medical or forensic evidence, as one judge put it, 'analogous to the process of incrimination in other criminal trials' (judge 1).

Some interviewees did consider that sexual behaviour with someone other than the accused might be relevant to *consent*. The only example which came to mind for a number of interviewees was one cited by the Scottish Law Commission, 'the orgy': 'the case of the kind of gang bang type of thing, where the defence might be that it was an orgy, would clearly be relevant, and that's allowed for' (fiscal 6). Fiscal 3 spontaneously referred to the possible relevance of evidence concerning the complainer and third parties to consent, indicating a certain commitment to character predisposition-to-consent.

I don't think it can be said in precisely the same way that evidence of some sexual contact between the victim and some other person would be quite so directly relevant to the question of consent in this case. Because, after all, you might well consent to some sort of sexual involvement with person A but not with person B. Depending on the nature of it, it might affect, I suppose, the likelihood of consent. If there were questions directed to show that the victim was 'loose' or 'easy' for want of a better word, then that might be relevant to the question of consent, so far as the likelihood of that consent goes.

Judge 4, by contrast, initially seemed to be referring to the idea of a disposition to consent on the occasion in question. He talked of a complainer going into a crowded pub and having a drink with man B, later having a cuddle with man C, and eventually going home with man D. He argued that all of this would be relevant by way of background circumstances for the jury and that these background circumstances have some relevance for the issue of consent: 'There are various steps to a rape, and one builds up a picture from the first contact.' But he went on to add, 'this sort of stuff, as often as not, comes out in favour of the complainer. All she was on for was for less. What was in her mind? Innocence followed by semi-unease?'

The majority of the defence argued either that sexual behaviour with third parties was relevant to consent, or took the view that such arguments were useful for persuading juries even if they themselves did not believe the 'predisposition-to-consent' connections that were being made.

> Well, again it boils down to the consent and belief in consent, and the example I gave you earlier on, about somebody doing something with one boy up a close, and then a few minutes later saying that she didn't consent to what the next boy did to her. That certainly seems to me something that if the accused and his defence witnesses are going to say that happened, then the girl should be given an opportunity to either agree or deny it. (defence counsel 1)

> The type of situation I can envisage where that type of investigation would be necessary is if information was provided by the accused that the victim, or the alleged victim, was so promiscuous with a number of partners that it would have a bearing. ... But I can't see any advantage at all in asking about a normal relationship with a third party, unless it's the type of offence where you are dealing with an underage female and there may be considerable importance, perhaps not to do with the guilt or innocence but to do with the mitigation. (defence lawyer 4)

Defence lawyer 2 was blunt:

> Well, I think it's only relevant to establish whether the complainer has led a promiscuous life, or whether they have led a moral life, or whether they have slept around. I think that is relevant and should be brought out.

This line of reasoning was totally rejected by advocate depute 2:

> Basically what they are trying to get across is, this is a loose woman. And that is totally unacceptable, but I think that's what lies behind the question. I think that's one of the things the section [of the legislation] was designed to stop.

It was also rejected by two defence respondents, although again the defence are faced with the dilemma of possibly using evidence they regard as 'dirty tactics' in order to get their client acquitted. Defence counsel 3 described a case in point, which also underlines the potential use of medical reports, mentioned in Chapter 6 and 7:

> A fellow of 18 charged with raping a girl of 14 – it doesn't matter all the details – she came over very pleasant, very nice girl and I had problems [with the defence case]. And there was a medical history, naturally, prepared on her by the police doctor who saw her immediately after the incident. And he wrote a whole lot of things in it, how it appeared to him – she had a mark on her leg – and at the very bottom of the report it said – remember she was only 14 years of age – she last had intercourse two weeks previously. Now obviously not with the accused. Now what do I do? It's something of a dilemma. And I discussed it with one or two colleagues and, of course, that section [of the legislation] has relevance, I thought. Because clearly in a jury's mind a 14-year-old girl would be assumed to be a virgin. Rightly or wrongly, they would assume her to be a virgin. And accordingly my defence of consent wasn't terribly good, because it's difficult for most members of the jury perhaps to accept that a 14-year-old is consenting to that kind of thing. And I don't have much doubt that if I had applied under that section [of the legislation], for permission to bring out this bit of the report I probably wouldn't have got it under that umbrella. ... In the event the sting in the tail is this. I said, 'No. I'll not do it. It's neither here nor there. If she's got a boyfriend, that's her business.' And I left it out. The jury went into the jury room, and they asked for the report. And of course you can't give them a part of the report. I went into the judge's chambers. I said nothing. I said I had no objection to the report going out and the prosecutor said he had no objection. I don't think he had read it, because I think if he had read it to the end and seen the last sentence he would have objected and I couldn't have done anything about it. And within five minutes the jury came back and acquitted. Now that illustrates the point ... they see she's no virgin, she's got sexual relations with somebody else two weeks ago – [they think] 'She's at it'. And that's it. And I think that's quite the wrong test. But as I say, it's a question of attitude.

Evidence about third parties can have general connotations of sexual character, 'bad repute' and the like, and here clearly overlaps with questions about the relevance of sexual conduct to the general credibility of the complainer. The reader is reminded that notwithstanding the aims of the legislation, a minority of respondents argued that promiscuity or 'bad sexual repute' did, and should, damage the general credibility of the complainer. (See under Sexual Character and Credibility at the beginning of the chapter.)

By contrast, sheriff 8 emphasised that sexual conduct had no intrinsic relevance to credibility; he did not see 'how sexual conduct in itself has a bearing on credibility any more than violent conduct would have a bearing on credibility'.

Nevertheless, it is clear that a number of the defence believed that past sexual behaviour with someone other than the accused could prejudice a jury sufficiently to change the outcome of the case, that is, basically to win their case. Defence counsel 3 was particularly forthright on this point. He asked, 'Why are we, both prosecution and defence, so concerned about an alleged victim's sexual history?' and went on to answer his own question as follows:

> The prosecution wants to keep that out because they know that most juries take the view that if a person has a sexual history, and it's an elastic matter whether it's promiscuous or not, but if a person has a sexual history – 'What is she complaining about? This is just another chapter in her sexual history.' And prosecutors know and feel that juries will take that view, so that's why they want to keep the sexual history out. Whereas obviously defence people, who share the same understanding of what juries' attitude will be, want it to go in. And I think it's absolutely reprehensible. But I don't think the legislation can possibly deal with it. I think what has to be made clear is that because a woman has had previous lovers, it's neither here nor there and should have nothing to do with credibility.

Several interviewees saw evidence such as 'past lover' as relevant to credibility in a more specific way, referring to evidence introduced to demonstrate inconsistencies in the complainer's testimony. Several respondents also referred to 'good character' claims, one giving the example of a complainer claiming she was a virgin when evidence that she had had sexual intercourse with someone other than the accused could be introduced.

EVIDENCE TO SHOW CONSENT WHEN IT IS NOT AT ISSUE

It was put to the interviewees that questions around the issue of consent seemed to be prevalent in the cross-examination of complainers even when consent was technically not an issue, for example, in age-related statutory offences which make certain behaviour an offence by definition, regardless of the willingness or otherwise of the young person. (This unnecessary use of the consent issue is a phenomenon that arose particularly in Sheriff Court trials, see Chapter 9.) This was a matter of concern because young complainers were thus exposed to the same repertoire of testing questions that occur in rape trials. All but one of the judges were not surprised. They were of the opinion that it was raised as a kind of 'early plea in mitigation', seeking to lessen the sentence. As one said:

> One normally expects the trial to bring out everything to do with mitigation – even if much of it is not relevant to guilt. The jury is entitled to the full colour print, not just the black and white version.

Another said:

> Of course consent is not an issue as to whether the crime was committed, and I would be disapproving if the defence asked whether she took the initiative.

But, he said, it may have implications for the credibility of the complainer 'if the Crown made out that she was lying there until pounced on.'

Similarly, amongst the sheriffs, the majority thought that it was an early mitigation point, that would have a bearing on the sentence, should the accused be found guilty. As Sheriff 1 said:

> to simply have a narration that a man of fifty was having sexual intercourse with a thirteen-year-old girl, it is perhaps thought that really, stated baldly, it would reflect very much worse on the accused, than if perhaps the circumstances of perhaps incitement on her part, or consent, show the whole circumstances.

And, for these reasons, he argued he would not want to rule out such questioning. Defence lawyer 2 said something similar but from a 'doing the best for the client' perspective:

> This is a ploy that is sometimes used by defence agents which you should be made aware of – it's my view that when one goes to trial for a client you don't always go to trial on the basis that it's either strictly guilty or strictly not guilty. It is sometimes of benefit to a client to go to trial in mitigation. That is, that one brings out facts during the course of the case that cannot be properly pled before a court if you just plead guilty, but can be elicited from a witness during the course of them giving evidence. And it might be the case that defence agents do this because they are going to trial on mitigation, on the basis that if they can get that out during the course of cross-examination, whilst they know very well that it's not a defence, they are also aware that if the sheriff believes for instance that there was consent involved here, that he may, when he's coming to sentencing, view it more leniently than he did or would do if that wasn't brought out.

He went on to say that he saw nothing wrong in doing that:

> because it's very difficult when you're submitting to a sheriff in mitigation, having pled guilty, it's very difficult indeed to impress upon a sheriff the fact that the complainer consented, in the same way that one would be able to do, if you actually had the complainer in the witness box and put that to them. It's much more convincing if you can get that from the complainer in the witness box.

Defence lawyer 4 said that he thought it was a fairly common practice, particularly if: ' the trial were going against you … then … from a mitigation point of view it would be relevant to at least investigate whether or not it was of consent.' The lawyer went on to say that 'the criminality element or the severity of the offence might be very much reduced' in those cases where the age of the complainer is close to the age of consent.

However there were several respondents who agreed that the purpose was mitigation but abhorred the practice because of the ordeal to which the complainer was then subjected. Fiscal 6 explained as follows:

> The purpose of a criminal trial is not always to establish guilt or innocence. Sometimes a trial is effectively a plea in mitigation. Now, it may well be that the defence are hoping for a sympathy verdict, or hoping to just hammer home the fact that this was something done consensually, albeit that technically that's not a defence. Clearly … that is a gross abuse of a witness's presence in court … it's just a sad legal fact … you see it with [driving offences] where there's an insurance company interest as well.

Sheriff 2, in sharp contrast to the majority of sheriffs interviewed said:

> this sort of questioning really does turn your hair white … one would have to be very, very firm as a sheriff when this sort of thing came up.

Their dislike for such questions was shared by a group of respondents who thought there were no grounds to ask them whatsoever. An advocate depute, a judge and a defence lawyer thought that such questioning was totally irrelevant. As the defence lawyer said:

> If I was sitting on the Bench and dealing with that, I would ask what the relevancy of those questions was. I don't understand why someone would want to lead that sort of evidence or try and extract it from the complainer.

Mitigation was not the only explanation respondents offered for the introduction of such evidence. Fiscal 4 at first thought that it boiled down to lawyers not really knowing the legislation, and that the same sort of thing often occurred in incest cases, but later changed tack slightly to say:

> There are [defence] agents who cloud the issues surrounding the law, either because they don't know the law themselves or I sometimes think they might have done it deliberately because juries have to take the law from the judge. But obviously once a person, that they probably think knows what they are talking about, has said it, it's difficult maybe to get that idea away from them, no matter how often the sheriff or the judge corrects what the agent has said. The way we handle sheriff and juries is sometimes different from the way we would handle a case in front of a sheriff, where you take it that he knows what the law is. Impressions and tactics in sheriff and jury trials are more important.

Altogether one sheriff, two fiscals and an advocate depute also thought that issues of consent were pursued in such cases because the lawyers simply did not know about the legislation.

BALANCING RELEVANCE AND PREJUDICE

The interviewees were asked whether, when on deciding the admissibility of evidence, the relevance of the information should be balanced against the way it might prejudice the jury, especially evidence with a well-known tendency to mislead. This prompted a range of answers, but little clear support for the idea that if a piece of information about the complainer was highly prejudicial, but of only slight although some relevance to the issues of the trial, then it should be excluded. (Although one judge in the observed cases explicitly discussed this problem, there is no such obvious requirement – or even power – to do so in the legislation itself.)

Judges offered a variety of responses. Judge 2 did not think it was a major issue at all although he acknowledged that 'all that is swimming around at the back of your mind, but essentially one's got to apply the words of the Act to the situation.' In general, the concern triggered by the word 'prejudice' is to avoid prejudicing the outcome of the trial by besmirching the accused, and risking an unfair conviction, rather than by besmirching the complainer and risking an unfair acquittal. For example, judge 3 remarked that 'trying to reach a conclusion on the question of the balance of relevance and prejudice is a lot like searching for the Holy Grail', which calls strongly for judicial discretion in 'assessing prejudice to the accused and the relevance in relation to the complainer.'

In discussion, the interviewers occasionally confused the issue by referring to 'prejudice to the complainer' as a shorthand for prejudicing the outcome of the trial through sexual history or sexual character evidence pertaining to the complainer. This was because of a concern to ascertain whether sexual history evidence might either produce a 'gut reaction' against the complainer on the part of the jury, or suggest to the jury that she is 'the kind of girl' who would consent, even though the evidence in question might technically be introduced in relation to some other issue. In either case, the effect would be to 'divert a jury from the proper issues in a case', in the words of the *SLC Report*,[3] and prejudice the outcome of the trial. Clearly, several interviewees believed that the outcomes of trials were commonly affected by sexual history evidence in these ways. However, the practitioners associated 'prejudice' only with the position of the accused and emphasised that their main job is not to protect the complainer. For judges, sheriffs and prosecutors the main job is ensuring a fair trial, while the defence are concerned with their client. Hence, responses such as that from judge 1 who said that he did not 'understand this whole business of the complainer being prejudiced.'

Judge 4 was of the opinion that 'relevance and prejudice is a misapprehension, there is no one criterion.' He went on to say that although the exclusions of the legislation were designed to deal with 'unnecessary and unjustified prejudice' they had to be read along with the exceptions where there was little room for considering prejudice. This was particularly so for the provisions dealing with 'explain or rebut' and 'the same occasion'. He said: 'I can't see under [141B (*a*) or (*b*) (i)] any place for the question of prejudice. The question is rebuttal and, if it is, then the court has no discretion in the matter. It does say, "The court *shall* allow" ... ' By reference to subsection (*c*), the 'interests of justice', he again made the point that the court has no particular duty to protect the complainer from prejudice. Regarding (*c*), 'it does mean justice in the functioning of the trial, and therefore justice to the accused and justice to the Crown, rather than to the complainer. A fair, proper prosecution and a fair, proper defence.'

Sheriffs and prosecution also offered a range of responses. Sheriff 5 did talk of a balancing act.

> Fairness is the crucial word. There is a danger both ways – of being unfair to the victim or the accused. So you have got to balance it. I think fairness is the test and the legislation as it stands does a good job of balancing that out.

But the most common response was to stress relevance.

> If it is relevant, or perceived to be relevant, then in a sense it doesn't matter if it is prejudicial, because that is why there are the rules about relevance and fair trial. (sheriff 6)

This view would also reflect the position taken by most of the defence. One more specific form of prejudice was discussed. The *MacPhail Report* discussed the fact that if sexual character evidence was introduced in order to cast doubt on the credibility of a complainer, then there was a danger that juries would see the evidence as having some bearing on the issue of consent. There was a range of views among interviewees on this issue. Not all judges, sheriffs, or prosecution saw it as a problem. And, as noted when discussing credibility, most of the defence felt it was artificial to separate credibility and consent. Judge 4 is an example of a judge who did not deny that conflation might occur but did not see it as something that had to be combatted.

> Usually credibility comes in, not as a consent problem but as a rebuttal matter. It usually comes in the 'explain or rebut' context, because she has said X. I don't feel it at all important to keep the credibility issue from the consent issue.

Some respondents did think credibility issues could have connotations of sexual character – and hence consent – yet many of those who did think conflation was a problem were pessimistic about any solution. Pessimism arose because of the near impossibility of making a separation in the minds of the jury between information about the complainer's sexual conduct, introduced as evidence of her lack of credibility, and a construction based on the same evidence of a disposition to consent. For example, this was the view expressed by sheriff 2:

> Although in a matter of analysis you can distinguish the two issues, but in the mind of a jury, in many cases, are they not going to be the same thing?

This acknowledgement that evidence introduced for the purpose of credibility was likely to be conflated with the issue of consent did not, however, necessarily lead interviewees to argue that sexual history evidence should not be admitted for the purpose of credibility in jury trials. Some interviewees did believe that the distinction between relevance to credibility and relevance to consent could and perhaps should be impressed on juries.

> It is up to the sheriff to charge the jury quite, quite carefully on the difference between credibility and consent. And it would be the sheriff's responsibility to do this.

> I would hope that the jury just wouldn't confuse credibility and consent ... I would hope it would be something which the judge would realise ... and direct them accordingly on it. (fiscal 6)

FLEXIBILITY IN THE USE OF EXCEPTIONS

The apparent elasticity of the exceptions was discussed in Chapter 6. Some interviewees were concerned about the lack of specificity in the 'interests of justice' but, with a few notable exceptions, were not worried by the research findings of how the exceptions were used. The subtle and indirect ways in which 'explain or rebut' was invoked, giving the defence room for tactical manoeuvre, including wide scope of 'inferential evidence', did not cause disquiet among many respondents, although some were uneasy about the relevance of the evidence in some of the examples given in the interviews.

Explain or Rebut

The judges shared a common view that the defence right to rebuttal is of fundamental importance to the trial, not least because it allows testing of the credibility of the complainer. The legitimacy of using 'explain or rebut' to do something much more complicated than knocking down one piece of factual information with another was asserted by a number of interviewees.

> One must look at the words in the statute. 'Evidence adduced' – it's not just factual evidence, but it is also inferential evidence. This may fall under the question of primary and secondary facts. One may be entitled to infer secondary facts from primary facts, and if one is entitled to rebut primary facts, then one would be entitled to rebut secondary facts as well. (sheriff 9)

However, defence counsel 3 argued that, precisely because sexual offence cases dealing with consent were all about inference, it was difficult to apply 'explain or rebut' in any rigorous way. Indeed, he saw it as an ineffective provison which was 'so elastic you can read anything into it'.

Speculative Questioning

One matter raised with respect to 'explain or rebut' was the extent to which the defence needed an evidential basis for the questioning they wished to pursue. It was commonly stated by interviewees that the general rules of evidence did not allow this, or indeed any other part of the legislation, to be a launching point for speculative questioning with no evidential basis. This was put most strongly by prosecution. However, there seemed to be two different aspects involved. On the one hand, fiscal 3 had this to say about the basis for a question about masturbation, which was put to a complainer in one of the observed cases, in order to 'explain or rebut' medical evidence of vaginal damage:

> I would regard it as barely proper and almost offensive unless they were doing it on a considered basis and in knowledge of medical evidence which they had available to them to say that, yes, the [medical findings] could be caused in that way, by masturbation.'

He was thus emphasising that questioning had to have an evidential starting point. However, advocate depute 2 expected that during an application to introduce prohibited evidence, the defence would not only explain the relevance of the questioning they were seeking to introduce but also declare 'what evidence they have got to back it up'. The general rule was, 'If you are a counsel, you can't ask a question for which you don't have some sort of basis. Anybody who does that is failing in his duty.' This seems to indicate that there should also be some evidential basis for the suggested alternative explanations. However, observation suggests that the defence were not always forthcoming on the evidential basis of their questions during the application dialogue. Some of the defence interviewees noted that they did not always abide by the rules but would follow a line of questioning whether they had any evidence or not:

> If the Crown doesn't interrupt and the judge doesn't stop you, and if you want to go along that trail you just carry on. Well you could end up against a brick wall. (defence lawyer 3)

Some had rules for breaking the rules:

> You can't go – eventually if you go away off beam you are going to be
> stopped. But you can sometimes stop yourself. If it's a young person,
> if it's somebody that is not intelligent, once again you have to be
> limited in speculation, but occasionally I think we all speculate. I
> suppose we all say to juries, 'You mustn't speculate' and then
> proceed to tell them exactly how to speculate. It's an open ended
> word. But I think you should not speculate on central issues. If you
> are going to attack on central key issues, if you are going to build a
> defence around a number of issues, they shouldn't be speculative.
> They should have something to support them. (defence counsel 3)

The defence counsel's main source of allegations against a complainer
is the account of the accused. The approach of the defence to such
allegations can vary as defence counsel 3 acknowledged:

> You can throw all the information that your client gives you at the
> complainer indiscriminately. And there are some people who do that.
> Your client says to you – whether it's [a case of] homosexual,
> heterosexual, under-age or what have you – 'He's "the local bicycle".'
> 'She's "the local bicycle".' 'This that and the other.' 'Everybody in
> town has had it off with them.' 'He hangs around in women's
> clothing.' – whatever you want, without bothering to investigate it,
> just throw it all in. You could do that if you want. Or you could say,
> 'Listen. I need some independent, reliable evidence that I can use in
> court if it comes to a conflict of evidence on this point.' Now, in the
> first scenario that is just putting everything your client tells you. If I
> have an adult, mature, moderately intelligent complainer I will
> perhaps be freer with my allegations. I would still want to have
> something [by way of evidence].

Disputes over the Status of the Medical Report

During discussion of the 'explain or rebut' exception in the interviews,
questions were asked about the status of information written down in the
medical report but not verbally introduced to the court by the prosecution, a question that had proved problematic in some of the observed
application cases. The problem was whether such information could
count as having been 'adduced' by the Crown. Clearly there were a range
of views about whether such material was open to rebuttal or alternative
explanations by the defence or not. Moreover, a number of prosecution
counsel suggested that perhaps the type of medical report requested
should be more specific than that produced by current practice. One fiscal
had this to say:

> Well I think there is a fundamental misunderstanding about the
> status of such reports. Police surgeons or pathologists do not do a
> report for the prosecution. It is, however, my report because I have
> commissioned it and the Crown Office has paid for it. But they don't

do it specifically for the Crown. They do a report on their findings, drawing their own conclusions. And it is there for the Court. Now it may contain stuff highly prejudicial to the Crown case, but that is tough. (fiscal 2)

This issue was taken up more specifically by advocate depute 2, who clearly did not think that just anything included in the medical report could be picked up on by the defence. He noted that a woman's contraceptive history was often included in the medical report and the defence might well seize on this.

> She's on the pill; therefore say the defence – without saying it – this means she's 'at it'. So if there's going to be any evidence about that, an application should be made ... I wouldn't lead that evidence. There should be an application. I would object to it, and if they try to take it from the medical report, I would object to that as well. They shouldn't take that at all.

Fiscal 1 believed that a problem would not arise since the test of relevance would be applied:

> They would still presumably have to argue its relevance in terms of the overall case. In other words, simply to say we are just trying to explain or expand on something that is in the medical report, and therefore we will ask about what she has been doing over the past five years, wouldn't be admissible. But if it was a particular point, then possibly yes.

Or as advocate depute 4 put it, 'the fact that it is there, has got nothing to do with its admissibility'.

The responses of judges and sheriffs generally confirmed this emphasis on relevance as the test of admissibility for medical information. While some of the defence acknowledged that such matters as contraceptive history could only be raised with an application, others generally felt that the medical report was 'up for grabs' and, although the rule of relevance applied, an application was not necessary and any controls rested with the prosecution:

> Now say you had the extreme example of a [written] medical report which was spoken to [during the trial] by a doctor but there was no reference at all to the [written] fact that the woman had three abortions. In cross-examination the defence are allowed to ask any questions at all. And if it wasn't relevant the Crown would have to object, and I think the objection would not be upheld if it was in the report. (defence lawyer 3)

The Same Occasion

The 'same occasion' exception was seen as largely unproblematic. For, although it could not be translated into precise time, which events were and which were not directly connected to the incident were generally straightforward enough to ascertain. Moreover, the actual circumstances of the case would dictate the relevance of evidence about the set of events leading up to the incident as the 'same occasion'.

The Interests of Justice

Concern about 'the interests of justice' exception came from a number of quarters.

> The weakness of this legislation is that it tries to take account of every situation. It tries to cover everything and then realises that it can't and that is why they stuck in the last general clause. (sheriff 9)

The same sentiment was expressed by sheriff 7:

> The interests of justice could be argued to be anything.

One defence counsel said:

> Because of that rider in the second subsection about, if the court thinks that despite the first section, there are reasons in the interest of justice to investigate it, because of that rider, I think that the legislation is a waste of time … lip service to feminism. (defence counsel 3)

Sheriff 2 suggested that the 'interests of justice' exception should have been linked to the other exceptions with an *and* rather than an *or* and that this would have prevented it being interpreted too loosely while also monitoring the other exceptions.

On the other hand, for some interviewees 'the interests of justice' exception was an essential component of the legislation. There were some cynical versions of this. Fiscal 6, believed there was value in the legislation and simply said that:

> In a way it's the only clause you need, and the others are explanations of situations where it would be contrary to the interests of justice.

However, fiscal 3's understanding also summed up the view of many of the defence when he said that the legislation was a 'well-intentioned response' to a problem which was more apparent than real and which had fortuitously, thanks to 'the interests of justice' exception, changed very little. He first noted that the legislation was excluding speculative attacks on character which in his opinion never took place anyway under common law and then went on:

> Likewise, looking at the [exception] provisions, it seems to me that such evidence was always admissible – questions were admissible, if they were relevant to credibility or whatever. And the new provision says that, notwithstanding the terms of the first part of the section, that such evidence will not be excluded if it would be contrary to the interests of justice to exclude it. And it seems to me that that takes us back to square one.

The position adopted by advocate depute 4 was essentially similar. He also thought that the legislation was basically redundant, simply providing a new procedure for existing practice.

> I think when it's applied for, it's so obvious to everybody that it is relevant ... when everybody is agreed then people are just looking for a formula to put it through on, and 'the interests of justice' is a great phrase to use. It gets thrown in basically because there's no argument.

Defence lawyer 1 had a slightly different interpretation of why the clause was used so often:

> They are the kind of words that leap immediately to defence agents' lips because they sound terribly impressive.

HAS THE LEGISLATION MADE A DIFFERENCE?

One of the questions put to practitioners was whether they felt the legislation had made any difference to what goes on in the courtroom. The response to this question was very much oriented by whether sexual character and sexual history evidence were seen as a *problem*. The minority who felt that there had been 'excesses' in the past generally felt that the legislation had done something to curb them. Most – but not all – of the majority who stated that the legislation had made no difference tended to think that there had been no need for the legislation to begin with. Hence, much of the discussion on impact was also bound up with statements on why the legislation had come about.

Three out of the five interviewed judges felt there had been an initial problem. While two thought there had been no need for the legislation in the first place, three felt there had been at least a degree of 'excessive' exploration of general background evidence about the 'highways and byways', as one put it, of the complainer's life. One said that there had been 'too much by way of attempts' on the part of defence counsel and another spoke of the judiciary being 'a wee bit casual unless there is a marker rule'. These three were satisfied that the legislation had made some difference, although one expressed the view that rape trials presented intractable and irresolvable problems. The idea that the main impact of the legislation was to be a 'reminder' was a theme echoed by other groups we interviewed.

For sheriffs, sexual character and history evidence was not really a Sheriff Court problem. They stated that they had never encountered attempts at delving into the sexual history, or attacks on the sexual character of the complainer, and that in any case there were few sexual offences going through the Sheriff Courts (in fact, there are more than is commonly perceived (see Chapter 4)).

There was no consensus between the three advocates depute, two of whom felt they lacked experience of sexual offence cases in which the legislation was relevant. One expressed the view that the opportunities for attacking the complainer in any shape and form were limited, and expressed a faith in the jury even, say, in a rape case involving a prostitute, to draw appropriate inferences from corroborating evidence of torn clothing or distress. The third advocate depute was very familiar with the legislation and its background. He took a very definite stance that the legislation had made no significant difference in the courtroom because it 'was to tackle a perceived evil which, in my view did not exist'. This misperception he attributed to the rape crisis lobby, who had been possibly influenced by the media, and who in turn were 'giving publicity to things in England'. His impression was that 'in England it was much worse, not only in that counsel tended to go for women in a way they do not here but that the phenomenon of light sentences for rape – an important background factor in certain crimes – might also be mainly an English problem.' He thus argued 'that in Scotland women never had been gutted and attacked horribly in court' and that 'people were not gratuitously attacking women'. 'It could only be done under certain controlled circumstances.' All that the new legislation did was to reaffirm the pre-existing situation: 'When it could be done now was in fact the only time it was done before.' This view, that it was in fact an English not a Scottish problem, was echoed by sheriffs, fiscals, and members of the defence.

Procurators fiscal said their potential experience of the issues involved is slightly split, in that they are involved in preparing cases for the High Court, yet their actual courtwork is confined to the Sheriff Courts where such evidence is less likely to appear because there is less at stake especially in summary cases. Although recognising in the abstract that sheriff-and-jury trials, notably sodomy and possibly assault with intent to rape, potentially raised problems, one said it was still essentially a 'rape problem'. Another, reverting to the more general 'England' theme said that Scottish lawyers did not tend to go in for 'subtle defences' which he associated with the relentless pursuit of single issues. Scottish defences had more of a pot luck quality raising a wide number of issues, with perhaps 'a few red herrings thrown in', so that it was impossible to tell exactly what line the defence would take.

However, the fiscals noted potential problems, for instance that, perhaps exceptionally, 'lawyers are willing to try anything to get their clients off and put complainers in as bad a light as possible', indeed that defence attacks might go in waves as a 'flavour of the month thing, where these things tend to get imitated'. Some scepticism was expressed as to the possible effects of any legislation in the area. One who welcomed anything that could be done in 'this era of the victim' to ameliorate her or his position, felt there could be a real gap between legislative intentions and actual consequences. A proponent of the 'England problem' nonetheless commented about the Scottish courts:

> If an experienced defence lawyer or defence advocate cannot smuggle in some of these sort of questions without asking them directly, he is not worth his salt ... in such a job, many lawyers are experts at rhetoric, empty or otherwise. So I do not think it would prevent questioning.

Others reiterated the theme that all the new legislation does is to reinforce the old rules in a statutory form acting at most as a 'reminder, deterring ill-considered or speculative attacks that should never have taken place anyway'. Equally, the 'interests of justice' clause ensures that 'all relevant questions on credibility, or whatever, will still be admissible as they always were, thus returning the situation to square one.' From this perspective, the legislation was deemed as a well intentioned human response to the feelings of victims that did not really alter the law.

The defence counsel were united in saying that the legislation had made no difference in the courtroom beyond formalising the existing situation, which was at least useful in 'letting everyone know where they stand', rather than defence just 'bashing on with their questions and waiting to be stopped by the judge or prosecutor', or as an aid to inexperienced practitioners. But one of them could not find even these virtues and stated that:

> Because of that rider in the second subsection about ... 'the interests of justice', I think that the legislation is a waste of time. (defence counsel 3)

Defence advocates were particularly vocal about the 'demand' politics of the reform. The legislation was described as a response to a demand to protect witnesses, especially women and children, and as a 'cosmetic' piece of legislation, 'so that members of Parliament can say to their women's lib constituents ...' and as 'lip service to feminism'.

There was an interesting clash of opinion between two defence agents who agreed – but for opposite reasons – that the legislation had made no difference. One reiterated the familiar point that attacking a complainer's character was not quite as widespread in Scottish criminal cases as people might have us think. The other began by stating that when he first started off in practice about 17 years ago there was a common practice of questioning female witnesses, particularly complainers, about their sexual history – and that it still was prevalent today: 'I haven't seen any noticeable change.' While he felt such questioning 'didn't always go over the score' in aggressiveness in the Sheriff Court, that reservation did not necessarily apply in the High Court, where the stakes were much higher and instructions given to solicitors and counsel could often be that the whole background of a woman's sexual history would have to be brought out. The reason for the legislation's lack of impact he gave as, 'the exemption clause which allows the judge to rule on what he thinks should be the general guidelines within which the questioning should be limited'.

There is then a substantial (although not universal) consensus among members of the legal profession that there is not now (if there ever was) a problem concerning the use of sexual character and sexual history evidence in the Scottish Courts. The confidence with which this is asserted does not square with the level of sexual history and sexual character evidence observed by researchers or picked up by the monitoring of clerks. It seems possible that legal practioners do not always recognise sexual history and sexual character evidence at the time and/or that they do not remember it as such. Alternatively, and this view was clearly articulated by some, sexual history evidence and sexual character evidence are seen clearly enough but they are seen as at an acceptable and unproblematic level which needs no remedy and/or they are seen as intractable.

CONCLUSION

The views of the legal practitioners help to clarify why sexual history evidence is still a feature of so many cases. The practitioners all stressed that the main test of admissibility of evidence is its relevance. However, they alluded to a number of pressures against strict tests of relevancy: the desire to give the jury a full unedited version of events and tactical reasons such as not being seen to object or intervene too often. More important perhaps is the fact that there were a range of views about what is and what is not relevant sexual history evidence. Practitioners were not always aware of the dissensus, believing rather that there is general agreement.

A minority of interviewees clearly continued to regard any sexual history evidence as relevant, and had little sympathy with the concerns expressed by *MacPhail* and the *Scottish Law Commission Report*. The majority had more specific ideas about when sexual history is relevant and believed that, on the whole, these represented the only times such evidence is put to a jury, hence the widespread view that there is not really any problem in the Scottish courts. The belief that only relevant evidence is generally admitted is paradoxical given that not all share the same criteria of relevance. The issue on which there was most consensus is that regarding past sexual relations between the complainer and the accused. Most regarded such information as relevant evidence, at least at the level of necessary background narrative to the case. Many either believed that past consensual intercourse is indicative of consent or they believed that juries believe this. Evidence of 'flirting with the accused' was also regarded by many as relevant to consent. However, ranked against those making these connections between certain sorts of behaviour and consent are a set of respondents who vehemently repudiated these ideas.

There was no more consensus on the relevance of sexual relations between complainers and third parties. For example, in each professional grouping there were practitioners who believed that evidence of promiscuity was relevant to a defence of consent. There were also a set of interviewees arguing that this is precisely what the legislation was designed to exclude.

Views on the extent to which there is a problem of harmful use of sexual history evidence are interwoven with understandings of its prejudicial effects on the outcome of the trial. The defence were the most certain that sexual history evidence swayed juries. From the perspective of many of the defence, 'throwing a smoke screen of immorality around the complainer' was a legitimate tactic and one they knew worked. Prosecution were aware of subtle defence tactics which besmirched the sexual/moral character of the complainer but there was no consensus on whether or how to deal with this, and judges typically declared that they were unlikely to intervene. There was no general support for weighing the prejudicial effect of evidence against its relevance.

Some disquiet was expressed about the open discretionary nature of 'the interests of justice' clause. Among those who, in contrast, saw it as the saving grace of the legislation were practitioners who believed that the legislation had been unnecessary in the first place and fortuitously changed nothing.

NOTES

1. Although court observation revealed a number of attacks on the complainer's character there were no retaliatory attacks on the accused. Fiscal 4 commented, 'you have to be very careful about doing that, because obviously if you bring out character of the accused in the wrong situation, then you might otherwise lose a conviction that you might have been going to get. I think there's an argument for objecting to as much as possible that does not appear to be directly relevant to what's before the court'. Most prosecutors, however, were wary of objecting.
2. Again proximity in time to the subject matter of the charge was seen as important.
3. *SLC Report*, para. 3, p. 14. It is worth noting that one of Heilbron's recommendations was a statutory affirmation that any attack on the character of the complainant warranted a counter-attack on the accused.

9

Breaches of the Rules

Sexual character and sexual history evidence about the complainer was introduced without application in many cases in both the High Court and the Sheriff Court. Sometimes such evidence was introduced by the prosecution as allowed under the legislation, although regarded as potentially problematic by some commentators, especially where it becomes the subject of defence cross-examination, as it often was. Whether or not defence questioning was responsive to Crown evidence, it has been classified here as a breach of the legislation if it involved sexual history or sexual character evidence introduced without an application. As noted in Chapter 3, there may be some ambiguity here when the defence is pursuing matters already introduced by the prosecution, and Chambers and Millar, and others clearly thought the legislation did not control normal defence rights here. The approach taken here is that the legislation did require an application to be made even for 'normal' cross-examination and, with one exception, this was the view of the practitioners interviewed. Sufficient information is generally given to identify those cases as they are discussed; therefore any reader dissatisfied with this classification can make their own comment.

Recording sexual history and sexual character evidence necessarily also touches on the question of what instances should count, as discussed in Chapter 4. High Court clerks recorded any instance during the trial of the following types of sexual history evidence concerning the complainer: sexual relations with the accused, sexual relations with others, prostitution, virginity, masturbation and pregnancy. Clerks were not, however, asked to record sexual character evidence as such. As well as recording whether or not an application was made, High Court clerks also distinguished whether this evidence was used by the prosecution, the defence or both. This was crucial to estimating levels of breach, because of the Crown's exemption from the new rules. An estimated 16 per cent of High Court cases were in breach of the legislation and the rate remained stable over the period despite an increase in applications; observation which also included sexual character evidence suggested a higher level of 21–8 per cent .[1]

The monitoring by clerks indicated that in 24 per cent of those High Court trials in which there was no application to introduce prohibited evidence, nevertheless such evidence was heard. Observation suggested that the situation was no better for solemn cases heard in the Sheriff Courts,[2] although a marked lower incidence of sexual history evidence was observed in cases heard by summary proceedings. Apparent breaches of the legislation did not typically result in intervention by either the prosecution or the presiding judge or sheriff. High Court clerks indicated interventions in less than 10 per cent of these cases and this tallied with findings from court observation.

Using detailed notes from court observation, this chapter focuses on defence questioning, while noting, where appropriate, the prosecution evidence that prompted it. In other words, the chapter describes the types of references to the complainer's sexual conduct that were involved in cases with apparent disregard for the legislation. As in Chapters 6 and 7, the cases are referred to by the number allocated in the research study, which allows the reader to check further details in Appendix 3. An obvious question to address is whether or not such evidence would have been admitted had an application been made. In examining the observed cases in more detail, it is useful to frame the picture by reference to the application cases discussed above, for two reasons. First, the application cases give some standard as to what should count as evidence requiring an application. This follows the guiding principle of the research to tend towards conservative criteria for identifying sexual character or history evidence. Second, even if the defence questioning without an application is recognised as a breach of the legislation, it might be argued that this is a mere technicality if much of this evidence would have been admitted had an application been made. This, of course, is not necessarily an absolute standard of propriety in itself, given some of the questions raised about applications, but it gives a measure of comparison. Specifically this has meant excluding for numerical purposes (while still noting) the more subtle modes of sexual connotation and innuendo that can build up – in Peter Fraser's words, quoted earlier, through 'a skillful line of questioning, without mentioning the word sex'. The figures for sexual character and history evidence given here do not include, for instance, several instances of the defence suggesting that young complainers were deliberately trying to appear older, suggesting sexual precocity, yet without asking about sexual character or behaviour directly; also excluded are five High Court cases where something bordering on sexual character or history evidence was introduced by the defence. Through comparison with cases in which applications were observed it is possible to conclude tentatively whether or not the evidence would have been admitted if an application had been made. Available data meant that this could only be done with respect to the High Court. Clerk returns indicate fewer applications in the Sheriff Courts, and none were observed.

OVERVIEW

High Court

Out of the 79 trials observed in the High Court, there were 22 that contained defence questioning concerning the complainer's sexual character or sexual history in the absence of an application to do so.[3] Most of the cases involved charges of rape or attempted rape. The inclusion of eight (058, 069, 074, 121, 123, 135, 139, 143) of these 22 cases requires additional justification since the evidence in question referred primarily to the complainer expressing a sexual interest in the accused rather than very specific sexual behaviour and, hence, might be regarded as not falling under the legislation. It should be remembered that an application to introduce evidence that the complainer had previously kissed and flirted with the accused was unsuccessful. And in all of these cases the questioning of the complainer contained elements of an attack on her character in sexual matters. In some of these cases, other sexual evidence was also involved. As is discussed below, on a more conservative interpretation of breaches of the legislation, informed by observation of applications, five of these cases would be excluded. (Five additional cases where something bordering on sexual history or sexual character evidence was introduced by the defence have been set aside as more doubtful breaches of the legislation.)

Sheriff Court

Solemn Procedure

Fourteen full trials heard under solemn procedure (with a jury) were observed. Sexual history evidence of the prohibited type was not heard in all of these trials. In two cases, no sexual history evidence was heard at all (020, 055) and in another it was confined to the subject matter of the charge (016). In two cases, evidence was introduced by the prosecution and not referred to again (010 – details of steady relationship with boyfriend; 081 – lack of hymen) and hence these cases do not involve prohibited evidence. The following discussion refers to those nine Sheriff Court solemn cases where sexual history evidence was used by the defence without reference to the legislation (012, 106, 120, 147, 148, 152, 159, 164, 166). It should be noted that there were no objections from the prosecution in any of these cases. As discussed below, three of these cases involved 'sexually interested' behaviour on the part of the complainer towards the accused leading up to the incident and would be excluded from a more conservative interpretation of breach of the legislation (120, 152, 166), although again the questioning contained elements suggesting that the complainer was 'not of good character in relation to sexual matters'.

Summary Procedure

There were 22 observed Sheriff Court cases heard under summary procedure. Four of these cases involved prohibited evidence introduced by the defence (004, 056, 112, 130) in breach of the legislation. There were an additional four cases that involved something bordering on sexual history or character evidence; in three cases the defence tried to present young complainers as sexually precocious without directly addressing sexual behaviour[4] (005, 094, 133), and a fourth involved alleged payment to the complainer for sex which was the subject matter of the charge (096). These cases are not counted as breaches of the legislation.

As in the solemn procedure cases that were attended, there were no applications made to introduce sexual history evidence in any cases heard under summary procedure. However, the legislation was the reason for prosecution objections in two cases (056, 112). The objections in both cases referred to section 346A (1) (*c*), 'sexual behaviour not forming part of the subject matter of the charge'. These cases will be discussed in more detail below.

EVIDENCE BY EXCLUSIONS

Most of the evidence which referred to the complainer's sexual conduct without reference to the legislation could be categorised under the third exclusion, 'sexual behaviour not forming part of the subject matter of the charge'. Direct references to prostitution, prohibited by the second exclusion, were very rare. However, there were more numerous instances of evidence that could possibly have fallen under the first exclusion prohibiting evidence showing or tending to show that the complainer is 'not of good character in relation to sexual matters'. Character evidence of this type appeared in both High and Sheriff Courts.

Sexual Behaviour Not Forming Part of the Subject Matter of the Charge *[s. 141A/346A (1) (c)]*

Sexual Behaviour with the Accused

High Court Cases. In 16 of the 22 relevant cases there was defence questioning about other instances of sexual behaviour between the complainer and the accused which were not the subject matter of the charge. Six cases involved a past relationship, one an alleged previous sexual encounter, one involved alleged sexual intercourse since the incident, three involved past 'sexually interested' behaviour, and five involved sexually interested behaviour leading up to the incident. Eight of these cases also involved alleged sexual behaviour with someone other than the accused or questions about virginity.

Six cases involved a complainer and an accused who had had a previous sexual relationship (019, 024,[5] 066, 071, 111, 171). Much of the evidence was introduced by the prosecution and the defence subsequently picked up on the evidence in cross-examination. The prosecution was establishing the background of the relationship between the complainer and the accused. In some cases, the prosecution asked about sexual relations in order to establish the effective breakdown of the marriage. The main purpose of defence questioning was to undermine the prosecution case that consent was absent. They were appealing to the notion that consent in the past makes consent in the present more likely, often also attacking the character and credibility of the complainer suggesting that she was 'that sort of woman'.

For example, in case 171, a rape case, the prosecution took evidence from the complainer that she had lived with the accused and that they had co-owned the house in which the complainer lived. The defence cross-examination began 'Perhaps I could start by asking what background relationship you had with the accused', and proceeded to ask a series of questions suggesting that the complainer had initiated the affair with the accused and demanded that he leave his wife and children in order to live with her. These questions were not explicitly about sex but bordered on suggesting 'not of good character in relation to sexual matters' and, embedded in the series of questions, was one explicitly about her sexual behaviour. The questions included: 'Did you at some stage make it known to him you were single and lived alone?' 'Did you not give him your telephone number and address and ask him to call as you were attracted to him?' '[Was it] not the case when he was visiting [the town] you called him and invited him for coffee?' 'Was it accepted you might go out for a drink?' 'You knew he was married?' 'You knew he had two children?' 'After that did you go back to your place and an affair commenced?' This last question amounts to asking whether she had sex with the man the first night that she went out with him. That is certainly how the complainer answered it as she said, 'not immediately that night' to which the defence repeated, 'I mean that night'. When the complainer again denied it, the judge intervened with the question, 'On a later occasion?' to which the complainer said she had. In case 024, the defence suggested that sexual relations had occurred the day before the incident in the half hour that the complainer was alone with her husband on his release from prison.[6] In case 019 the fact of marriage was also used to work against the presumption that sex would not occur voluntarily during a time of menstruation.

In terms of breaches of the legislation it is important to distinguish between past sexual relations, and relations arguably part of the same occasion as the charge, since the exclusions cover only the former. In cases involving an accused and a complainer who were ex-partners (019, 024, 071, 171), or who had had a sexual relationship of some duration (066, 111), defence investigation was not limited to a time period immediately around the incident in question. In case 066, it was the prosecution who initiated detailed questions about the precise number of past occasions of sexual intercourse, how recently these had occurred before the event, and whether or not oral sex was involved (which was also part of the incident). In this case the judge made reference to the legislation, and questioned the prosecution about pursuing this line of evidence, thereby raising the possibility of further exploration by the defence. The prosecution simply said 'the approach I take is so tied up that the questions should be allowed'. The defence did return to these questions, repeating each one. There was no further intervention on the matter. In case 111, the complainer, aged 17, had in the past had an affair with the accused which involved 'three in a bed' sessions with his wife, this too being an aspect of the incident. The judge intervened to ask more questions about the 'threesome', and the issue of previous intercourse with the accused was elaborated upon.

If the defence in these cases had sought permission to question the complainer about the history of her sexual relationship with the accused, there is little doubt that they would have been successful. They would not have properly fallen under the 'same occasion' exception since they referred to incidents quite separate from the charge although, as noted in Chapter 6, one successful application was made using this exception to investigate the relationship between a complainer and accused who were ex-partners. The 'interests of justice' would be the most likely exception employed here. Observed applications that sought to explore the prior sexual relationship between the complainer and the accused were always successful and generally had the support of the prosecution and some-times followed evidence led by the prosecution acknowledging the previous sexual relationship. Moreover, following successful applications, questioning was not limited to the immediate period around the incident and sometimes took on the quality of a character attack as happened in case 171 without an application.

The other relevant High Court cases without application involved a specific, alleged previous occasion of sexual intercourse, as in case 176, (where the defence put it to one of the two complainers that she had had consensual sexual intercourse with one of the accused earlier the same evening as the alleged rape) or, more usually, alleged 'sexually interested' behaviour towards the accused on the part of the complainer. In three cases the alleged past incident was one quite separate in time from the events which were the subject matter of the charge (074, 121, 123) and details of time and place were not always specified. In all but one (121) of these cases, these allegations were denied by the complainer. These cases are fairly similar to the case discussed in Chapters 6 and 7 in which the defence made an application to the judge to introduce evidence that the complainer had been kissing and flirting with the accused five or six weeks previously. This application was objected to by the prosecution on the grounds of irrelevancy and refused by the judge. In one case (074), evidence was introduced by the defence after the complainer's cross-examination, to suggest that she had already had sex with the accused on the same evening as the incident. The complainer obviously had no chance to comment. Applications to put an alleged prior or subsequent incident of sexual intercourse between the complainer and the accused to the complainer were generally successful and it is not clear why no application was sought and why this was not put to the complainer in case 074.

In five cases (058, 069, 135, 139, 143), attention was focused upon the complainer's 'provocative' or 'sexually interested' form of behaviour in the events leading up to the incident in question. In all the cases, the argument was usually based on kissing and cuddling or dancing with the accused, or entering into some other sort of behaviour which was supposedly indicative of sexual interest in the accused. In all these cases this bordered on suggesting that the complainer was 'not of good character in relation to sexual matters'. Similar questions were also asked in the observed cases involving an application to introduce prohibited evidence. But no application was made just on the basis of 'sexually interested' behaviour leading up to the incident, although this was part of some applications. It is not clear whether the questioning discussed here would be generally regarded as requiring an application or not. In calculating evidence in breach of the legislation, these cases are excluded from the more conservative estimates. In 069 the accused claimed that he had had sexual intercourse with the complainer since the incident but this was never put to the complainer. In case 143 the defence were attempting to rebut the medical evidence of virginity with questions concerning the complainer's sexual precocity. Comparison with cases in which applications were heard does not clarify whether these cases would have succeeded since, for each case, both a similar successful and an unsuccessful application was observed.

Sheriff Solemn Cases. Similar use of 'sexually interested' behaviour was made in half of the Sheriff solemn cases referring to sexual behaviour between the complainer and the accused (120, 152, 166). These cases involved charges of assault with intent to rape. As in the equivalent High Court cases, the behaviour was arguably part of the same occasion as the charge; that is, it formed part of the events leading up to the incident which was the subject of the charge. In the Sheriff solemn cases the sexual behaviour involved was kissing, cuddling, fondling, and other behaviour which was used to show that the complainer fancied the accused, and therefore, by implication, consented to what later took place. Some examples of this are: 'Is the position not simply this, Miss ... , you indulged in kissing and cuddling with this boy throughout the whole evening, that you were quite willing for him to give you those kisses on the neck, and that you had a further kissing and cuddling session in the bus shelter on the way home?'(166). 'You followed him, with your drink, into the men's toilet, and certain intimacies occurred?' (152). 'Earlier, when he wanted to smuggle you into his room so you could have sex, you tried to get in the back way, through the kitchen. And when that failed you went to the cemetery, for sex?' (120).

Sometimes behaviour which was not unambiguously sexual was presented as evidence of sexual interest. Glances cast across a room at the accused, and repeatedly walking past the accused (even if he was standing next to ladies' toilets), were used by the defence in this way. Also suggestive dialogue between the complainer and accused is construed as an indication of sexual interest. For example, in a Sheriff solemn case involving charges of assault with intent to rape the defence put it to the complainer that, '[The accused] joked about your dress, saying "that's some dress, is it supposed to button up the front or the back?" and you said "that depends on my mood."'(152). The defence went on to suggest that this exchange was tantamount to sexual foreplay.

When comparing these cases and cases with applications, it has to be noted that in the case of the latter, such questioning more often appeared in cross-examination over and above the material addressed in the application, rather than within the subject matter of the application itself. In one case (049) such a line of questioning took place in spite of the application to ask the complainer about kissing and flirting with the accused, having been refused. Legal professionals' discrepant views of the relevance of such questions are discussed in Chapter 8. However, it is likely that many practitioners would regard cases, in which the sexual history of the complainer is restricted to the development of the acquaintance between the complainer and the accused leading up to the event, as being hardly in breach of the legislation. Hence, on a more conservative inclusion of cases of breach these three Sheriff solemn cases would be excluded.

In three of the six Sheriff solemn cases referring to behaviour between the complainer and the accused (012, 106, 159) the behaviour was said to have occurred on a quite separate occasion either prior to or subsequent to the charges laid out in the indictment. These cases involved charges of indecent assault (012, 159) or shameless and indecent conduct (106). For example, in case 012, the defence suggested that the 14-year-old male complainer and the accused had met a number of times in the past, and that the complainer always initiated sexual activity by asking the accused to masturbate so that he could watch. In case 159, the defence maintained that mutual 'fondling' had occurred over a substantial period of time, and that the female complainer had once tried to seduce the accused, by pulling up her skirt and saying 'come on in', that intercourse was then attempted, and would have occurred if not for the arrival of someone else. In case 106, which involved three complainers, the defence tried to show that two of the complainers had participated in sexual behaviour with the accused since the incident in the indictment. Here, the defence alleged that the complainers had, individually, met up with the accused in a 'gay' cafe and accompanied him back to his flat, and spent the night. Again if the defence had made recourse to an application in these cases it is probable that they would have been successful. The defence might have appealed to both 'explain or rebut' or the 'interests of justice' exceptions, as occurred in a number of similar applications.

Sheriff Summary Cases. One summary case involved references to sexual behaviour with the accused other than that outlined in the charge. In this case (130), involving charges of indecent exposure and indecent assault, the complainer had met the accused earlier on the same day. The defence suggested that at that time they had kissed and cuddled and started touching each other, and then made an arrangement to meet up again that night for agreed intercourse.

Sexual Behaviour with Someone Other than the Accused

Whereas the defence introduced evidence of sexual relations between the complainer and the accused primarily to suggest consent, but also to undermine the credibility of the complainer, there were also a number of uses of sexual relations between the complainer and others. Again there were parallels between cases in which applications had been made to introduce such evidence. Questions concerning the complainer's sexual activity without reference to the accused appeared in 13 High Court cases. In six of these cases virginity was at issue. In three of the cases the defence asked the complainer if she had ever had sexual intercourse or if she was a virgin prior to the incident (070, 162, 176). In one case the defence made much of the medical evidence that the 15-year-old complainer was not a virgin (095). And in two other cases the defence countered medical evidence of virginity by lines of questioning suggesting the complainer was sexually precocious and seeking sex (074, 143). In cases 074 and 143 and also in cases 135 and 139, sexually interested or provocative behaviour with someone other than the accused was alleged.

Two additional cases involved evidence of sexual behaviour with others, introduced by the prosecution to strengthen their case (as with virginity in 143 and 074) which was then picked up and used by the defence to strengthen their case (069, 136). In two similar application cases, one application (080) was granted to ask about virginity on the basis that it would test the consistency of the complainer's statement that the incident was the first time by asking for an explanation of her lack of hymen. The other attempt to ask about a damaged hymen (077) failed on the basis of being speculative questioning. Both these applications involved the 'interests of justice' exception and the former also 'explain or rebut'.

In three High Court cases, all involving charges of rape (011, 019, 066), sexual behaviour with others was introduced and used in an attempt to show alternative explanations for injury or signs of sexual intercourse, while also attacking the credibility of the complainer. In cases 011 and 019, the defence tried to show that the complainer's bruises and genital tenderness were due to sexual activity with someone else. In 066 sexual behaviour with others was explored by the defence to account for the forensic findings of semen (although this alternative source was actually ruled out by forensic findings).

Sexual history evidence was also used to suggest alternative sources of medical evidence in Sheriff Court trials. There were three examples of this among the solemn cases. In an indecent assault case (147), the defence tried to show that the vaginal injuries sustained by the complainer were due to masturbation (childhood sexual abuse was also suggested). The same possible explanation was put to the complainer as the reason for her lack of a hymen in a statutory offence case (164) (s. 5 of the Sexual Offences (Scotland) Act – indecent behaviour towards a girl between 12 and 16 years old). In this case the defence also elicited information from another witness concerning whether the young complainer had ever suspected she was pregnant. In an assault with intent to rape case (166), the defence tried to show that love bites on the complainer's neck were 'old', and therefore unlikely to have come from the accused. This case also involved eliciting information about a previous pregnancy.

In one summary case, sexual history evidence was used to indicate an alternative source of evidence. In case 056, again a statutory offence (s. 4 (1) of the Sexual Offences (Scotland) Act 1976 – unlawful sexual intercourse with a girl under 16), it was suggested that pregnancy was due to sexual intercourse with someone other than the accused.

As was discussed in Chapter 3, putting alternative explanations for medical or forensic evidence was envisaged by the Scottish Law Commission as a circumstance involving the legitimate use of sexual history evidence. Observation of applications documented a number of appeals to the 'explain or rebut' and 'interests of justice' exceptions on these grounds. Such circumstances were also (along with 'the orgy'), among the few involving legitimately introducing evidence of sexual conduct with third parties envisaged by interviewees. Therefore, if applications had been made in these cases, they would probably have been successful.

However, there is an issue of what evidential basis the defence have for suggesting alternative explanations for medical or forensic evidence. When an application is made then there is some opportunity for the basis of the proposed questioning to be examined. The legal professionals interviewed generally agreed that speculative questioning without any evidential basis, was not really acceptable, although it sometimes happened. It is not that the defence have to prove their case but they must have some basis for their questions. At the very least there has to be a medical basis for the starting point of speculation or some factual basis about the complainer, showing not just an abstract possibility, but some evidence that the alternative explanation, as suggested by the defence, is possible. For example, to suggest masturbation as an alternative source to vaginal injuries is only proper if the defence has the testimony of a doctor that the injuries are consistent with masturbation. More strongly, to suggest sexual intercourse between the complainer and another as an alternative explanation for evidence should also require that 'the other' testify to the sexual intercourse, or some alternative supporting evidence be given such as a record of last intercourse taken by the doctor in the medical report.

However, observation of applications indicated that the fact that an application was made was not a guarantee that the evidential basis of proposed questions was carefully scrutinised. The application cases demonstrate that sometimes the evidential basis of defence questioning was thin. Moreover, a number of applications argued that the questioning was necessary to demonstrate an alternative explanation for medical or forensic evidence (for example, finding an alternative source of semen when the facts of sexual intercourse were not at issue) and the purpose seemed to be an attack on the complainer's credibility and/or to suggest consent. This was also the likely purpose in the cases described here. However, in the cases where there was no application, the defence did not make any statements justifying their actions.

It is still possible that, had applications been made, in some cases they would have been successful on the grounds that the proposed questions were relevant to showing an 'alternative source' of evidence although in fact the questions would have served a different purpose. An 'alternative source' argument might have been made, for example, in case (066) where the complainer was asked very detailed questions about her relationship with her boyfriend and the dates and times of sexual intercourse. However, such a justification for the questions could have been challenged if either the prosecutor or the judge had been prepared to intervene. While these dates were close to the time of the alleged offence, (as in an observed application (134) see Chapters 6, 7 and 11) there was also clear forensic evidence that semen found after the incident could have come from the accused but not from her boyfriend. The defence clearly knew this but nevertheless pursued the questions possibly because they helped to damage the credibility of the complainer by suggesting that she was 'not of good character in relation to sexual matters'. Observation of application cases suggests that if he had been challenged on this, the defence might simply have produced a more acceptable account such as testing the consistency of the complainer's answers with respect to the medical report. On the other hand, the questioning might have been disallowed in a formal application.

Evidence referring to 'sexual behaviour with someone other than the accused' often had an indirect bearing on sexual character. This happened in two rape cases[7] without applications (074, 135) and in a case of attempted rape (143). For example, in case (135), the complainer was said by the defence to be that night 'looking for a man', allegedly putting her hand down someone's trousers and commenting what a 'big boy' he was, allegedly being 'all over' a number of men, and engaging in lewd forms of banter. While the defence motive can only be inferred, it seems that these were attempts to discredit the complainer as a credible witness and to suggest that she was the sort of person who was liable to consent to intercourse, notwithstanding her allegation of sexual assault.

In none of these cases was the defence one of mistaken belief in consent on the part of the accused.[8] Indeed, case 135 was the only case out of the four where the accused was actually present to observe this allegedly sexually provocative behaviour with others, and, even in this case, the defence made no suggestion of a mistaken belief formed by the accused on the basis of his observations of the complainer's conduct. Rather, in all of these cases, the point seemed to be to suggest some basic disposition for sex either in general, and/or on the occasion in question. In one other case (139), the defence put to the complainer that she was kissed by a friend of the accused in a pub prior to the incident, apparently to suggest a willingness to engage in sexual activity. In the previous chapter several interviewees were cited asserting that this type of character attack not only should not, but simply would not, be allowed to happen. Others argued that evidence of flirtatious behaviour and/or of general promiscuity was relevant and should be allowed. When evidence of this nature was the subject of an application it generally had mixed fortunes and it is possible that if a formal request had been made to introduce such evidence it would have been excluded as irrelevant in at least some of these cases.

Incrimination

A special defence of 'incrimination' was lodged in two Sheriff solemn cases (147, 148). This special defence, by its very nature, involves evidence of sexual relations with someone other than the accused, so it is not unreasonable to expect that during these trials there would have been an application. Indeed, the legislation provides subsection 141B (1) (*b*) (ii) for this purpose, but no reference to it was made. In neither of these two cases did the defence seek to use the special defence to challenge either the medical or forensic findings, or other prosecution evidence. Rather it was used more in an attempt to establish that the complainers in both cases had some prior liaison with someone other than the accused, on an occasion other than that charged on the indictment. And in at least one of the two cases (147), the defence of incrimination was not really about incrimination as such; there was no suggestion that the alleged events happened but someone else was responsible for the evidence incriminating the accused. As was observed in three application cases, incrimination seemed to be thrown in to give added legitimacy to attempts to introduce questions which might undermine the complainer's credibility.

In case 147, the 'incrimination' thus turned out to refer to an alleged incident with a third party two years previously that, in turn, was supposed to have provided the now-nine-year-old complainer with the necessary information to invent a charge against the accused. The first question asked of her by the defence was, 'You've told us about the things that happened. These happened in the woods with [the incriminee] didn't they?' Through this leading questioning, the defence was in effect trying to establish that the complainer had accrued some sexual knowledge from a previous incident with the incriminee, and that she had then used this knowledge to claim something had happened with the accused. In this particular case, the cross-examination of the complainer was extremely short, and apart from the above question, the matter was not referred to again during her cross-examination. However, in the cross-examination of other witnesses the defence introduced and developed the issue of incrimination. The complainer's aunt (who was also the aunt of the accused, and of the incriminee) was asked, 'Did you ever hear your mother say anything in relation to the girl's person?' Although this was objected to by the prosecution on the grounds that it constituted hearsay evidence, it was overruled by the sheriff, when the defence explained that the witness's mother was dead. The witness replied, 'My mother said [the complainer] had disappeared with [the incriminee] and when she came back she was covered in love-bites.' This alleged incident with the incriminee had taken place two years prior to the charges outlined in the indictment (when she was aged seven). Further direct questions were asked of the incriminee when he took the witness stand. 'Have there ever been times when you pulled [the complainer's] pants down and put your finger inside her?' 'Did you not once say to [the accused] that you had screwed [the complainer]?'

In the second case involving a defence of incrimination (148), the cross-examination of the complainer contained many direct references to her sexual past with her stepfather, which was in fact the substance of separate charges due to be heard in the High Court one month later. The complainer was asked by the defence, 'You've had some problems at home with your mum and stepdad [the incriminee]. Your mother has been involved in this, and has in fact assisted your stepdad?' 'You know that you are going to another court on … regarding the things that your stepdad did to you and since this started there has been nothing but talk about these sexual things. And the truth is that this case started when your stepfather tried to get [the accused] involved as well because he knew [the accused] was giving you money?' Subsequent similar questions were posed in such a way as to suggest that the stepfather was trying to spread the blame to include the accused as well as himself. The mother of the complainer was asked, 'Do you recall yourself participating with your husband (the incriminee) in sexual abuse of your daughter?' 'Did you not witness incidents of a sexual nature between [the complainer] and your husband?' 'Do you not remember saying that [the complainer's] period was a week late and that as far as you were concerned it was [the incriminee] who had made her pregnant?'

Had there been an application in case 148 it is likely that it would have been successful and the 'incrimination' exception could have been used for this purpose. However, in case 147 any investigation of the defence line during the subsequent application dialogue might have forced a shift in the grounds of application from a defence of incrimination to an attack on the complainer's credibility. It is possible, however, that the application would still have been successful.

In two summary cases, the legislation *did* prompt some prosecution objections to the introduction of evidence of past sexual behaviour with someone other than the accused. Among other things, it was suggested, in both cases, that the complainer had become or suspected she was pregnant by someone other than the accused. During the cross-examination of the stepfather of the 13-year-old complainer in a charge of unlawful sexual intercourse (112), the defence asked why the complainer was in care. The witness replied, 'Because she made an allegation against me'. The defence asked, 'What sort of allegation?', to which the prosecution objected on the grounds that it would contravene s. 346A (1) (c). The defence argued that he was not trying to elicit evidence about the complainer's sexual behaviour, but about the nature of the allegation.

The prosecution retorted, 'But that [sexual behaviour] is exactly what you are going to show'. To which the sheriff said, 'Well, we won't know that until we hear the answer'. The objection was therefore overruled and the court heard that the complainer had alleged that her stepfather (who was not the accused in this case) had had sexual intercourse with her. A second prosecution objection referring to the legislation occurred later in the same case when the complainer was asked, during cross-examination, whether her recent stay in hospital was because she was pregnant. The sheriff stated, 'If the girl had been the victim of sexual behaviour her age necessarily makes it unlawful'. The defence stated that he acknowledged the point made by the prosecution, but thought that ' ... it might be remedied by s. 346B (1) (*c*)' ('the interests of justice'). The objection was again overruled, and the defence established that the complainer did suspect that she was pregnant and had gone to the hospital for a scan. The pregnancy issue was pursued, and other witnesses were asked if they knew she had visited hospital for this purpose. Pregnancy was also made a major issue in the defence summing-up. The prosecution appeared to have given up, as, when the complainer was asked such questions as, 'Do you have a boyfriend?' 'Have you ever stayed over[night] with him?' 'What sort of things did you do with him?' he did not raise any objections at all. In both these cases if an application had been made it may have been successful, since in each case the sheriff apparently took the view that no application was necessary. However, there is no doubt that the defence questions concerned matters prohibited by the legislation and were arguably contrary to the aim of the reform.

Pregnancy was also an issue in summary case 056. Investigations commenced when it was discovered that the 14-year-old complainer was pregnant. She named her uncle as the father of the child, and he was charged with unlawful intercourse under s. 4 of the Sexual Offences (Scotland) Act 1976. The defence argued that the accused had been wrongfully blamed, and that the complainer's motive for the false allegation was that she was trying to protect herself and the real father. First, the complainer was asked whether she had ever had sexual intercourse with anyone else. Second, it was suggested to her by the defence that she had had intercourse with someone other than the accused at the time of the conception, who was the real father. There were no objections made at this point. However, the legislation was the reason for a prosecution objection during the testimony of another witness. (It is not uncommon for sexual history evidence to be elicited from witnesses other than the complainer. This is particularly so when the complainer is a young girl.)[9] In this case, the defence asked the mother of the 14-year-old complainer, 'Were there any indications that [the complainer] had sexual relations?' The prosecution objected at this point, stating that the question was irrelevant. The objection was, however, overruled, and the defence continued with the question 'Did you have any indications that [complainer] had previous sexual relations before this incident?'. The prosecution objected again, stating that section 346A 'prohibits evidence regarding promiscuity'. The sheriff then sustained the objection. Had the prosecution objected at the outset or had the defence made an application at the outset then it is not clear whether the questioning would have been allowed. As in many cases, the picture of the sexual past of the complainer which the defence introduced by their questions was undoubtedly intended to undermine her credibility as a witness.

Sexual history evidence appeared to come out inadvertently in case 130, an indecent exposure and indecent assault case, during the cross-examination of a 'first report' witness. This witness was testifying to the distressed state of the complainer, and said, 'I think she also said that she had been raped the year before'. There was no prosecution objection, (despite this constituting hearsay evidence), and the defence went on to question in more detail, 'Did she say who had done it?' The witness replied that she believed the complainer had said her stepfather. The defence went on, 'What did she say about being raped the year before by her stepfather?', etc. Subsequently, during the examination of a police witness, the sheriff intervened to ask whether this witness had any information about the complainer being raped by her stepfather. In summing-up, the defence reminded the sheriff that, 'Allegedly, there was some sort of sexual misconduct in the past, and this, I think, reduces her credibility as a reliable witness.'

Sometimes evidence of the complainer's sexual history with someone other than the accused was introduced in a neutral fashion, as factual background detail brought up by the prosecution to establish the complainer's status and address as living with someone, married, unmarried, number of children, identity of fathers of the children, etc. In some cases, this information was used by the prosecution in a much more focused way, for example, to establish an ex-husband as a natural confidant. However, once such evidence had been introduced by the prosecution, it was often taken up by the defence and put to other uses. This happened in both the High Court and the Sheriff Court. One notable example of such use was in a rape case, (058), where the defence attempted to construct a motive for the complainer to lie. Here, the defence suggested that the complainer was afraid that her jealous cohabitee would find out she had had consensual intercourse with the accused. More commonly such evidence is elaborated by the defence to impugn the character of the complainer. Hence this use of such evidence is discussed under the heading of 'not of good character in sexual matters.'

Prostitute or Associate of Prostitutes [s.141A/346A (1) (b)]

High Court

Sexual history evidence appeared without an application in one High Court case involving prostitution (in the usual sense of a person's main income-generating occupation) (011).[10] This case involved, in addition to rape, a number of other charges – assault and abduction, assault on a police officer, and various weapon offences associated with the gun, knife, and sword that the accused had had in his possession and used to threaten the complainer. The fact of the complainer's occupation was used in a number of ways. The prosecution stated that the complainer was 'used to a little rough and tumble' to emphasise the seriousness and truth of the crime as indicated by her distressed state. The defence suggested that her line of work gave an alternative source for her bruises and other injuries. In the summing-up, the defence also suggested that she displayed insufficient resistance to being threatened with a shotgun, 'She is not a housewife, she is a streetwise prostitute, and could have made an attempt to go for the gun. Why not?' Whereas the complainer had suggested that the incident had included a range of sexual acts due to the problems that the man was having with impotence and a small penis, the accused attributed his impotence to the fact that the complainer was, he alleged, 'soaking wet' from other men (despite, as she pointed out, the fact that she always used a condom). Both prosecution and judge insisted on the fact that prostitutes were entitled to the same legal protection as everyone else, and, indeed, the prosecution put it to the accused that he thought he could get away with raping a prostitute, to which he replied, 'No, sir'.

The other main issue was payment. The prosecution asked if money had been received from the client (the accused) and established that it had not, thus suggesting that the incident had not been a normal prostitute/client exchange. The accused's story was that he had never been to a prostitute before, and he believed that it was possible to have sex free with a prostitute if he 'used his charm' – a belief which was confirmed for him since he claimed the entire event had been consensual and free despite his admitted use of the weapons. The final verdict was guilty to a firearm licensing offence (the accused claimed that he had been out bird-shooting when he was apprehended in the city centre an hour after the alleged incident at 11.30 p.m.). In this case had an application been made to question the complainer about her prostitution in order to establish an alternative source for her injuries, then it would probably have been granted. Since the fact of the complainer's prostitution was essential to the narrative of events, the prosecution had to lead evidence of her prostitution and was unlikely to object to further questioning by the defence.

Sheriff Court

There were no Sheriff court cases involving prostitution in the usual sense. However, in three of the nine solemn cases discussed here (106, 120, 148), the defence suggested that the complainers were either offered or received financial payment from the accused for sex.[11] Clearly the defence intention in these cases was to suggest consent, even when consent was technically irrelevant to the charges involved.

In an assault with intent to rape case (120), it was suggested that the complainer had accepted £2 from the accused to accompany him to a nearby cemetery for sex. In case 106, in which the charges were shameless and indecent conduct, it was alleged by the defence that all three of the (male) complainers were regularly paid in return for sexual favours from the accused, and that all three had conspired against him and brought charges when he refused to part with any more money. In case 148, a statutory offence involving a 14-year-old girl, it was established that she regularly received substantial amounts of money from the accused (who was her uncle), and further suggested that she regularly went to him specifically to cadge money in return for mutual masturbation.

There were no summary cases involving prostitution but one of the four cases discussed here involved payment for sex, or, perhaps more to the point, payment to keep quiet about it (130).[12] In this case of indecent exposure and indecent assault, the accused, after the offence, offered the complainer £10 not to tell the police. However, as he did not have that amount of money on him at the time, he asked her to meet him two days later when he promised to pay up. The defence line seemed to be that the suggested meeting indicated a bargain between the complainer and accused. (This was not the only sexual history evidence involved in this case.)

There were only two cases of observed applications in which prostitution was an issue with which comparisons can be made. One unsuccessful application concerned the taking up of prostitution by the complainer some time after the incident that was the subject of the trial, and is not relevant to the cases discussed here. The other involved the defence suggesting that the male complainer in a sodomy case was in fact a 'rent boy'. The judge in this case indicated that an application was hardly necessary. Suggestions that the complainer was a 'rent boy' or 'loose woman' were also made irrespective of the application in a number of application cases. It is very likely that if the defence had chosen to make an application to put it to the complainer that there had been a history of sexual favours for money between the complainer and the accused then permission would have been granted.

Not of Good Character in Relation to Sexual Matters
[s.141A/346A (1)(a)]

Statements such as, 'This is a lady whose door opens to one, two, maybe three or four men', (066), by the defence counsel in a case involving rape and other charges, do seem to be quite clearly the sort of character attack most practitioners believe no longer happens. It is possible to give many more examples of defence statements at least on the borderline of sexual character innuendo. For example, in another rape case, 074, the complainer was said to frequent a fish and chip shop, 'a regular haunt', where she engaged in lewd and suggestive banter with the boys who worked there. The complainer in this case was also alleged by the defence to have told one boy that 'he would get his nooky' if he arranged her a date with another boy.

Those judges, sheriffs and prosecution interviewed who said that there was very little problem in this area believed that the defence would refrain from attacking the character of the complainer because that would entitle the prosecution to retaliate by attacking the accused. However, there were hardly any objections and certainly no counterattacks in any of the observed cases. Moreover, such formulations did not only come from the defence. In case 139, a rape case, the accused's statement that the complainer was 'that kind of girl' was reformulated by the judge as saying that the complainer had been 'flaunting herself' and was 'pretty bold'.

Whether or not a complainer was a virgin, was an issue in a number of cases involving young female complainers. Sometimes, virginity might be used as evidence of 'good character' by the prosecution and its absence as evidence of 'bad character' by the defence, although the prosecution did not always lead this evidence because of the possibility of a subsequent counterattack by the defence. But irrespective of character, virginity becomes an issue because of the view that prior virginity makes consent less likely, or creates a presumption of non-consent which the defence wishes to attack. Commonly, evidence of virginity introduced by the prosecution, either verbally or by Crown production, usually the medical report, was later explored in cross-examination. It has been noted that interviewees, particularly judges, believed that complainers had a tendency to 'hold themselves up' as being particularly virtuous and hence to leave themselves open to attack. The cases we observed did not fit with this but involved complainers simply responding to direct questions about their sexual experience. In a rape case, 176, the defence asked the 16-year-old complainer, 'Were you a virgin that night?' although the Crown had said nothing about virginity. If forced to make an application, the defence may have produced some justification for this, but, on the face of it, the questions were inadmissable.

Questions alluding to the sexual habits or predispositions of the complainer were regularly asked of other witnesses by the defence. These questions were of the variety: 'Was she the kind of person to chat up strangers?' and 'Does she often go out looking for men?'. This was often coupled with references to dress and demeanour. In both High and Sheriff Court cases, the aim of these sorts of questions seemed to be to show that the complainer was 'that kind of girl', one who is sexually bold, and of loose sexual character. One particularly noteworthy example of this kind of evidence was elicited from a defence witness in a Sheriff solemn case involving charges under s. 5 of the Sexual Offences Act (indecent behaviour towards a girl between 12 and 16 years old). Reproduced here is the *entire* defence examination:

DEFENCE: Do you know [the complainer]?
WITNESS: Yes, a while ago I did.
DEFENCE: When was that ?
WITNESS: About two years ago.
DEFENCE: Was she a friend of your family?
WITNESS: No, she was a friend of my friend's daughter.
DEFENCE: What sort of girl was she?
WITNESS: A pleasant girl.
DEFENCE: Did you ever see her distressed?
WITNESS: Once. She thought she was pregnant and didn't want to tell her father or mother.
DEFENCE: Was she injured at all?
WITNESS: No.

There was no cross-examination by the prosecution. One can only assume that this witness, who had very little knowledge of the complainer at all, was brought on to the witness stand solely in order to talk about this pregnancy (which was the first and only time that it had been mentioned during the trial) (164).

Evidence referring to the complainer's sexual behaviour was sometimes introduced in a neutral fashion and then used to suggest 'bad character' by the defence. In cases in both the High and the Sheriff Court, the prosecution established the complainer's status as either single, engaged, married or involved in a steady relationship. This factual information, which gave an indication of the complainer's life style, was often something that was picked up on and reiterated by the defence, although with a different emphasis. For example, in the Sheriff solemn case involving s. 5 of the Sexual Offences Scotland Act (referred to above) the defence said, 'You are single, but you have had boyfriends?', the complainer replied 'No, not really', to which the defence said, 'Come now, presumably you had many boyfriends when you were growing up?'(164). Another example of this type of questioning is, 'You're not married. Have you always lived with your parents, or have you ever lived with someone else?'

Similarly, evidence concerning masturbation, previous full-term pregnancies or abortions, particularly if the complainer is very young or unmarried, has implications for sexual character. Indeed much alleged sexual behaviour, whether with the accused or others, whether flirting or sexual intercourse, can be used in a way which suggests sexual 'bad character'. As in application cases, non-sexual matters such as drinking habits, dress and other aspects of life style were also used in a way which suggested a certain sort of sexual character. Repeated reference to character indicators accumulated, during the course of the trial, resulting in the construction of a sexual character, in much the same way as a reputation is built up.

The use of non-sexual signifiers conveying 'bad sexual character', was typically most prolific in the defence summing-up. 'Dress' was most frequently used, for this purpose. For example in a rape case the defence addressed the jury thus, 'Ask yourself, did she intend to pick up men, deciding that a taxi driver was good enough?', and, 'She had gone out to a disco, ... looking for men ... purring around ... very well dressed for it ... wearing an attractive, provocative dress to show her figure to full advantage' (058). The 'that's what type of girl she is' suggestion simultaneously impugns her character and suggests consent.

This use of dress or other such indicators suggesting sexual character is rarely challenged. However, another rape case, (135), was notable for the judge's very sharp interrogation of a defence witness whose testimony returned several times to a particular item of clothing, a tee-shirt, worn by the complainer, which, he claimed, was very sexually suggestive. First, the witness said that it carried the slogan, 'These are my mounds', then, he modified this to say that it had a picture of a mouse which had led to lewd conversation about holes and mouse-holes, etc. The judge insisted that the tee-shirt be looked at since it was a Crown production. The tee-shirt was inscribed with a picture of a dog, a well-known cartoon character. The judge was extremely scathing about the testimony of this witness, but made no reference to the legislation.

Another defence tactic is to implicate the complainer by introducing character evidence concerning the life style of his or her associates – 'setting the scene' as it were, by placing the complainer in association with other witnesses whose own sexual character and/or life style is brought into question. The first series of questions asked of the mother of the complainer in a Sheriff solemn case involving charges under s. 5 of the Sexual Offences Scotland Act (indecent behaviour towards a girl between 12 and 16), case 148, illustrate this vividly:

DEFENCE: I understand that you were married at 16 and you were carrying [the complainer] at that time?
WITNESS: Yes.

DEFENCE: Shortly afterwards you left your husband and started living with Mr [name]?
WITNESS: Yes.
DEFENCE: Your marriage and relationships have all been quite problematic?

Commonly, in cases involving young or adolescent girls, there is an attempt, by the defence, to typify the complainer as 'sexually provocative' or 'precocious'. Again this seems to be for the purpose of discrediting the complainer and suggesting that she consented to the sexual activity (even though in many of these cases consent is not technically at issue). For example, in a summary case involving charges of lewd and libidinous practice (004), one particular line of questioning was relentlessly pursued in cross-examination of the complainer and other witnesses in the trial. Broadly, this was to suggest that the 13-year-old complainer was (and always had been since earliest childhood) flirtatious and sexually 'precocious', and that the sexual activity in the charge had been initiated by her in order to satisfy her 'avid sexual curiosity'. It was also suggested by the defence that she preferred the company of adult men to women, and that she had developed and maintained a particular pattern of behaviour which she exhibited whenever men were present. This 'direct action' included 'going up to men, sitting on their knees, and ruffling their hair'. In the same case, the prosecution had questioned the mother of the complainer about her daughter's hobbies and interests. The mother replied that she had 'normal' teenage interests – pop records, pop stars, clothes, make-up and, latterly, boys. This was picked up by the defence in his summing-up as 'an unnatural interest in boys for one so young – an obsession in fact'. Although the legislation was not referred to during the trial, this last statement was enough to earn a reprimand from the sheriff at the end of the trial, who told the defence to 'move with the times', that 'children of her age usually experiment with make-up', and that 'to show an interest in boys is normal, nay preferable'.

In summary cases involving s. 4 of the Sexual Offences (Scotland) Act (unlawful sexual intercourse with a girl under 16 years old), there were also attempts to typify the complainers as precocious and as inviting sexual encounters.[13] This was commonly done with reference to the complainer's appearance (physical development, types of dress, e.g. tight jeans, high heels, make-up, hairstyle), demeanour (confident manner, swearing, drinking or smoking habits, and, in one case, chewing gum), and sexual knowledge (provocative behaviour, lewd conversation, boyfriends). Such typifications carry with them character implications. Many of the above examples bear out what one defence advocate was prepared to admit, 'you try to get away with anything which you think the jury will use in assessing the credibility of the complainer'.

It has been noted that questions put to the complainer about sexual behaviour often carry connotations of being 'not of good character in sexual matters'. One case is cited at greater length in order to illustrate the multi-purpose nature of questioning and the cumulative effect in creating an impression of the complainer which could prejudice the outcome of the trial. The style of questioning in this case was fairly typical of the defence questioning of young complainers in rape cases. However, the questioning was quadrupled because there were four accused and hence four defence advocates acting for the accused. It was atypical in one other respect. A guilty verdict was passed and this was most likely to have occurred because one of the four accused corroborated the rape charges against his co-accused. The trial was in the second half of 1989; that is about three and a half years after the legislation came into force.

The complainer in the following quoted extracts was 15 years old at the time of the offence. The events took place when the girl went to a party with her mother who was, by her own testimony, very drunk. The charges also involved another rape, that of the girl's mother and the relevant accused was found not guilty of this charge. Questions about sexual history were put to both complainers. It was put to the mother that she had had consensual intercourse with the accused the same evening prior to the events in the charge. The extracts given here concern the young complainer.

The defence made a vigorous attempt to create a 'smoke screen of immorality around the complainer', as one of the interviewees described it. Repeated suggestions that she was trying to look older than she was and that she was looking for a sexual adventure were made to the complainer, put to her by each of the four defence counsel. This was often done through questions about non-sexual matters, although questions about her sexual history and sexual intentions were also present.

1ST DEFENCE:	Were these four men known to you?
WITNESS:	No.
1ST DEFENCE:	Were they known to your mother?
WITNESS:	No.
1ST DEFENCE:	Were they known to your father?
WITNESS:	No.
1ST DEFENCE:	And yet after your father had gone, you and your mother stayed in a house with four strange men?
WITNESS:	Well, women were there as well.
1ST DEFENCE:	Yes, but four strange men. A set of complete strangers?
WITNESS:	Yes.
1ST DEFENCE:	What time of night was it?
WITNESS:	Don't know.
1ST DEFENCE:	What time did the pub close?
WITNESS:	Almost 11.

1ST DEFENCE:	So it was around 12 a.m. when you and your mum arrived in the house of these strangers?
WITNESS:	Yes.
1ST DEFENCE:	What did you think was going to happen?

. . . .

1ST DEFENCE:	I'll just put it quite simply. Intercourse only took place between you and him in the other house and you were quite willing?
WITNESS:	No.
1ST DEFENCE:	You were lying in bed, with your legs wide apart. Were you a virgin that night?
WITNESS:	Yes.
1ST DEFENCE:	How often did you have intercourse that night?
WITNESS:	Three.
1ST DEFENCE:	Only three? Do you mean like going up and down? I can't hear you. How often were you penetrated?
WITNESS:	Five times.
1ST DEFENCE:	Was it very painful?
WITNESS:	Yes.
1ST DEFENCE:	You received medical treatment as a result, from your own doctor. Were you bleeding from your private parts?
WITNESS:	I don't understand.
1ST DEFENCE:	Did you experience bleeding from your vagina that night?
WITNESS:	No.
1ST DEFENCE:	You weren't aware of any wetness in your private parts?
WITNESS:	I don't know. Because I've not done it before ... I don't know.
1ST DEFENCE:	You told us you were a virgin but you never experienced any bleeding.
2ND DEFENCE:	Did you get dressed up?
WITNESS:	No really.
2ND DEFENCE:	Did you have make-up on?
WITNESS:	Yes.
2ND DEFENCE:	I think we can see that in the photos. Lipstick, eyebrows, etc. To go to pictures you were wearing high heels?
WITNESS:	Yes.

3RD DEFENCE:	So you got changed into dress, make-up etc?
WITNESS:	No, I already had my dress on.
3RD DEFENCE:	When you were sitting on the couch, did you have make-up on?
WITNESS:	No, I put lipstick on later.
3RD DEFENCE:	Where did you think they were going?
WITNESS:	Pictures.

. . . .

3RD DEFENCE:	So you weren't so bothered about the man who put his

	arm round you? You were up dancing with him?
WITNESS:	Yes.
3RD DEFENCE:	You were sitting on couch together?
WITNESS:	No, we sat down together.
3RD DEFENCE:	But you left a space conveniently beside you?

4TH DEFENCE: You were dressed up to look much older than 15 years old?

. . . .

4TH DEFENCE:	What happened to your dad this night?
WITNESS:	Don't know.
4TH DEFENCE:	Oh, come now. He was told by someone to go away because you and your mum wanted to go to party and he wouldn't be welcome.

. . . .

4TH DEFENCE:	Weren't you interested to see your first grown-up kitty for a carry-out?
WITNESS:	No.
4TH DEFENCE:	How many put money in the kitty?
WITNESS:	Don't know.
4TH DEFENCE:	Did you see the carry-out bought?
WITNESS:	No.
4TH DEFENCE:	Were you the last one out of the pub?
WITNESS:	Yes.
4TH DEFENCE:	Wasn't it you who put money in the kitty?
WITNESS:	No.

4TH DEFENCE: See, I'm going to suggest to you the overall picture of that night is that you were pretty drunk, you had sex, you sobered up and felt dirty and complained of rape. Isn't that why we're all here today?

. . . .

4TH DEFENCE:	Didn't you permit [accused] to fondle your breasts?
WITNESS:	No.
4TH DEFENCE:	And put your hand down his shirt?
WITNESS:	No.
4TH DEFENCE:	It is the sort of thing a drunk woman would do. And the sort of thing a drunk woman would regret when she woke up.

. . . .

4TH DEFENCE:	Do you know what a condom is?
WITNESS:	A contraceptive.
4TH DEFENCE:	Was there any talk between [accused] and you about a contraceptive?
WITNESS:	No.
4TH DEFENCE:	Might you have forgotten?
WITNESS:	No.

CONCLUSION

Although the defence did not attempt to justify the relevance of sexual history evidence – indeed, had no need to do so given that they made no formal application to introduce the evidence and were generally unchallenged – it was most commonly used in both High and Sheriff Courts to strengthen the defence line that the sexual activity was consensual and/or to undermine the credibility of the complainer. Basically the defence tactics were the same in cases with and without an application.

Consent was suggested by using past sexual activity as if setting some sort of precedent for the present, combating a presumption of non-consent. The most obvious examples of this were the cases where the complainer and accused had been lovers or partners in the past. But the same purpose seemed to lie behind the introduction of an alleged history of flirting with the accused. This happened in cases involving lesser charges than rape – including both solemn and summary Sheriff Court cases involving such charges as assault with intent to rape, indecent assault, the statutory offences, and lewd and libidinous practices. But much of this evidence would probably have been allowed on application.

Sexual history evidence was also used to show a general disposition to consent in cases where there had been no prior sexual liaison with the accused. Some of the examples discussed under the heading 'sexual behaviour with others' and many of those under 'not of good character in sexual matters' serve to illustrate this. Here examples are given of apparent attempts to portray complainers as sexually adventurous, liable to be interested in sex and hence consenting. The defence in such cases was always that the complainer consented not that the accused had a mistaken belief in her consent. One of the defence advocates interviewed explained very frankly that such a defence was more difficult (see Chapter 8).

Much of this evidence suggests consent by besmirching the character of the complainer – 'that's the kind of girl she is' – and undermining her general credibility as a witness. The above text offers examples of this in both High Court and Sheriff Court cases. Under the heading, 'not of good character in sexual matters' are included examples of cases in which the complainer's sexual character was impugned by evidence of behaviour and characteristics which are not in themselves obviously or unambiguously sexual. Although the interviews suggest that there is no clear agreement that such evidence is covered by the legislation, it is serving the same purpose for the defence as the sexual history and sexual character evidence, which the legislation explicitly prohibits.

In cases 147 and 148 the special defence of incrimination was used in a way that largely focused on the complainer's credibility, since in both cases the suggestion was that the complainer had used her previous sexual encounter with someone else as the basis of a false allegation. Disputes about medical or forensic evidence (in three of the 22 High Court cases three of the nine Sheriff Court solemn cases, and one of the four summary cases discussed in this chapter) seemed to be occasions for attacking the credibility of the complainer rather than occasions for demonstrating an alternative source of key medical or forensic evidence.

It has been noted that much of the evidence introduced without an application would probably have been admitted had an application been made. The fact that the procedures were not followed nevertheless is arguably a serious matter. There was no formal occasion on which to question the defence as to their intentions or to limit their lines of questioning. Moreover the conclusion that much evidence would have been permitted on application is not based on an abstract reading of the legislation or on an attempt to apply the intentions of the legislators, but on observation of practice. The fact that much of the evidence introduced in breach of the legislation could have been done legitimately, is of little comfort if there is cause for concern regarding successful applications. Chapters 6 and 7 on applications suggest that this is the case. While some applications seem to exemplify the type of exception to the exclusions anticipated by the policy makers, some do not, in ways which might be regarded as contradicting the aims of the reform. Observation of applications suggests that the relevance of evidence to the issues in the trial was not always carefully scrutinised and opportunities to limit irrelevant and prejudicial questioning were not always taken.

Observation of both application and non-application cases suggests that the prosecution is implicated in practices which allow more sexual history and character evidence than the legislators seem to have intended. The High Court clerks found overall that sexual history evidence was introduced more frequently by the defence than the prosecution. However, the prosecution led sexual history evidence in most of the observed cases. Defence advocates were often adept at reinterpreting sexual history evidence introduced by the prosecution: for example, by turning the prosecution suggestion, that a newly married and pregnant woman was not likely to consent to casual sex, into circumstances which allegedly had led her to make a false allegation in order to account for her behaviour to her husband, or, by turning the prosecution evidence, that the complainer normally abstained from intercourse during menstruation, into the very time at which the complainer would choose to have an illicit affair. Only exceptionally did the prosecution make any attempt to intervene or counterattack when the defence pursued lines of sexual history or sexual character evidence which were obviously prejudicial to the prosecution case and of dubious relevance to the issues in the trial.

NOTES

1. The first estimate includes any case marked by the clerks as containing defence use of evidence in one or more of the following regarding the complainer: sexual relations with the accused prior and since the occasion of the charge, sexual relations with someone other than the accused, prostitution, virginity, masturbation, pregnancy. See Table A2.3 for more detail. The lower of the estimates based on observation include these items and also sexual relations with the accused on the occasion of the offence but not specified in the charge and any blatant attacks on the complainer's sexual character. The higher estimate includes cases where the defence introduced sexual history and sexual character evidence by focusing on the complainer's allegedly sexually interested or provocative behaviour towards the accused leading up to the incident that was the subject of the charge.

2. Observation documented some defence questioning on sexual matters in nine out of 14 solemn trials and four out of 22 summary cases. No applications were observed in the Sheriff Court. (This total does not include several instances of the defence putting the case that the complainer was deliberately trying to appear older, suggesting sexual precocity without overtly asking about sexual character or behaviour.) But the number of observed cases are perhaps too small to safely translate into an estimated rate of breaches of the legislation. These Sheriff cases compare with 42 cases which contained defence questioning concerning the complainer's sexual conduct out of an observed 70 cases in the High Court. In 20 of these cases there was an application.

3. Three of these cases were before the elaborated High Court clerks' form came into use and therefore there is no matching information from the clerk, and in one case the clerk return was missing. Of the remaining cases nine were confirmed by the clerk.

4. Sexual precocity was the substance of the defence case in 004 but the more blatant approach resulted in this case being a clearer breach of the legislation.

5. Indeed the clerk who completed the form for case 024 marked it as involving an application. However, from our observation, what occurred in this case was that both counsel had agreed before the trial commenced that evidence would be led which could contravene the legislation. During the complainer's cross-examination the defence did refer to the legislation before proceeding but this was done in the presence of the jury and without further discussion. This is the only case where a clerk's judgement and observation do not concur on whether or not there was an application.

6. The fact of marriage was similarly used in 140, which has not been included in the 22 cases breaching the legislation since the references to sexual behaviour were less explicit. The defence argued that the complainer was led by a desire for reconciliation to initiate a 'winching session' with her ex-husband. The defence also suggested as in case 019, that the fact that they had been married worked against the presumption that sex would not occur voluntarily during menstruation, arguing the accused 'had seen it all before'.

7. This also happened in a third rape case (013) classified as a more marginal breach of the legislation and not counted in the 22 cases discussed here. The complainer was said to have taken off her skirt when drunk and in the company of men (not including the accused).

8. Mistaken-belief-in-age did creep into some cases but not mistaken belief in consent. In case 74 the defence attempted to raise a defence concerning the accused's belief in the complainer's age. Here the complainer was 15 years old and the accused were 13 and 15 years old. The complainer was described by the defence as an 'older woman' who had a 'predatory nature' because she allegedly pursued one of the accused. (The complainer was also described by the defence as 'a consummate actress and a pathological liar' in reaction to her denials of his questioning.)

9. Mothers were asked questions such as whether their daughters had gone out with boys or if they had ever known their daughter to have an older boyfriend. Further examples are discussed under the heading, 'Not of Good Character in Relation to Sexual Matters'.

10. One other High Court case (032) involved sex for money but was not a breach of the legislation as this was integral to the charges and led by the prosecution without any further use by the defence.

11. In an assault with intent to rape case (016), where the complainer was an alcoholic, it was suggested that she prostituted herself to subsidise her drinking. Because this was not put in a blatant way, this case has been categorised as a more marginal breach of the legislation and is not discussed further.

12. This was also a feature of the lewd and libidinous practices case, 096, classified as a more marginal breach of the legislation. The (male) complainer and his friend were asking for odd jobs and met the accused who told them to come back the following day and assist him with clearing building debris. Both boys did go back, and the offence occurred when the accused called the complainer away from his friend. In cross-examination, the defence insinuated that the complainer was aware, 'being a street-wise lad', of the accused's intentions the first time that he met him, and challenged him on returning to the accused on the following day. 'You spend quite a lot of time on the streets, hanging about in the [docks] area. You've seen quite a few things, no doubt, fights, stabbing people. You know how to look after yourself'. The defence suggested that the boy recognised 'the signs' of what was going to occur, but thought he would be able to get 'a fair price', hence he did not try to get away.

13. This happened in four cases involving s. 4 of the Sexual Offences (Scotland) Act (005, 094, 112, 133) but because this did not involve explicit sexual history or sexual character evidence, these have been classified as more marginal breaches of the legislation. Only case 112 is counted in the four cases of breach of the legislation as it involved additional explicit sexual history evidence.

10

Enforcing the Rules

The research indicates instances in both High and Sheriff Courts where the legislation appears to have been openly breached or ignored (see Chapters 6, 7 and 9).

Monitoring in the High Court indicated that 16 per cent of all trials (24 per cent of trials without applications) contained evidence of one or more of the following used by the defence without reference to the legislation: sexual relations between the complainer and the accused, sexual relations between the complainer and someone else, and the complainer's prostitution, virginity or masturbation. Using the same indices but also paying attention to evidence concerning the complainer's sexual character, court observation of High Court trials indicated a higher rate of 21–8 per cent of all trials in breach of the legislation and an additional number of trials in which questioning bordered on the prohibited areas.

Court observation in the Sheriff Court documented questioning on sexual matters in six of the 14 solemn trials and four of the 22 summary trials which were in breach of the legislation. A slightly greater number of cases were observed in which questioning bordered on prohibited sexual history or sexual character evidence.

Breaches of the legislation also occurred in trials where applications had been made. On the one hand, there were those cases where there had been an *unsuccessful application*, yet the defence nonetheless subsequently managed to introduce the excluded evidence (see Chapter 7). On the other hand, there were cases where there was a *successful application*, but the evidence was used by the defence in ways that overstepped the bounds specified in the application. Here, questioning strayed into areas that were either not outlined by the defence in the application, or that fell outside the limits of questioning set by the bench and agreed to by the prosecution (see Chapter 7).

Sexual history evidence prohibited by the legislation appeared not only in relation to rape-related offences – rape, attempted rape, assault with intent to rape – but also in trials involving sodomy, lewd and libidinous practices and behaviour, age-related statutory offences (i.e., s. 3, s. 4 and

s. 5 of the Sexual Offences (Scotland) Act 1976 and s. 80 (7) of the Criminal Justice (Scotland) Act), and clandestine injury.

Yet the research also showed that such breaches seldom provoked objections by the prosecution or intervention by judges/sheriffs. It might, therefore, be legitimate to ask why such breaches seem to be rarely reacted against by prosecutors or judges.

THE LACK OF INTERVENTION

Even using the crudest tests of what counts as inadmissible sexual history evidence, the rarity of judicial interventions or prosecution objections to such evidence comes over very strongly. There were exceptions to this general lack of reaction, but they are striking precisely because they were exceptions.

In the High Court trials without applications, there were a total of five judicial interventions in three trials, and four prosecution objections in two trials. There are no interventions recorded by the clerks in Sheriff solemn or summary cases, although researchers noted two Sheriff solemn trials with prosecution objections referring to the legislation (see Chapter 9). The lack of prosecution and judicial reaction constituted an important subject of enquiry, and raised two related questions. First, why was there such a glaring lack of intervention? Second – and perhaps the nub of the issue – whose duty is it to enforce the legislation?

In the interviews, a number of possibilities were explored which could account for the overall lack of intervention. Could it be due to a straight-forward lack of awareness of the existence of the legislation? Certainly there were times when the use of sexual history evidence was so blatant that this seemed to be the only possible explanation. Were there associated problems to do with the assimilation of its contents? For example, were practitioners aware of the full range of offences covered? On a different tack, were there tactical and/or pragmatic reasons for the lack of objections? For instance, the possibility that the Crown may deliberately not object if, for example, the witness appears to be coping with the questions, if the answers are potentially damaging to the defence, or the evidence would have come out anyway? Or, since it would seem that much evidence would probably have been allowed on application, did it seem pointless to demand going through proper procedures? How do courtroom personnel perceive their role in relation to the legislation? How do they see their relative duties and responsibilities? Could the lack of objections/interventions be due to ambiguities surrounding whose duty it is to enforce the legislation? And finally, what about the possibility of seeing prohibited questioning when there was none in the eyes of the legal personnel concerned, albeit that they were mindful of the legislation? Could the lack of intervention be due to inherent differences of opinion

over what is prohibited evidence and what is not, and what is relevant to
a particular case and what is not? And if there are differences can these be
explained by the sexist assumptions of some practioners concerning the
appropriate behaviour of women and men, as opposed to the more open-
minded approach of others? Interviewees also raised other sorts of considerations. Hence, the two main questions – why lack of intervention? and
whose duty to enforce? – were explored against the backdrop of a broad
set of issues, ranging from the interpretation and application of statutory
rules, ideas about incompetent and/or irrelevant evidence, intervention
strategies and adversarial techniques, to a 'feel' for particular cases drawn
from courtroom experience.

In actual fact, there was no single clear-cut answer to these sorts of
questions. It is important to state at the outset that a range of views were
encountered on many of these issues. On some things, there was a broad
consensus, on others there were a range of responses. Some divisions were
along professional lines. For instance, the view that responsibility for
enforcing the legislation lay primarily with the Crown was one commonly
held by judges and sheriffs. It was not, on the whole, a view shared by
most prosecutors who insisted on the role of the judge/sheriff. Other
issues provoked reactions that cut across professional boundaries, resulting in groupings of defence, prosecution and judiciary sharing a common
perspective on one or two or more matters, yet, on other matters, holding
views which were in direct opposition to each other. Often, the answers
that were given by individuals to particular questions or sets of questions
seemed inconsistent with their answers given to similar sorts of questions
in another part of the interview. Whilst this is not unusual in interviews, it
did make it rather difficult to get a clear sense of individuals' reactions.
Another set of differences centred around individual approaches to the
issues under discussion. Whilst some interviewees were fairly flexible and
open in their approach, others were more dogmatic with strongly held,
inflexible views and opinions.

Knowledge of the Rules

General Awareness

It was made clear that, as a matter of policy, all Scottish judges and
sheriffs are formally circulated with details of new legislation. In some
instances, this is with accompanying guidelines. The judiciary are circulated with updates of Renton and Brown,[1] the *Scots Law Times* and the
Scottish Criminal Case Review which highlight new legislation. All of the
judges and sheriffs interviewed said that they had been aware of the
legislation since its inception. (Two judges and four sheriffs stressed that
they had followed the debate about sexual history and sexual character
evidence long before the legislation had reached the drafting stage.)

Several sheriffs thought it a distinct possibility, however, that many defence lawyers and what one termed 'career fiscals' might not be fully aware of all aspects of the legislation.

Prosecutors, like judges and sheriffs, are also alerted to new legislation by a system of circulars and instructions issued from the Crown Office. They too receive copies of the journals. However, most prosecutors interviewed wanted to explain that they end up being selective as to which legislation, out of the plethora that reaches them, they pay the closest attention. Selectivity is dependent on the type of legislation and its relevance to the type of work done, and also by 'pragmatic arrangements' such as locality and type of offence most often encountered.

Advocates were given the opportunity to comment on this legislation when it was going through Parliament (see Chapter 3). As advocate depute 1 said, 'there are lots of ways that you become aware of what's happening'. The comments provided by the Faculty of Advocates would 'be available for everyone to see and ... would be reported to the faculty meeting so people who were at the meeting would be aware of it as well.' All advocates depute and fiscals however, emphasised that they are expected, as part of their professional responsibilities, to keep abreast of new legislation, 'in the same way as if we were in private practice.' In this regard, according to one fiscal, they are 'lawyers first, civil servants second'. A number of other prosecutors made the same point, that is, that they regard their work as not substantially different from that of a lawyer in private practice. On the whole, they felt that this was no more evident than in the preparation of particular cases, wherein they would acquaint themselves with all legislation relevant to that case. According to a fiscal:

> As lawyers, we are expected to keep ourselves up to date with changes in the law in our own field ... we have to be aware of what is passed in our own area ... So just as I would if I were practising on the defence side ... so also as a fiscal.

It is up to defence counsel and solicitors in private practice to keep up to date with new legislation. All of the defence counsel and lawyers said that they were aware of the legislation prior to its inception, were familiar with its contents, and said that they have it in mind when preparing for a trial involving sexual offences. Although as defence counsel 1, said:

> Nobody memorises it and comes along quoting all the subsections. People just bring along a photocopy so that they can refer to it specifically.

Assimilation of Contents

According to those interviewed, then, it would be difficult not to know about the *existence* of the legislation. However, the research was concerned not only with general awareness of the legislation, but also with factors that may have affected the assimilation of its contents. The rules on sexual history evidence were introduced in a bulky Miscellaneous Provisions Act which contained a vast and diverse range of other reforms to both criminal and civil law. Miscellaneous Provisions may be, by their very nature, difficult to assimilate – did this mean a slow take-up of the rules? With just a handful of exceptions, the interviewees felt that the fact that the legislation was contained in a Miscellaneous Provisions Act did not obscure nor detract from its assimilation in any significant way. The reason given for this was that they are used to legislation being passed in this manner. Sheriff 3, commenting on what he termed the 'rag bag' quality of such Acts summed up this view when he said he found it, 'very, very aggravating to get important legislation filtered through under such a Bill, but we are very used to Miscellaneous Provisions.'

A second possible problem of assimilation may be the wide scope of the rules in excluding evidence of the complainer's sexual behaviour with the accused as well as with others, and in covering such a wide range of offences, and therefore in applying to lower courts as well as the High Court. Observation had suggested that sometimes it appeared that prosecutors and sheriffs were simply unaware that the new law covered the offences they were dealing with. (One prosecutor expressed great bafflement about what a researcher was doing at a trial involving a male complainer, and, once enlightened, wondered whether in fact he might have objected to defence cross-examination on the complainer's 'homosexual tendencies'.) Whilst most interviewees said that they were aware that there was a wide remit in terms of offences, there were a significant number (over a third) who were not aware that homosexual and age-related statutory offences were covered. This was based on the widely held view that it would be, 'highly unlikely that the same sort of questions [as in rape and rape-related offences] would arise in those sorts of cases' (Judge 1). An example of this view was provided by defence lawyer 1, recalling a case involving homosexual offences:

> I certainly didn't use the legislation … but I would be surprised if I didn't have a go at the complainer on the basis that he was promiscuous. It probably didn't occur to anybody to use the legislation … I'm sure that we led out with that, or cross-examined him on the basis that he was promiscuous, not much more than a rent boy.

Later on in the interview he returned to this example and said:

> It wouldn't have occurred to me to make an application, because I think of it as legislation designed to protect women from improper questioning about their past, rather than protecting boys or men.

Those that *were* aware that the legislation covered a wide range of offences also believed that incest was included. When told that it was not, most were surprised, and expressed the opinion that it must have been an oversight by the legislators.

Generally, there was the widespread view that the legislation covered only the 'more serious sexual offences.' For example, five sheriffs, three fiscals, and two defence lawyers said that they would not have the Act in mind when dealing with cases heard under summary procedure. Others said that they would. A slightly different version of the perception of the legislation as having a limited scope is the view (most commonly held by Sheriff Court personnel) that sexual history evidence simply does not appear in the types of cases that typically come up for trial in the Sheriff Court. Therefore, many Sheriff Court personnel would not have the legislation in mind when conducting trials concerning those sexual offences that are heard in the Sheriff Court. Defence lawyer 3 explained his position thus:

> The use of these provisions is limited to the High Court, because normally the other offences – indecent behaviour, indecent assault – very seldom involve previous history, because they are usually one-off situations. It's a girl going along and somebody coming and touching her or something, which is normally never a consent sort of situation.

Although there are divergent views concerning the extent of the overall remit of the legislation, the fact that some interviewees believed the use of such evidence to be much more circumscribed could be one possible explanation why, in certain types of cases – that is, homosexual offences, statutory offences and the so-called 'less serious' sexual offences – prohibited evidence is introduced without objection.

THE DUTIES OF PROSECUTORS

Laying Out of Relevant Evidence

All interviewees were firmly agreed that the most important duty of the public prosecutor is to lay out all of the relevant evidence in the case. This is essential 'for there to be a fair operation of the criminal justice system.' As judge 1 said:

> Their duty is to lay out all of the relevant facts before the jury and to present the case as impartially as possible.

According to advocate depute 4:

> A prosecutor's job is to place all the evidence, warts and all, before the court. If ... I've got information which is contrary to my case I will lead it. That's part of legal theory. It's very important – the prosecutor's job is to place everything before the court which is relevant.

Here, clearly, relevance is crucially important. However, as discussed in Chapter 8, there is not always agreement on what is and what is not relevant. This disagreement is reflected in skirmishes between the prosecution and defence over what the prosecution is obliged to lead. For example, note the following exchange in an application (002) founded on the 'explain or rebut' exception:

> JUDGE: I do not understand this application. It implies that the Crown is going to lead evidence that the complainer frequently entertained men in her room ... Is the Crown proposing to do this? Parliament has indicated its disapproval of such questioning. Would the Crown therefore question on this?
>
> DEFENCE: The Crown has a duty to place all relevant evidence before them to the jury.

In this case the prosecution did not accept the relevance being claimed by the defence. However, an obvious consequence of the prosecution's professional duty is that in some cases, 'relevant facts' will include evidence which is favourable to the defence. Indeed, some interviewees maintained that, rather than being merely a consequence of the main professional duty, this in fact constituted a clear duty in itself, to convey information or evidence that would be favourable to the defence where he or she is aware of its existence. As advocate depute 2 said:

> You can't keep things back. If there is a witness that we know about that is helpful to the defence we have to tell the defence that. Even if we don't call him, we have to make the witness available if he is on the indictment. At least tell the defence where this witness is. And if he's not on the indictment we really should tell the accused's agents that there is this witness who has something to say.

The Crown Exemption

The legislation exempts the Crown from the prohibitions. The *SLC Report* deemed that the Crown need not be covered by the prohibitions since the problems associated with the use of sexual character and sexual history evidence did not arise in relation to prosecution questioning generally and that such evidence would only infrequently be relevant for Crown purposes (see Chapter 3). The research documented that in some cases it was the prosecution who introduced sexual history evidence, and that it was sometimes taken up by the defence, with or without application. Sometimes, the evidence led by the prosecution is similar to the tests of a complainer's credibility or character that are more typical of the defence. The following, from case 156, is a good example of this:

> PROSECUTION: Had you had intercourse with anyone before this incident?

> COMPLAINER: Yes, the Saturday before ... with my fiancé. He's now my husband.
>
> PROSECUTION: Where was this?
>
> COMPLAINER: At [friend's] house.
>
> PROSECUTION: Was that the first time you had intercourse with him?
>
> COMPLAINER: Yes.
>
> PROSECUTION: Had you had intercourse with anyone else?
>
> COMPLAINER: No.
>
> PROSECUTION: Are you sure?'

If this evidence is clearly relevant, then this is not a departure from legal propriety but the opposite. For, as the interviewees made clear, it is a prosecutor's duty to bring out all of the 'objectively' relevant facts. The problem, as the interviews indicate, is that not all practitioners would agree such questions were actually relevant and hence necessary.

In another case (124) involving a number of homosexual charges, the prosecution introduced the suggestion that the male complainer was in the habit of 'hanging around the bus station'. Taking this up, the first question asked of the complainer by the defence was, 'The advocate depute asked if you frequented the bus station?'

Sometimes it might be positively useful for a prosecutor to bring in the sexual history of a complainer (although, as the following example illustrates, this may be done in a rather distasteful manner). In one non-application case where the complainer was a prostitute (011), the prosecution argued that her distressed state after the incident had to be taken as a very strong sign that she had in fact been raped and threatened with a gun, precisely because a prostitute would be 'used to a little rough and tumble'. Therefore the incident must have been qualitatively different from the sexual interaction she was accustomed to.

On the whole, however, prosecutors did not rely overmuch on the traditional presumptions of sexual 'good character' evidence, as many had feared (see Chapters 1 and 3). Chambers and Millar had suggested that questioning on 'virtue' was:

> ... nevertheless questioning on sexual experience ... [and] sexual history evidence. By introducing sexual history evidence the prosecution allows the defence [on application] to lead evidence on this subject to explain or to challenge the prosecution evidence.[2]

But for these very reasons, pragmatism might counsel against such a prosecution strategy. As advocate depute 4 said:

> It wouldn't have occurred to me. Even in the preparation of a case, I couldn't think of any circumstances ... to say, 'Let's present this person as a paragon of virtue.' That's asking for trouble, in a way, to set yourself a standard. The higher you try and pitch a particular position, the easier it is to knock it down. It's better to proceed on the basis of a truthful account rather than to introduce matters that don't

have a direct bearing. Whether you are a Sunday-school teacher and
you have never had sexual intercourse before or not – to introduce
that simply invites people to go away and investigate whether or not
that was true. And then you have a credibility issue.

As described in Chapter 7, it was often defence constructions of
complainers' evidence as implying 'good character' claims that led to
character attacks, rather than the prosecution deliberately presenting the
complainer as 'of good character'. At the same time, the prosecution's
questioning in observed trials was not as scrupulous in avoiding 'good
character' evidence as interviewees suggested.

Responsibility to the Complainer?

Most interviewees were emphatic that the prosecution did not have, what
one judge termed, any 'direct' responsibility to the complainer. However,
some 'indirect' responsibility was identified as a consequence of prosecution being in the public interest. Certainly all were in agreement that the
prosecution does have some general responsibilities towards all the witnesses, such as preventing them unnecessary distress in the courtroom.
Thus, some prosecutors did see themselves as having *some* responsibility
to the complainer, although it must be made clear, this was not a uniquely
'special' duty, but rather part of a wider one to all witnesses. As advocate
depute 1 said:

> The prosecution has a duty to prosecute in the public interest and
> that of course to some extent involves a duty to the complainer ...
> which involves to some extent protecting the complainer's interests
> when that is necessary.

A slightly different answer along the same lines was given by fiscal 4
who said:

> I think our duty to the complainer is part of our overall duty to the
> public. To be there to protect the public interest. The complainer is
> a member of the public and I will not allow a complainer to be
> browbeaten if I can stop that within the rules of evidence.

There were a small minority who thought that a public prosecutor had
no obligations to the complainer at all as that would involve an inherent
and total conflict with her or his public duty to lay out all of the facts of the
case impartially. Most felt that the duty to 'place all relevant facts before
the court' would be no excuse for a failure to object to defence use of
irrelevant and prejudicial information. According to a fiscal, 'we oughtn't
to be allowing [defence] tactics to dictate what we do.' Some interviewees
who were not prosecutors also thought that the prosecutor may feel
'morally bound to protect the complainer's interests' in the trial, particularly if the complainer was subjected to 'harassment', 'haranguing' or
'irrelevant cross-examination'. Sheriffs in particular, took the view that

the approach of some prosecutors had been affected by the fact that sexual offence trials (specifically, the 'ordeal of the trial' for the complainer and some much publicised sentencing disparities) were currently a subject of much public attention. Sheriff 1, for example, said:

> I'm quite sure that the prosecution would do everything to avoid the complainer unnecessary distress ... I'm sure that it is a matter, particularly in the present day climate, which procurators fiscal are very modulated to.

Sheriff 3, on the other hand, felt that 'the current obsession with the rights of the complainer' has been to the detriment to the rights of the accused, which, he felt 'under our adversarial system, are much more important'.

WHEN IS OBJECTION/INTERVENTION APPROPRIATE?

There are divergent attitudes to the role of statutory rules. Are they to be applied uniformly to every case according to strict due process/rule of law in a formalist manner? Or are the rules there to be used instrumentally only when 'appropriate', as and when the prosecutor or judge or sheriff sees fit? As some of the prosecutors said, they at times may be working against the 'no smoke without fire' presumption, and to jump up and object to some sexual history reference by the defence could well draw more attention to it and, in smothering it, lead to the impression that there is a 'real' story being suppressed. According to one fiscal, 'One doesn't want to be seen jumping up and down all the time. It can be detrimental to your own Crown case.' A defence counsel said that it is a useful defence tactic to provoke the prosecution into objecting:

> You spring a fast one, you open up a line. The prosecution jumps to his feet and objects. That is a low blow, because the jury sees it and says, 'Wait a minute, the prosecutor is trying to conceal something' ... but the damage is done from the prosecution point of view, because the jury sees that you are opening up a line which embarrasses the prosecution and that is a trick we use in all kinds of crimes ... a fairly strong incentive not to object.

Equally pragmatically, the prosecutor could decide not to object, either on the one hand because the defence line may ultimately assist the Crown case, or on the other hand because it is already too late as very often 'the damage lies in the question, not the answer.' As one fiscal said, in cases where there was not a Crown objection to 'dodgy' questioning by the defence, it was probable that:

> the Crown have made their own decision not to object for some other reason ... Especially in a jury trial, you don't want to be seen to be objecting too much. You may even feel that the evidence coming out is inherently unlikely, or is likely to put the accused in a bad light by

> virtue of raising it, and so you may even decide to let it go on the basis
> that it's likely to do more harm than good to the accused person.

Sometimes the prosecution calculation might be that this sort of evidence was going to come out anyway, so better that it be 'got over with' and minimised rather than kept hidden, only to be dramatically revealed by the defence. A number of those interviewed held this view.

Research findings regarding granted applications were put to the prosecutors – that on the one hand, defence questioning seemed at times surprisingly detailed and, on the other, it sometimes strayed beyond what was specified in the application. There was a range of responses to these findings. Some prosecutors said that clearly they would not feel able to object once the judge had allowed a line of questioning, even if the subsequent defence questioning was overly detailed and elaborate. Others said equally strongly that they would object if they felt that the questioning was overstepping the boundaries set during the application. One advocate depute said that the place where he would tackle 'overstepping' and 'any allusions made by the defence' [regarding the complainer] would be during his summing-up speech, where he would 'warn off' the jury.

Advocate depute 4 here touched on the possibility of seeing questioning as being prohibited when, in actual fact, it was not. In a somewhat unusual and non-literal reading of the legislation, he argued that what he termed a straightforward question to the complainer about her sexual behaviour did not need an application. Illustrating this point by means of a hypothetical example, he suggested that if there was semen on a complainer's bed which could have been up to 72 hours old, then it would be fair to ask the complainer if she had had sex in that bed with anybody else in the last 72 hours. He maintained that an application need not be made to ask that sort of question.

> If you turn round and start making allegations and seek to prove that,
> or seek to elicit from her that she did do that, then clearly you are
> making the attack which needs the legislation. But ... because she
> could turn around and say, 'no', and if you say, 'thank you', and
> move on, and don't seek to contradict her, you are making no attack.'

By the same argument, no objection would be needed. In this view much is therefore dependent on how the question is asked and the answer that is given (what if she had said 'yes' for instance?). It is interesting that a practitioner firmly held a view in such contradiction with the literal reading of the legislation. Among other things, the law clearly states that the court shall not admit questioning designed to elicit that the complainer has engaged in sexual behaviour not forming part of the subject matter of the charge (see Appendix 1).

Used properly, objections can be an important tactical device, according to those interviewed. The secret of success often lies in the timing of an objection. On the one hand, it is often normal practice to let a defence line of argument run for a bit to see where it is going before any prosecution objection or judicial intervention is made. On the subject of judicial interventions, judge 2 said:

> It is in nobody's interests to jump in too quickly. One should take a careful line, watching for the next question.

He went on,

> One doesn't want to start interrupting all the time ... the questioning may well be for a purpose which will become clear. After all, the judge doesn't know what the questioning will be.

On the other hand, it may be better to object as soon as possible. In the Sheriff Courts, the actual timing of a prosecution objection can be crucial. As one fiscal said:

> If it is a jury trial, the objection must come as soon as possible, because once heard it will never be forgotten. So the objection must come as soon as possible after, so the judge could order that the jury put a particular bit of information out of their minds. If it is a summary trial, however, it doesn't really matter when one objects. The sheriff will hear it under reservation anyway, and you are just minuting your objection.

There are also occasions when sexual history evidence comes out by accident, for instance in a case (in our preliminary work) where a lesbian relationship between the complainer and a main witness in the case emerged through the routine prosecution identification of productions. Asked to identify all the items of clothing labelled as 'hers' – meaning what she was wearing when the incident occurred – the complainer replied, 'no', that the bra belonged to her friend. What should the prosecutor do on occasions such as this? As one of the summary cases (130) showed, such accidents may easily be exploited (see Chapter 9). One witness's statement that the complainer had previously been raped became the basis of the defence remark that the 'sexual misconduct in the past ... reduces her credibility as a witness'.

WHOSE DUTY TO ENFORCE LEGISLATION?

What the Prosecutors Say

The interviews revealed three distinct positions on whose duty it is to enforce the legislation among the prosecution. Some prosecutors differentiated between, on the one hand, drawing attention to the legislation – either done by objecting to a line of prohibited questioning and/or by provoking an application – and, on the other, dealing with an application once it had been made. These were seen as two essentially different responsibilities falling within the separate domains of the prosecution and the judiciary.

Here, the 'onus' for drawing attention to the legislation fell primarily on the prosecution, although what followed was up to the judge. Here, the prosecution and judiciary are held to be working in conjunction with each other regarding the enforcement of the legislation. One proponent of this view said:

> It's like any other piece of legislation ... or any rule of law which says what is or isn't admissible ... If a question is asked by the defence and is not objected to, the judge in most cases will probably rarely intervene unless it's something blatant ... It follows that we should be seeking to enforce and to take objection. Once you make the objection and argue the case out, then it's really up to the judge what attitude he takes. At the end of the day, he's the final arbiter as to whether this should be enforced or not ... .the duty of the prosecution initially is to object to questioning if its objectionable. Then it's up to the judge to rule on it. But the judge has got to be invited to make the rule.

A fiscal who held this view said that he would 'at all times' be 'bearing in mind the position of the complainer who has been given statutory protection, to some extent, by this piece of legislation', and would therefore be on the lookout for contraventions.

Advocate depute 4 was firmly of the opinion that it was the prosecution's duty to deal with questioning which strayed beyond the bounds of an application.

> I think any prosecuting Counsel would be sitting ready to object if the defence moved over the bounds of the application, because the defence has made his application and given his reasons and by definition he is bound within what he has said he is going to do. If he wants to do something else he will have to apply again.

Another fiscal said, 'I would be failing in my duty if I did not object' to straying questions.

Other prosecutors held a view which was somewhat different, albeit slightly. Again, prosecutors and judiciary were seen, in general, as having separate spheres of responsibility. The difference was that, when confronted with evidence or questioning prohibited under this particular legislation, these separate responsibilities would merge and sometimes blur.

An advocate depute summed up this point of view when he said he understood the balance of responsibility, 'with regard to this particular legislation', to be *shared* between Crown and judge, but 'with probably a greater duty on the judge.' Usually, he said, 'it's always the prosecutor's responsibility ... In normal [operation of rules of] evidence, the judge should sit there and even if he says. "I don't think that's relevant", if the prosecutor chooses not to object, I don't think the judge has any particular role to intervene.' However, he thought that this legislation altered the normal operation of rules of evidence since 'there is a statute here forbidding certain things to be done, unless the Court is satisfied.' He went on:

> Because there is a statutory requirement I think the judge ... has been appointed by Parliament to do this job and I think he has a duty as much as the prosecutor has a duty, at his hand, to stop it.

Then there is the completely different view, held by a number of prosecutors interviewed, that there is another option open to them which circumvents the need to object in open court. This can be done informally, according to one fiscal, 'just by conversation between ourselves and the defence over the table.' He went on:

> The fact that no formal objection is made doesn't mean to say that there's not been a conversation about it and an agreement reached.

This practice, it seems, is not restricted to either the High or Sheriff Courts, although the advocate deputes interviewed were divided in their views over whether it did or did not occur. According to advocate depute 1:

> If it looked that the defence were coming on to that sort of state, I would probably drop them the wink that they should be making an application, rather than have to get up and object to the matter in open court. I might just whisper across the table to them, 'if you are following this line you should make an application', or something like that. ... I always think it's better to try to have these matters dealt with without having to resort to objection and so on.

Advocate depute 4 put it this way:

> It could be that the defence has said to the prosecutor, 'I am going to go into this to a degree', and the prosecutor says, 'Oh well, I don't mind that.' And they have said to one another, 'Do you really think that goes so far as to need an application?' ... If there had been a dispute, there certainly would, and maybe in strict theory so it did, but the prosecutor has said, 'Well, it's touch and go whether it needs it or not and as I'm not objecting, we'll not bother'. So ... everybody knows its going to happen and the strict need for an application then is doubtful. Because people do conduct business to some degree in that kind of commonsense approach.

He went on later in the interview to talk of 'shorthanding', that is, saving time by not going through formal procedures, which everybody knew were unnecessary, since everybody could see that the evidence was relevant. Once again this, however, relies on there being agreement as to the relevancy of the particular evidence – a general consensus that does not, in fact, exist (see Chapter 8).

However, the third and most widely held view was that the legislation is primarily 'the court's business'. Here, the prosecutors saw the burden of responsibility, both in terms of enforcing the legislation and dealing with applications, as falling on the presiding judge or sheriff. Indeed many were surprised that this could be perceived otherwise. Those that held this view justified it by referring to the wording of the legislation in the exclusions section, s. 141A, '*the court* shall not admit or allow ... ' and in the exceptions section, s. 141B, 'the court shall allow' which they felt was absolutely explicit. According to one fiscal:

> I think quite clearly the court means the judge or the sheriff. Neither the fiscal nor the advocate depute is the court, the court is the judge of whatever sort.

The prosecution's contribution to the application dialogue in case 060 exemplifies this 'minimalist' position:

> It is not clear to what extent the Crown ought to interfere in such an application. It is not the Crown's business to be seen to protect the complainer. The application is perhaps the court's business.

This last position clearly relies to a great extent on a judiciary who are, at the same time, actively interventionist and willing to assume responsibility for the enforcement of the legislation and the admissibility of evidence both during an application and, during the trial in general.

What the Judiciary Say

Although there were again a range of views, judging from the court observation of trials and from the interviews, many judges and sheriffs do not see enforcement as their responsibility either. In the main, judges/ sheriffs conceive their role as adjudicating on procedural issues only if they are raised by prosecution or defence. The position of the interviewees was very clear on this. The judicial role in the course of the trial is essentially passive, to respond to objections but not to initiate. Sheriff 9 summed up this conceptualisation:

> The function of the judge in Scotland is as an umpire. He only speaks when he is appealed to. If the defence thought to bring evidence, and the prosecution objected to that evidence, you would consider the question to see whether it matches the section [of the legislation]. And if it did, uphold the section. And then give your judgement.

Or, as one judge put it, 'one must sit back and be impartial.' And another, 'normally speaking, one leaves it to the other side [the Crown] to object.' And a sheriff:

> The judge keeps quiet. It's up to the prosecution to raise the legislation ... the proper way for a sheriff to behave on the Bench is to listen to the prosecution, listen to the defence, and to adjudicate on matters in dispute when [the legislation] is raised.

Judge 4 said he applied the same attitude as that for litigation, 'It is for counsel to intervene' and to invoke the legislation, although he expressed the view that 'there is a strong tendency for the Crown not to intervene.'

Sheriff 4 gave different reasons why, as a rule, he does not intervene. Although he felt quite clearly that it was the sheriff's job to enforce the rules, he was nonetheless chary of intervening because:

> any occasion where I've intervened I've made a cock-up of the whole thing. I don't intervene now, I let them [prosecution and defence] get on with it.

Only two sheriffs held views which were in some sense compatible with that given by some prosecutors, that the responsibility for invoking the legislation should be shared. Sheriff 1's version – although predominantly that of an 'umpire' – was most in tune with this view. Accordingly:

> one would hope one would be quick enough to intervene. Sadly, one very often isn't, and one does rely on the party who is to be prejudiced by the piece of incompetent evidence no doubt to be keeping a weather eye open, and to hope that between both of you, you would stop it.

Sheriff 2 felt that, 'the general approach to the whole law of evidence is that it is up to the opponent, as it were, to object to evidence which he claims is not admissible.' However, with regard to evidence prohibited by this legislation, his view 'would be that if I found this sort of questioning going on, I would hint to the fiscal would he not care to object, so that he or she made a positive decision about it and didn't just overlook it. But if the fiscal said, "I don't propose to object to this", then I think I would let it in.'

It may well be that the 'umpire' position is the prevalent Scottish mode in comparison with judicial interventionism south of the Border. At least this has the advantage of preventing judges/sheriffs from embarking on explorations of the complainer's sexual history which, Chapter 7 noted was one of the major problems documented by Adler in relation to the English law. Observation in the Scottish courts revealed relatively few instances in which judges did take up such questions from the defence with enthusiasm.

One judge and two sheriffs did not agree with the 'umpire' characterisation and, in fact, regarded themselves as actively interventionist. They felt this was positively sanctioned by the legislation, which, according to one of the sheriffs was 'peremptory'. Judge 3 was firmly of the opinion that the prosecution are 'a bit wet' about objecting in cases where the defence ask questions which may impugn witnesses, and consequently sees the judge as:

> having a clear duty ... to stop counsel from asking questions which might be objectionable or utterly irrelevant, whether the prosecution objected or not. If one relied on the Crown all the time, one would be in a sorry state.

He did make a distinction, however, in terms of the types of cases which would warrant intervention calling for an application. Obvious cases which would not warrant an application, he said, were those involving a husband and wife or co-habitees. In such cases, 'it would be ridiculous' to demand an application, because one would have to send the jury out ... the Crown would have to be called in ... and it does cost money.'

But what of the balance of responsibility when an application was being made? By and large, the judges and sheriffs said they would look to the prosecution when an application was being made. Certainly, researchers observed applications where the judge expressly asked for the prosecutions' point of view before deciding on whether or not to allow the evidence. As judge 2 said, the onus to object was on the Crown at all times, but particularly when an application was being made: 'If the Crown says nothing, or makes no objection, then it is a fairly good start to having an application granted.' This was a common sentiment. Most agreed with it, saying that it would only be in rare cases that they would disregard the stand taken by the prosecution. One explanation for this reliance, given by some of the judges/sheriffs was that this is very often because they do not know the full facts of the case, whilst the prosecution obviously does.

Enforcement – A Duty Gap?

Whose duty is it to enforce the legislation? There seems to be a grey area here. Certainly, there were cases where it appeared that the legislation was being disregarded. Given what was said in the interviews, it seems that enforcement is falling, as it were, between two stools, between the prosecution on the one hand, and the judiciary on the other.

There is obviously a certain structural problem here, when, for example, a 'passive' prosecutor meets an 'umpire' judge/sheriff. If there is no objection by the Crown and no intervention by the bench when prohibited evidence is introduced, then it makes it very easy for the defence, as one fiscal so aptly put it, to go 'sailing through.' This is a problem that does not go unrecognised by the prosecution, yet why is enforcement not stepped up? Perhaps the rather desultory tone of one fiscal's response offers a clue:

It's probably up to us to provoke an application, but ... I do agree ... that we do appear to be reluctant to do anything and indeed we may be passive in this legislation. It could be said, I suppose, that we might do something more about it ... but I am quite sure in this legislation that we do nothing.

Obligating neither, the new prohibitions have no natural agent of enforcement. If, as Kelsen tells us, laws are primarily addressed to legal officials, here it would seem, these rules are marked 'address unknown'.

NOTES

1. R. W. Renton and H. Brown, *Criminal Procedure According to the Law of Scotland* (edited by G. H. Gordon, J. Maclean and C. H. W. Gane and more recently by Robert Wymss) (Edinburgh: W. Green, 1983, 5th edition).
2. J. Chambers and A. Millar, *Prosecuting Sexual Assault*, (Edinburgh: HMSO, 1986), p.139.

11

The Trial as an Ordeal:
Rules and Procedures in Practice

The extent to which sexual history and sexual character evidence was used, with and without the appropriate procedures, has been presented in Chapters 5, 6 and 7. This chapter offers a further illustrative picture of the way in which the general legal-evidential procedures discussed in Chapter 2 translate into questions put to complainers in the courtroom. While it has been acknowledged earlier that normal rules and conventional practices can produce a considerable degree of necessary ordeal, the question that was not addressed was whether the ordeal suffered by complainers was greater than necessary. The material presented indicates that there is a case for arguing that the extent of the ordeal suffered by the complainer is over and above that required by the normal rules.

In shaping the experience of a witness, normal cross-examination procedures, in themselves a testing business, interact with illegitimate practices such as sexual history and character evidence admitted and pursued without permission. In what follows, ways in which normal procedures can become particularly harassing practices are referred to as well as more obvious abuses of those procedures. Rape cases, as expected, provided the most extreme examples of obvious ordeal and for this reason most of the illustrations are drawn from such cases. Hence the chapter is initially structured by reflecting on the consequences for complainers of normal procedures and typical types of evidence discussed in Chapter 2.

CORROBORATION AND THE DEFINITION OF THE CRIME

The basic corroboration rule of Scots criminal law, that facts have to be substantiated by two independent sources, has obvious merits. However, it is often noted that in sexual offence trials, on-the-scene witnesses – a common source of corroboration in some other offences – are largely absent. This, it is said, accounts for the pressure on the complainer and the difficulty of proving the charge beyond reasonable doubt. What has to be corroborated in turn, depends on the specific definition of the crime. In rape cases what is at issue is whether sexual intercourse took place against the will of the complainer. The prosecution leads the complainer's evidence about how sexual intercourse took place against her will and calls on subsequent witnesses to substantiate her account. Not all elements of the crime may be contested. For example, a common defence in the case of rape involves acknowledging that sexual intercourse took place but arguing that it was with consent. But whatever the defence line of argument, the defence is constantly attempting to dis-corroborate or distract from elements of the prosecution evidence.

In a rape case, the possible sources of corroboration, as well as eye and ear witnesses are evidence of semen, injury, damaged clothing and distress after the event. Observation of rape cases revealed that these factors can take on prominence even when they are not logically required for corroboration and/or when their corroborative value is slight. It would be a very rare case in which the prosecution felt able to present evidence on all of these fronts. However, the defence makes capital out of the absence of evidence. For the case to have proceeded to the stage of the trial, some evidence which appears to corroborate the complainer's account will be a part of the prosecution case, but rarely the whole gamut of possible sorts of corroborative evidence. Nevertheless, the defence routinely tried to suggest that the *absence* of such factors as semen, injury, damaged clothing was in itself evidence indicating that no assault occurred. Moreover, questioning in these areas sometimes became a way of harassing the complainer and generating a confusion of largely irrelevant detail by the defence. This adds to the ordeal of the complainer and helps the defence case.

Semen

The presence or absence of semen was often discussed as an important sign of sexual intercourse. This is misleading as research on rape shows that penetration is often slight and ejaculation is rare. The definition of rape does not require ejaculation and only some penetration. Thus, while it is plausible to treat the *presence* of semen in the vagina as evidence of penetration, the converse is not. The prosecution did not usually take the opportunity to inform the jury that the absence of semen was in fact characteristic of rape rather than a counter indication. When the defence make much of the absence of semen, such an explanation would often be helpful to the jury.

The frequent concern with semen is also puzzling because in the overwhelming majority of cases the defence argument was that what took place was not rape but normal sex. Hence, the act of sexual intercourse was not in dispute and therefore signs of sexual intercourse were not essential corroboration, nor could their absence be a significant lack of corroboration. It seems that the interest in semen has simply become a convention in rape trials, perhaps because semen is one of a very limited number of possible physical signs, all of which are routinely investigated regardless of circumstances. Routine questioning about a sexual matter which is of little or no evidential significance can be an unnecessary ordeal for the complainer.

Injuries, Force and Resistance

The presence or absence of injuries took on considerable significance in many observed rape and rape-related cases. Injuries were treated as key signs of the absence or presence of consent, hence defence questions such as, 'Is it not the case that you let him do this? There was no mark on you, him or your clothes. You were willing?' (case 058). Again an emphasis on injuries is potentially misleading as research reveals that rapes frequently occur without visible physical injury. In the observed trials the prosecution very rarely informed the jury that the absence of injury was characteristic of rape cases. Again this would be helpful to the jury when the defence suggest that the absence of injuries indicates the absence of rape and the presence of consent.

The emphasis on injuries may also create the impression that if force was absent then rape did not occur. It was noted earlier that Scots law does not require, as part of the definition of rape, that force was used. Yet it is an assumption easily perpetuated when we find juries presented with definitions of rape such as the following from our research: 'Rape is overcoming the female's resistance by physical violence or by using a lethal weapon' (011); 'The essence of the crime of rape is force' (013); 'Rape is carnal knowledge without consent. ... sexual intercourse must have been forcibly against will' (052). Even a scrupulously accurate judicial statement can be subverted in advance in the defence summing-up. Thus in one case (058), the judge's statement: 'If everything had been with her consent and then suddenly he was about to insert his penis and she says 'no', then that does constitute rape; consent must be at the time of penetration', was prefaced and perhaps undermined by the defence's prior statement: 'She, for some reason panicked and asked him to stop.' The situation even as the defence described was therefore rape. (The outcome of the case was a 'not guilty' verdict.)

Possibly the Scots law definition in terms of 'overcoming the will' rather than the abuse of consent further privileges force as part of the crime itself. Yet even if legal definitions are clarified or altered, force may still linger on as a test of rape because, as the above quote says so clearly, 'force is the *evidence* ... of the want of consent'. In the crudest sense, it is evidence in that it leaves physical traces, the bruises, soreness, marks of struggle, that are privileged as the indelible signs of rape, left behind for others to see. Physical force is evidence, second, because the fact that the man has to use force to succeed in his object of sexual intercourse is taken as evidence, within the situation, of the woman's lack of consent. *Force* defines non-consent from the man's point of view. The man's responsibility to establish a woman's mind in any other way is not a focus. Conversely, attention focuses on the woman's *resistance*, as the outward sign of her positive will not to consent. This resistance may be manifested in saying, 'no', in shouts and screams, and of course, in the physical fight that she puts up.

Questions put to complainers, particularly by the defence in cross-examination sometimes suggest that merely saying, 'no' is not enough – it has to be shouted and physically reinforced. It is as if women's non-consenting words are not to be taken seriously and they could only say, 'no' through physical means. Typical examples of questions which try to suggest consent by pointing to a lack of resistance are: 'Why did nobody hear screams?', 'Why were there no visible signs of struggle?', 'Why were you not injured nor the accused?', 'Why did you not poke him in the eyes or kick him between the legs?' These questions are often put to the complainer in a hectoring fashion, a tactic documented by Chambers and Millar,[1] which unfortunately still persists. Questions such as these also appeared during the defence summing-up when they are put in a rhetorical fashion to the jury.

Chambers and Millar also commented on instances in which the defence tries to suggest to the jury that 'real' victims would try to resist their attacker 'to the last'. Again this tactic persists. In case 049 the complainer described how she was woken by having her head banged against the wall and was then raped.

DEFENCE:	Did you struggle at all?
COMPLAINER:	What do you think?
DEFENCE:	Did you express surprise at that question? How did you struggle?
COMPLAINER:	I don't know.
DEFENCE:	Were you doing your physical best to fight off this man who was brutally assaulting and raping you?

The defence advocate returned to this theme several times in his lengthy cross-examination. On the third occasion he asked about why she did 'not fight effectively':

DEFENCE:	How do you explain no marks on the accused?
COMPLAINER:	I am flaming four feet flaming ten, that is why.

State of Distress and 'First Report' Evidence

The complainer's state of mind at the time and the degree of upset caused are also taken as indicators of lack of consent. These are usually elicited through questions to the complainer like: 'How were you feeling at this time, or immediately afterwards?' The latter is corroborated in the 'first report' account when it is a 'recent complaint'.

'First report' evidence is very important in sexual assault trials. This is the evidence from the first person whom the complainer told that she had been assaulted. The immediate question such evidence raises is hearsay – is the witness allowed to actually repeat the words the complainer said or must evidence concern only the real evidence of her state (distress, torn clothes, the fact that the complainer said 'something'). As noted in Chapter 2, the question is usually resolved in terms of whether or not it was a *de recenti* statement, that is, made very soon after the event. This evidence is admitted in relation to the complainer's credibility, either as real evidence of the truth of her claim or as showing consistency. Yet, once again defence frequently turns this around, so that the absence of such 'first report' corroboration becomes evidence in itself that no rape occurred:

> ... it has become the normal practice for the court to look for some sort of evidence that the complainer first made his or her allegation against the accused shortly after the event. Far from being simply a matter of positive evidence in support of the credibility of the complainer, the *absence* of any early complaint has become regarded as a positive point in favour of the defence ... [2]

The 'first opportunity to complain' works on the presumption that the worth of any 'first report' witness decreases if the complainer did not act on the first chance. What constitutes an 'opportunity' may be highly contentious. When a complainer is still in a car with her attacker after the attack and the car is overtaken by a police car, does this really amount to an 'opportunity'? The other question is whom a complainer might speak to. The fact that a complainer has not spoken to the first person she saw sometimes counts against her. This is often countered by the notion of the 'natural confidant(e)' – that a mother or a close friend or a ex-husband (in one of our cases) would be the chosen person to speak to about such a private and horrific matter. One judge even spoke sympathetically, if archaically, of a woman's 'natural modesty' that would prevent her speaking to just anyone. However, this too may go against a complainer who *fails* to confide in one of these 'natural confidant(e)s'.

In the following example of a rape case in which the accused was the complainer's uncle, the defence's efforts to attach significance to the delay in reporting the rape are combined with attacks on the credibility of the young complainer. The extract follows a series of detailed, quickly fired questions about the events after the incident:

COMPLAINER: Can't remember.
DEFENCE: Well don't just stand there saying things off the top of
                          your head, Teresa. [uses complainer's first name

which we have altered for purposes of anonymity].

DEFENCE: And you made tea after all these bad things had happened?

COMPLAINER: Yes.

DEFENCE: Were you crying when you handed the keys in?

COMPLAINER: No, I had washed my face.

DEFENCE: Didn't you ask for help from a neighbour or run in to a neighbour's house?

COMPLAINER: No.

DEFENCE: Why not?

COMPLAINER: Don't know.

DEFENCE: You do know, Teresa.

COMPLAINER: No.

DEFENCE: Because nothing happened.

COMPLAINER: That's a lie.

DEFENCE: Why did you not tell the ice-cream man?

The reliance on 'first report' accounts of the complainer's state after the event also presumes that visible distress is normal following rape or sexual assault. Adler discusses research querying whether there is such a thing as a 'normal' reaction. Some victims may show evidence of acute anxiety, emotional breakdown, and disruption of normal patterns of behaviour. Others, 'appear calm and collected, showing little external evidence of distress which may reflect shock and disbelief'.[3]

CREDIBILITY AND RELIABILITY

Attacking the credibility and reliability of key prosecution witnesses is a standard part of the art of the advocate for the defence. For example, if a prosecution witness has consumed alcohol around the time of the incident, then the defence typically suggests that their judgement was impaired. In observed trials, generally the defence devoted more time and creative energy to attacking credibility than reliability. This was particularly the case for the defence attentions devoted to complainers in rape cases in which the defence story was one of consent and false allegation.

Illustrations of typical attacks on credibility are not singled out here as many have already been given. In Chapters 6 and 7, it was noted that defence advocates successfully applied to introduce sexual history evidence by stating the need to test the complainer's credibility. Illustrations are given there of how this translated into actual questions put to the complainer. In Chapter 8 which reported on interviews with defence advocates, examples are given of advocates discussing their discrediting tactics. Chapter 9 dealt with sexual history and character evidence introduced without use of the formal procedures. Again examples are given of ways in which sexual history and character evidence were used to attack a complainer's credibility. In Chapters 6, 7 and 9, illustrations are given of ways in which the defence discredit the complainer by questions about life style which cumulatively create the impression of a 'bad sexual character'. In a rape trial the majority of attempts made by the defence to indicate that the complainer consented are simultaneously an assault on her credibility. The final example at the end of this chapter illustrates this interaction.

THE ASYMMETRIC ADVERSARIAL SYSTEM

Statements from witnesses, physical artefacts and written reports are the contested signs of crime. With these signs forming the building blocks, prosecution and defence present their cases. The trial is a contest of accumulation, construction and demolition of characters and stories. But the prosecution and defence are not equally free to pursue these constructions. As noted earlier, the prosecution must prove the Crown case 'beyond reasonable doubt', whereas the defence may concentrate on casting doubt on the prosecution case, introducing red herrings and confusion, without the need for proof. The rules require that the prosecution puts all relevant evidence before the jury, whether or not it contradicts the testimony of key prosecution witnesses while the defence only call witnesses that strengthen their case and need not put the accused in the witness box.

In the course of a trial, typifications of characters are constructed, including presumptions about their motives, and stories are built up about the events. Character presumptions and stories can combat or contribute to each other's logic. While both prosecution and defence participate in this, the defence invariably do so with greater gusto. It is in their client's interest to knock down and reshape the prosecution case, painting alternative scenarios for the jury, and they have more creative manoeuvre to do so. The prosecution task of laying all relevant facts before the jury places a natural limit on the creative art of advocacy.

While both prosecution and defence advocates bring prior experience of presenting evidence in ways which they believe will impress the jury, the defence have a much freer rein. It is the defence who more often conjure up popular stereotypes in their character constructions, like the 'loose woman' or the 'precocious, seductive girl'. For the prosecution, discrediting defence witnesses is only embarked on when professional judgement deems it appropriate; for the defence discrediting key prosecution witnesses, particularly the complainer in a rape trial, is stock-in-trade. While the prosecution task does not require weaving contradictory pieces of evidence into a coherent narrative, the defence frequently attempt to impress the jury by doing so, often trying out several, sometimes contradictory, narratives in the course of one trial. Indeed, many of these stock narratives do not rely on good/bad stereotypes but on a repertoire of received ideas about plausible conduct.

In rape cases, the most common defence story is one which presents the characters and events as consistent with a narrative of consensual sex followed by a false allegation. A small repertoire of stories is reused and reworked around each case. The standard motives for false allegations include, the woman panicked and was ashamed after the event, she feared discovery by husband or boyfriend or parent, she was caught in a tissue of lies. Sometimes the role of the 'first report witness' may be recast by the defence as part of the 'caught up in a web of lies' routine. Here the complainer is presented as distressed but inarticulate or indecisive in speaking to someone. It is the confidante who produces the formulation 'Did he rape you?' and, before she knows it, the complainer finds herself being interviewed by the police, etc. These stories do not necessarily rely on the standard stereotypes of 'good' and 'bad' women.

Defence advocates typically make use of every opportunity to introduce, develop and reiterate aspects of the defence story. This can be done in ways that simultaneously belittle prosecution witnesses by attacking their credibility. For example, rather than allowing a witness to deny an incident or event by asking a single question, the defence advocate will ask a series of questions about specific details, simultaneously providing an ordeal for the complainer and unfolding the defence story to the jury. The following example is the result of the defence's successful application to put the accused's allegation of consensual sex to the 15-year-old complainer (176).

DEFENCE:	Is it not the case when you were upset, you sat down to be consoled?
COMPLAINER:	No. I was pulled on to his knee by him.
DEFENCE:	Did it not happen, you were upset and put your arms around him and were crying?
COMPLAINER:	I wasn't crying.
DEFENCE:	You were being comforted, sitting on his knee?
COMPLAINER:	He was not comforting me. I did not sit on his knee.
DEFENCE:	You were washing dishes. He came up behind?
COMPLAINER:	Yes.
DEFENCE:	You were enjoying his attention.
COMPLAINER:	No.
DEFENCE:	You were leaning against him?
COMPLAINER:	No.
DEFENCE:	You had on jeans and a T-shirt. Your jeans were too big, quite loose at the waist?
COMPLAINER:	Very.
DEFENCE:	He put his hands in your jeans.
COMPLAINER:	No.
DEFENCE:	While still at the kitchen sink you agreed to him slackening off buttons on your trousers?
COMPLAINER:	What?
DEFENCE:	While still at the kitchen sink you agreed to him slackening off buttons on your trousers?

COMPLAINER: No. [researcher notes – complainer is obviously very
                surprised by this line of questioning.]
DEFENCE: At the same time you tried to take down the zip of his
                trousers?
COMPLAINER: I totally deny that. [researcher notes – complainer
                sounds shocked.]

THE NECESSARY ORDEAL?

The Example of Case 134

Given the strong emphasis placed on the paucity of corroborative evidence in rape trials, it is interesting to examine a case in which there was,
unusually, an on-the-scene witness who heard and saw some of the
events. The outcome of this case was also atypical, a guilty verdict. This
was probably greatly aided by the strong corroboration but also by the fact
that the accused made what his defence advocate privately referred to as
a 'poor showing' in the witness box under an unusually lively attack from
the prosecution.

However, what is striking in this case is that despite the strong
corroboration evidence introduced by the prosecution, the complainer
was still subjected to standard defence attempts at dis-corroboration,
creative defence use of the absence of all possible corroboration, attacks
on her credibility, and the defence construction of a story of consent and
false allegation. In all these respects it was a typical case. It is particularly
interesting, however, because the rigorous pursuit of these lines of defence could not be justified by the usual argument that it is simply the
complainer's word against that of the accused.

This was a case of attempted rape. The defence story was that the
complainer was annoyed with her boyfriend, that she fancied the accused
(whom she knew only as an acquaintance), invited him to have sex with
her on the way to find her boyfriend, and then changed her mind,
probably because she realised they were being watched, and started to
scream. The police were contacted by two ear witnesses and the complainer then became trapped in a set of false allegations. This was a
defence elaboration and partial reconstruction of the facts that emerged
from the complainer's account: she went to meet her boyfriend whom she
expected to be at home; when he was not there she looked for him in a
particular pub where she was bought a drink by the accused whom she
knew, and where she chatted to the accused; the accused said he had seen
her boyfriend in another pub and offered to accompany her; *en route* he
dragged her down an alley and attempted to rape her.

The defence tried to construct indicators of consent from the fact that
the woman was bought a drink by the accused (the complainer said that
she did not drink this drink), and from the fact that she chatted to him and

left with him. The length of time she spent in the pub was a matter of dispute, with the complainer saying 15 minutes, and the accused saying about half an hour. The defence put it to the complainer that she had in fact put her arm round the accused and encouraged him. This was done through a repeated and leading series of questions.

DEFENCE:	Did you get friendly?
COMPLAINER:	We were talking.
DEFENCE:	You put your arms round him?
COMPLAINER:	No.
DEFENCE:	Were you not angry that your boyfriend was not there?
COMPLAINER:	Yes.
DEFENCE:	You were pleased to see [accused]?
COMPLAINER:	No.
DEFENCE:	Didn't you get really friendly with him?

The defence advocate returns to this theme later after making an application.

DEFENCE:	Did you not suggest going up the lane?
COMPLAINER:	No.
DEFENCE:	Did you encourage him?
COMPLAINER:	No.
DEFENCE:	Were you not happy to go up the lane?
COMPLAINER:	No.
DEFENCE:	You were upset you hadn't met your boyfriend?
COMPLAINER:	Yes.
DEFENCE:	You were pleased to see [the accused] and encouraged him to go with you?

The story is built up both through challenging and reinterpreting the signs of the crime and recasting the events as signs of consent. The defence also used the standard tactic of turning any gap in the conventional repertoire of signs of rape, or attempted rape, into a sign of consent. In this case it was lack of injuries and damage to clothing that were given significance by the defence. He put it to the jury that if the accused had such a strong hold on the complainer's wrist and if she struggled as much as she claimed, then her wrist specifically would have been injured, and her clothes more damaged than they were. The defence advocate contested all the key pieces of corroboration presented by the prosecution, for example, querying the reliability of the eyewitness by suggesting that there was insufficient light, and by suggesting that the semen found on the complainer's skirt came from her boyfriend not the accused. The defence desire to pursue the possibility that the semen in fact came from the complainer's boyfriend formed the ground for a (successful) application. In addition, the defence also tried to cast doubt on the complainer's credibility in a number of ways.

DEFENCE:	Did you tell the doctor yourself?
COMPLAINER:	He asked questions.
DEFENCE:	Did he ask about periods? Questions about whether you were on the pill?
COMPLAINER:	Yes.
DEFENCE:	And that you had a boyfriend?
COMPLAINER:	Yes.
DEFENCE:	And the last time you had intercourse with your boyfriend?
COMPLAINER:	Yes.
DEFENCE:	Is it possible you said you had intercourse that day?
COMPLAINER:	No, I never saw him that day.
DEFENCE:	Doctor said you told him you had intercourse with [boyfriend].
COMPLAINER:	No.
DEFENCE:	Is he lying?
COMPLAINER:	Yes.

The 'Is he lying?' is a deliberate tactic used by defence advocates when questioning prosecution witnesses about someone whose veracity is assumed to be beyond question. The line of questioning boxes the witness into a corner in which there seems to be no choice but to agree that somebody, whom most people regard as a source of truth, is lying. This is one of many standard ways of discrediting a witness.

The case as a whole illustrates the wide licence available to defence advocates, in terms of the interpretations and alternative explanations of evidence that they may offer in the course of one trial. In the case discussed above, much defence time was devoted to trying to suggest that the complainer had a sexual interest in the accused as part of the story that events happened with her consent. At the same time, the defence put considerable effort into the alternative source of semen argument in an attempt to establish that very little of a sexual nature had happened with the accused in any case. Perhaps the most creative defence reinterpretation of events was the attempt to transform the significance of the on-the-scene witness's testimony by suggesting that the complainer had consented, but then protested because she was aware of being observed.

CONCLUSION

Observed cases confirm what other authors have indicated, that the complainer's ordeal in the court may be exacerbated if she cannot give the 'correct' responses to questions about semen, injuries, resistance, and about her 'first report' and state of mind after the event. Yet these acceptable answers are based on a very limited perception of the phenomena of rape and sexual assault. The absence of any of these indicators of crime is seized on by the defence and turned round into a sign of consent. Observation also indicates, however, that her ordeal is not necessarily less if she is able to give the 'correct' responses. Clear evidence of semen, injuries and distress after the event is not the end of the story. The defence will then set about challenging, casting doubt on, or trying to reinterpret these signs. For example, by suggesting an alternative source for injury or for the staining or damage to clothing, or by saying that the injury or damage is insufficient given the complainer's account, the defence typically builds towards a story of consent and false allegation. And, to reiterate, no independent evidence has to be brought by the defence to back up these claims. The laws of evidence – particularly the need for corroboration – and the definition of rape provide only partial explanations for how questioning about such issues as semen, injuries, force and resistance, unfold in the courtroom.

Sexist assumptions about the rules of sexual conduct were certainly in operation at times. The defence made free use of the double-standard in sexual conduct which divides the moral universe of women, but not men, into 'the good' who are not seeking sex and 'the bad' who are. By manipulation of this moral universe, the accused become the victims of seductive and mischievous women and girls. Moreover, the use of sexist assumptions was not confined to the defence. For example, it seemed to be taken for granted that the question, 'Did the accused attempt to establish consent?' had no relevance, while the question, 'Did the woman do everything she could to state her non-consent?' was treated as unproblematic. This is illustrated by the definition of rape offered by the prosecution in his summing-up in case 092. 'Rape occurs when a woman is penetrated, taken against her will; making it clear she doesn't want it to happen.' This definition seems to suggest that a woman who is silent because she is afraid to protest is having 'normal sex'.

The asymmetrical adversarial system allows the defence scope for using a range of techniques to discredit complainers. While many of these techniques are neither unique to sexual offence trials nor used exclusively on female witnesses, their use enhances any defence attempt to construe the complainer as of 'bad sexual character'. The worst excesses of the adversarial techniques used to unnerve confuse and discredit witnesses have been documented by Adler, Chambers and Millar, and Edwards among others. Such techniques are taught as part of the art of advocacy and are a 'natural' feature of the evidential contest. Although there is considerable scope for reducing unnecessary suffering through higher standards of adversarial conduct, as long as the adversarial system persists, the trial is something of an ordeal. The asymmetrical nature of the adversarial system also gives the defence considerable creative freedom. In doing so, the confident use that the defence makes of sexist assumptions reflects their understanding of the jurors' ways of thinking. The defence believes, it seems rightly, that jurors are comfortable with a moral universe which divides women into 'good' and 'bad'. The high acquittal rate in rape cases generates a sense that their tactics work.

Complainers in sexual offence cases, are frequently confronted with such creative defence manoeuvres, as the suggestion in case 134, that the complainer consented to going down an alley for sex and only panicked when she realised she was being watched. Such reinterpretations of events are particularly common in cases in which consent is at issue. Complainers may find the construction of such stories a shocking and bizarre experience. Out of the blue all sorts of possibilities are suggested. Yet the prosecution rarely tackle these defence stories directly, perhaps not seeing it as their job to do so. Sometimes additional evidence would need to be sought in order to rebut the allegations of the defence. But in re-examination, it would often be possible for prosecution advocates to emphasise ways in which the evidence does not fit easily with the defence story, as well as presenting ways in which it does support their own case. Atypically, this was done in case 134 when the prosecution attacked the credibility of the accused and addressed the unlikeliness of the story. As well as gaining points in the evidential context, this may have given some satisfaction to the complainer.

Creative defence stories occurred whether the complainer was male or female if consent was put at issue. Observation indicated that the defence used consent as a form of defence, albeit a mitigation plea rather than a straightforward defence, in offences involving girls under 16 and homosexual offences involving boys under 21, although consent was irrelevant to the definition of the crime. In the case of jury trials, it may be that the defence presumes jurors to be guided by a lay sense of justice when reaching their judgement rather than by the law.

The trial will remain a particular ordeal when consent is at issue and standard tactics require the complainer to prove the absence of consent: a situation produced by the interplay between adversarial technique, crime definition, rules of evidence and sexist assumptions. Prohibiting evidence of a complainer's sexual history or sexual character from the trial potentially removes an area of unnecessary humiliation and embarrassment. However, as earlier chapters have indicated this has not been achieved as the legislation intended.

This chapter has concentrated primarily on rape offences. However, the other offences should not be forgotten. For statutory age-of-consent offences, the phenomenon of the 'early plea in mitigation' was discussed in the context of interviews with practitioners. The focus on the issue of actual consent in such offences makes them far more like rape trials, and is even more inappropriate precisely because of the youth of the complainers. As for trials for homosexual offences, the character-blackening associated with imputations of prostitution is no less humiliating and discrediting than for women – yet there is little awareness that the legislation intends to protect them equally.

NOTES

1. G. Chambers and A. Millar, *Prosecuting Sexual Assault* (Edinburgh: HMSO, Scottish Office Central Research Unit Study, 1988) p. 201, emphasis added.
2. David Field, *The Law of Evidence in Scotland* (Edinburgh: W. Green & Son, 1988) p. 201, emphasis added.
3. Z. Adler, *Rape on Trial* (London and New York: Routledge and Kegan Paul, 1987), pp. 12–13.

12

Conclusions Drawn from the Research

THE PARTIAL SUCCESS OF THE LEGISLATION

The aim of the law reform is to minimise undue investigation of complainers' sexual lives while continuing to admit all the evidence necessary for justice to be done to the accused. Particular types of evidence are to be excluded – sexual history and sexual character evidence – unless it had genuine relevance to the key issues of the trial. The aim is not to suspend the normal rules of evidence in sexual offence trials but to remove the anomalous admission of sexual 'bad character' evidence in such trials and to prevent abuses of these rules. The reform stems from concern about the harmful effects of such evidence, the unnecessary ordeal for the complainer and the possible prejudice to the outcome of the trial.

Some limited success can be claimed for the legislation on the following grounds: the research showed that very blatant attacks on the complainer's sexual character were rare and were not permitted by judges when the procedures were followed; similarly, blatant instances of suggesting that because a complainer was promiscuous then she or he was a liar were rare and not permitted; some important boundaries between the acceptable and the unacceptable were drawn through the new procedures; in general, the procedure of making an application provides a forum for questioning the defence about their proposed use of evidence and for placing limits on their questioning.

However, the research indicates that the legislation falls short of achieving the aims of the legislators. Although some evidence is being excluded through the legislation, much does persist. Indeed the description given by Chambers and Millar of the pre-reform situation remains relevant to current practice:

> Questioning on moral character and sexual experience, in particular with regard to relationships with specific men, was undertaken by both prosecution and defence … It was apparent that the prevailing view of counsel and judge was that a woman's sexual experience was important to the issue of consent and that questioning on these topics was therefore justified. In attempting to understand the complainer's

experience at trial, defence tactics were of paramount importance. These included accusations of lying, insensitive and persistent questioning, harassment and intimidation.[1]

Overall, complainers were asked questions concerning their sexual conduct in about half of the sexual offence trials involving juries; some questioning was obviously very upsetting to complainers; some evidence was of the type that the reform sought to exclude. The acquittal rate, particularly in rape cases, remains extremely high at 78 per cent (not proven or not guilty verdicts). Sexual history and sexual character evidence is often heard in jury trials of sexual offences other than rape and in both High and Sheriff Courts. However such evidence is rare in cases tried under summary procedure. Nevertheless, the extensive coverage of the types of sexual offences written into the legislation was a wise extension beyond the trials of rape in which the problems of such evidence are seen most acutely.

Three general problems can be identified which affect the achievement of the aims of the legislation. In addition, there are a couple of background factors which necessarily limit general satisfaction with the legislation. These are introduced briefly here and discussed in more detail later.

Problem One

Sexual history and sexual character evidence are *still* used without reference to the legislation, that is, the rules are not being followed.

Problem Two

Sexual history and sexual character evidence which are admitted legitimately can be of the type and/or have effects that the legislators aimed to exclude, that is, the rules are being followed but not with the anticipated achievement of aims. As part of the aim of excluding undue intimate and possibly embarrassing questioning, two specific evidential constructions were to be excluded – the complainer is promiscuous and therefore a liar; the complainer consented to sex with A and B and therefore consented with C. While there is no suggestion that the legislation failed to the point where such evidence was straightforwardly admitted on application, this type of evidence did appear in other forms and permitted questioning which had the same effects. In other words, following the letter of the law is not achieving the spirit of the law.

Problem Three

There is one factor contributing to the prevalence of sexual character evidence which was addressed by the policy makers but then left untouched by the legislation in its final form, that is, the need to control subtle character attacks. The legislation falls short of achieving its aims in relation to a recognised and anticipated problem.

Background Discontent and Resistance

It must also be recognised that, while the general aim is to prevent gratuitous investigation of complainers' sexual lives, it was never intended to exclude all that was regarded as illegitimate by the most vocal pressure groups calling for reform, namely the Rape Crisis Centres, nor was the intention to take on board all the concerns expressed in feminist academic writing on the law. At the same time, it must be remembered that, at the time of the reform, some members of the legal profession expressed the view that the reform was completely unnecessary (a view reiterated in interviews). For some members of the legal profession then, there was and is no recognition of any of the problems identified in this report. This extent of lack of consensus at the time of the reform meant there was always a danger of disappointment with the legislation, whatever its effects.

PROBLEM ONE: THE RULES ARE NOT BEING FOLLOWED

The presence or use of prohibited evidence without reference to the legislation, is partly, perhaps largely, a matter of procedures not being followed. Most, although not all, of the prohibited evidence which was introduced by the defence without an application may well have been admitted legitimately had an application been made.

Considerable insight into this apparent disregard of the procedures was given by the practitioners themselves. Lack of awareness of the scope of the rules was not a general problem, although it was a factor in some cases. Over a third of practitioners were not aware that homosexual and age-related statutory offences were covered by the rules, and sheriffs were inclined to regard the rules as mainly relevant to the High Court. On the other hand, many practitioners thought the rules covered incest cases and saw this as an omission when told they did not.

By their own testimony, defence practitioners sometimes break rules for pragmatic reasons and there is a danger that neither the prosecution nor the presiding judge/sheriff will enforce the legislation, each seeing it as the responsibility of the other. The pragmatic neglect of rules and the problems of enforcement could allow evidence which would never have been admitted otherwise to slip through. Although comparison with successful applications indicated that this was not typically the case, the introduction of such questioning or evidence by way of an application provides the formal opportunity to check the admissibility of the evidence and to place limits on defence questioning.

What redress is there when rules of evidence are breached? Normally, when this concerns the accused, there is the possibility of an appeal to a higher court. The prosecutor and complainer have no such option. There will be no appeal cases on the kinds of breaches of the legislation described here.

PROBLEM TWO: THE RULES ARE NOT ACHIEVING THE AIMS

The second problem is much more serious and complex, with contributing factors which also have a bearing on the neglect of procedures. A series of factors undermine the effectiveness of the application as a point of resistance to the use of irrelevant sexual history and sexual character evidence to the key issues of the trial. These are discussed first and then attention is turned to the Crown and judicial exemption.

The Permeability of the Application Barrier
The Ineffectiveness of the Wording of the Legislation

One set of factors concerns shortcomings in the framing of the legislation, more specifically the effectiveness of the wording in achieving the aims. The wording of the exceptions helped to create a situation in which the type of evidence that the legislation aimed to exclude could in fact be admitted. In the reports and consultations leading up to the reform it was clear that the aim was to exclude evidence that was not relevant to key issues in the trial, and certain clear instances of what would not be relevant were discussed.

It was also strongly stated that certain sorts of assumptions could no longer be regarded (if they ever had been) as a basis of relevance – suggesting a complainer is promiscuous and therefore a liar, and suggesting that because a complainer had consensual sex with A or B, that they therefore consented to sex with C. The aim was to prevent bogus connections being drawn between sexual character (or sexual conduct construed as indicating a certain character) and the key issues concerning the credibility of complainers or the likelihood of consent. However, the exception subsections of the provisions were not worded in terms of relevance to issues nor did the legislation specify that the defence had to show relevance in the application.

Debate during the reform process focused particularly on the 'interests of justice' exception because of concern with the discretionary leeway it gave to defence arguments and the amount of discretion it left to judges. In fact, all the exception subsections of the provisions, not just 'the interests of justice', have proved sufficiently open-ended and discretionary to allow the admission of evidence of little relevance or probative value. This has happened in spite of the fact that judges, sheriffs and prosecutors profess themselves to be primarily concerned with the relevance when deciding the admissibility of evidence. Not only does the legislation not require relevance to be considered, in some circumstances it works against it being taken into account. The wording specifies that 'the court shall allow' questioning or the admission of evidence if the exception subsections of the provisions apply. This wording combined with the wording of the 'explain or rebut' subsection, in particular, gives the defence an opportunity to argue that the exception subsection applies, without addressing the relevance to the case. In combination with the fact that the Crown is exempt from the restrictions on sexual history evidence, this places the defence in a strong position to pick up any such evidence led by the prosecution with little need for justification.

Establishing that the words of the statute apply is not always an uncontentious business. Frequent arguments were observed with reference to the 'explain or rebut' exception. In order for the 'explain or rebut' to apply, the defence must first indicate the part of the prosecution evidence that is the subject of the explanation or rebuttal (the wording refers to 'evidence adduced, or to be adduced' by the prosecution). However, there were disputes over precisely what was or would be adduced by the Crown.

Written materials supplied by Crown witnesses but which were not put before the court could be particularly contentious subject matter. In one application, the defence was refused permission to introduce material which appeared in the precognition taken from a Crown witness, and in another they were allowed to use material from the medical report which was a Crown production. In both cases the prosecution objected and declared they had no intention of leading the evidence.

What has and has not been led by the Crown is also necessarily a matter of negotiation and dispute because, as one practitioner put it, 'evidence adduced' is not just factual evidence but is also inferential evidence. Hence, there is scope for considerable dispute as to what was implied by the prosecution evidence. It is in the interest of the defence to attribute inferences of 'good character' in sexual matters to the main prosecution witness and a number of observed cases illustrate the eagerness with which the defence seize on any possibilities to do this. Whenever at all plausible, the actual questions asked by the prosecution are construed by the defence as sexual 'good character' claims in order to provide a 'straw woman' or indeed 'straw man' to be knocked down. This seems a specious manner of outflanking the exclusionary rule.

Another contentious issue associated with 'explain or rebut' concerns whether or not the defence should also specify the basis they have for an alternative explanation or rebuttal. There is a danger that the defence may use the subsection to gain permission to seek alternative explanations by asking speculative questions. For example, commenting on a successful application to rebut evidence of vaginal injury, by asking the complainer if she ever masturbated, one practitioner suggested this was speculative questioning as the defence had no prior indication from a doctor that the injuries were consistent with masturbation. A fairly similar application was refused on the grounds that the questioning was speculative. In general, however, the defence was not required to specify the evidential basis for their rebuttal or explanation.

These disputes illustrate the lack of consensus at the level of applying the words of the statute and the possibility of contradictory judgements across cases. They also illustrate the leeway given to the defence by the flexibility of 'explain or rebut'.

The Absence of Time Restrictions

The prohibition in the legislation covers sexual behaviour between the complainer and the accused but the Scottish Law Commission made it clear that such evidence would normally be relevant, and admitted under one of the exceptions, except if it referred to a chance encounter many years before. No time limits are specified in the legislation. Sexual history between the complainer and the accused is routinely admitted in practice, without any time limits being placed on the questioning. This means that a complainer can be, and is, asked questions about a sexual relationship which lapsed years previously. Questions can be deliberately embarrassing and unnecessarily detailed.

The Enforcement Gap in Applications

Factors associated with the wording of the legislation do not explain why so much sexual history evidence is admitted on application. The high success rate of applications is also due to ambiguities about whose responsibility it is to test whether the exceptions do indeed apply. As with other parts of the trial, during an application the policing of the legislation can fall between prosecutors, who do not feel it is their role to object, and judges who take their cue from the prosecution. Some prosecutors do not feel it is their job to query or challenge the defence during an application. By remaining silent they can achieve the effect of allowing the application to succeed, since some judges will not refuse an application if the prosecution have no objections.

The traditional way of discussing the use of sexual history evidence in the courtroom is to focus on the excesses of the defence. The research did find many instances where defence tactics and routines were much as painted. Cross-examination in rape trials – and other sexual offences – continues to produce examples of the 'art' of the advocate which involves the harassment and vilification of witnesses. However, the research indicates that the lack of reaction to defence tactics is a factor which should not be overlooked in understanding its ineffectiveness.

Lack of Concern with Probative Value or Prejudicial Effects

Questioning that often seemed weak in relevance and sometimes poorly based, in fact was allowed on application, yet with much potential for connotations of sexual 'bad character'. This potential was often exploited in subsequent cross-examination. Yet as currently framed, the legislation gives little leeway for the probative value of the evidence to be considered, and weighed against its potentially prejudicial effects.

The first of the provisions refers to evidence that 'shows or tends to show' that the complainer is 'not of good character in relation to sexual matters' and hence sets up a potentially wide-reaching exclusion covering the 'character effect' of much sexual and non-sexual evidence. However, the exceptions are prefaced by the phrase '*notwithstanding* the terms of [the first] section', which thereby seems to cancel out this breadth when it comes to admitting evidence requiring only that the court be 'satisfied' that the evidence falls under the wording of one of the exceptions.

Not surprisingly then, while the judiciary interviewed indicated their concern with relevance when deciding the admissibility of evidence, there were no standard routines of investigating its probative value. Balancing probative value against prejudice was an explicit concern of a judge in only one observed case.

Lack of Consensus Concerning Relevance

Consistent judgements of admissibility are unlikely, even if relevance to key issues in the trial is used as a test because, as the interviews revealed, there is little consensus on when sexual history and sexual character are relevant. Moreover, there is a minority view which persists in deeming as relevant to credibility and/or to consent, all of the types of sexual history and sexual character which the legislation seeks to exclude, and is thus clearly out of sympathy with its fundamental principles. Inevitably then some applications will be successful even if the proposed evidence contradicts the spirit of the legislation. However, this brings the matter full circle to the actual wording of the legislation itself, because this can only be done when the proposed evidence is seen to fit under one of the exceptions, which in turn, are very widely drafted.

Shifting Connotations of Evidence After Application

Evidence allowed as a result of an application in one form, later in the trial took on the form of evidence the legislation had aimed to exclude. The defence sometimes brought out quite different connotations of evidence in their cross-examination to those introduced during the application. Evidence which was admitted on the grounds that it was relevant to the complainer's credibility frequently changed in form or emphasis during cross-examination. In the observed appeals to credibility, the defence often claimed that the proposed questioning would be a test of the *consistency* of the complainer. It was argued that an inconsistency might be revealed by investigating the sexual life of the complainer, for example, suggesting chastity but having sex. Fortuitously, it so happened that the means of exposing untruthfulness was through an investigation of sexual life.

When the defence is one of consent, sexual history evidence introduced in a neutral form can then be used to suggest the type of connections between sexual behaviour, character and consent that the legislation aimed to exclude. Tests of consistency were often the outcome of the defence attributing implications of 'good sexual character' to prosecution evidence. As noted above, the ready attribution of 'good character' can be a device for outflanking the exclusions of the legislation. The construed 'good character' was to be tested by introducing sexual history evidence. What the jury heard were questions about a complainer's sexuality. Through the defence questioning and summing up they were encouraged to draw further conclusions about sexual character and the likelihood of consent.

The reformers were aware of the danger that certain evidence introduced with reference to credibility might then be heard as having relevance to consent, but the discussion focused on direct character attacks without reference to tests of consistency.

When consent was the leading reason for introducing evidence, again what was presented or accepted as the primary relevance was not all that was brought out in cross-examination. If the defence was given permission to ask questions about the complainer's past relationship with the accused because this was relevant to consent, then they might also use this as a way of suggesting she was not of 'good character', asking for example, how soon they had sex after they first met. Allegations of sexually interested or sexually provocative behaviour towards the accused were a typical part of the defence questioning with the effect of suggesting promiscuity, lack of credibility and likelihood to consent.

A common culmination of the defence case was the declaration by the defence concerning the complainer's motive or source of inspiration for making a false allegation of sexual assault after a consensual sexual act yet the defence very rarely indicated any intention of using the sexual history or character they sought to introduce in this way. The defence routinely constructed false allegation scenarios from almost any detail of sexual history. There were a number of accounts that were sufficiently repeated to be called standard – young complainers made false allegations out of remorse and guilt and to conceal 'the truth' about their sexual activity from parents or other adults; sexually active women similarly made false allegations to conceal 'the truth' from their partners; women who were ex-partners of the accused did so out of jealousy or a desire to seek revenge.

Tests of consistency with reference to sexual behaviour are an ordeal for the complainer because any investigation of this intimate aspect of life is potentially embarrassing. When such questions are also used to suggest promiscuity, a predisposition to consent with anyone anywhere and a lack of credibility as a witness, then such questions are inevitably an ordeal. Adolescent complainers are particularly vulnerable, being both less resourced to withstand this ordeal and particularly easy targets for certain standard character constructions by the defence.

The Crown and Judicial Exemptions

The Crown Exemption. The Crown exemption means that the prosecution can introduce sexual history or sexual character evidence as they see fit. At the time of drafting the legislation, the Scottish Law Commission sought views on the possibility of extending the prohibitions to include the Crown. There was little support for this within the legal profession and this remains the case. The reformers anticipated that the prosecution would only lead relevant evidence although there was dissent on this point from Rape Crisis Centres. Also Chambers and Millar criticised the prosecution use of 'good character' evidence such as virginity.

In some observed cases it was the prosecution who led evidence which caused their key witness, the complainer, to be embarrassed and subsequently harassed and intimidated by the defence. Sometimes this was the result of the 'good character' constructions which concerned Chambers and Millar. When consent was at issue in observed cases, sometimes the prosecution led evidence of the complainer's allegedly moral sexual behaviour, such as virginity, chastity or fidelity, in order to strengthen their case that the complainer did not consent. However, as Chambers and Millar observed, this was a dangerous strategy as the defence was liable to counterattack vigorously. Observation also indicated that the prosecution can also be wrong footed by their Crown productions, for example, in cases where the defence cross-examines details of the complainer's sexual history which are irrelevant to the case, but which are contained in the productions for 'administrative convenience'.

In some cases, the prosecution seemed to doubt their own witness and to view their sexual history as being relevant to either credibility or consent. The prosecution has a duty to put all of the relevant facts before the jury whether or not they support a conviction. However, for the prosecution, as with the defence case during an application, there are factors which mitigate against screening out sexual history and character evidence of very limited relevance. There is no injunction on the prosecution to weigh the probative value of such evidence or to consider its probative value against its prejudicial effects. Nor is there consensus on when sexual history is or is not relevant. As with other groupings of legal personnel, their ranks include a minority who regard most sexual history or character evidence as of some relevance. Hence in some cases the prosecution will introduce sexual history and sexual character evidence which is distressing to the complainer, highly prejudicial and of slight probative value.

'Judicial Exemption'. While Adler's study of the English legislation found that the judiciary often intervened to ask questions of the sort prohibited by the legislation, this was not found to be a general problem in Scottish trials. In only two observed cases did a judge or sheriff participate in such questioning. However in two observed cases the judge raised the possibility of a defence of mistaken-belief-in-consent in summing-up, despite the fact that the accused had not been questioned on this matter.

PROBLEM THREE: THE RULES DO NOT TACKLE AN ACCEPTED PROBLEM

Innuendo and Not of Good Character (in Relation to Sexual Matters)

A key objective of the legislation was to break the link between sexual immorality and credibility and, hence, to outlaw the notion that because somebody was sexually promiscuous they were also a liar. It has already been noted that this aim can be sabotaged by the introduction of sexual history evidence through other successful appeals to credibility. But a more common form of damage to this intention can be done by the routine use the defence makes of attacks on a complainer's character which are not explicitly sexual yet nonetheless have sexual connotations.

It is in the interests of the defence to suggest simultaneously that the complainer is both a liar and the type of person who would have sex with anybody anywhere. Many were adept at employing cumulative questioning during the course of cross-examination, using non-sexual character evidence as the building bricks in the construction of a 'bad sexual character' 'You are often out late? You drink regularly? You were wearing a low cut dress? Have you ever taken drugs? Are you in the habit of swearing? You are an unmarried mother? Where were your children? Do you often go to this type of pub? How would you describe the discos you go to? You went to a disco alone? You were happy to get into a car with a strange man?'

Interviews made it clear that there was no consensus among legal practitioners concerning whether such strategies do contravene rules of evidence. Some conceded that they might be dealt with under the exclusion, 'not of good character in sexual matters', others thought not. The Scottish Law Commission's original draft Bill clearly did cover 'bad character' precisely because of the difficulty of distinguishing sexual character and general character, but it was amended to refer specifically to sexual character. There is no general will amongst the legal profession to see such attacks stopped despite their prejudicial effect. A number of defence interviewees freely admitted that they would do what they could to suggest that a woman was of 'easy virtue' precisely because they believed that juries were swayed by it.

A generally held view among practitioners was that the defence was inhibited from making character attacks on complainers because they would then face the prospect of the prosecution in turn attacking their client's character. This was not borne out by observation of trials.

FEMINIST ISSUES NOT TAKEN ON BOARD

Previous sexual acts with the accused are regarded as being relevant to consent by many (but not all) legal professionals who argue that if a complainer has consented to sex with the accused in the past, then it is more likely she or he will have consented on the occasion in question. The Scottish Law Commission gave tacit support to the view that consent in the past suggests consent in the present. Critics of this reasoning, particularly Rape Crisis Centres, argue that it gives credence to the view that a woman who has had sexual intercourse with a particular man then enters into a permanent contract, rather than recognising that sexual intercourse has to be negotiated on each and every occasion. For example, the judicial statement (case 167), 'There is no reason why a husband should assume his wife is not consenting to intercourse unless she makes it abundantly clear to him she is refusing consent', presents marriage as making a wife available to her husband without any need on his part to check whether or not she wants to have sex. From the perspective of the feminist critique of such views, the legislation has done nothing to challenge the persistence of a view of women which is ultimately inimical to at least some of the aims of the legislation.

In addition to asking about any past relationships, the defence often suggests a recent history of sexually interested or provocative behaviour on the part of the complainer towards the accused. Again, not all legal practitioners accepted that such evidence was relevant but the majority saw it as indicative of consent. Clearly many defence advocates believed that juries could be convinced of consent by presenting such behaviour between the complainer and the accused as dancing together, drinking together, having an intimate conversation, kissing, cuddling, engaging in lewd banter as evidence of an interest in sex, suggesting sexual intercourse is a natural conclusion. In rape and rape related cases, the defence typically suggested consent through this route.

In observed cases this did not result in intervention or counterattack by the prosecution that such behaviour is not always followed by sexual intercourse and need not be intended or interpreted as a desire for intercourse. To treat such behaviour uncritically as indicative of consent is perilously close to condoning the view that if a woman engages in sexual behaviour that is short of sexual intercourse – kissing and flirting – then she is 'leading the man on' and cannot expect to be believed (either at the time or later) when she says, 'no'. The legislators and the legislation made no attempt to tackle this view. However, if the defence is correct, such views help considerably in gaining acquittals for their clients and thus work against the aim of reducing wrongful, not proven, or not guilty verdicts.

Clearly sexist assumptions about male and female sexuality are played on by defence advocates in their attempts to portray complainers as women who have consented by either having already had sex with the man in the past or by appearing to seek sexual adventure. As previously indicated, the defence conjure up a moral universe in which women, not men, are divided into 'bad women' who seek sex and 'good women' who do not. Such sexist attitudes are manipulated successfully because they remain prevalent in our society as well as in our courts and hence impress jurors. Clearly it is not only the defence who are implicated in the perpetuation of such stereotypes and stories in the courtroom. Stereotypes and stories succeed because of their cultural resonance. Feminist discussion on sexism in the courtroom is divided between authors who would characterise sexist attitudes as an interference in the course of justice and those who see the normal and supposedly neutral legal procedures as in fact being biased against women. While there is some truth in both positions, the facts do not fit either perfectly and it seems that both are too simplistic.

In a rape case, the normal rules of evidence and conventional procedures in combination create a situation in which there is a 'correct' answer to questions about semen, injuries, resistance, and who was told what and when after the event. Because the reality of rape does not generally fit the 'correct' answers then women are set up to be challenged. However, it is not clear whether to characterise this as the result of a bias against women, although this may be the effect. Most legal personnel would probably regard the emergence of such 'correct' answers as an unfortunate consequence of the limited range of available evidence in sexual offence trials. However, such questioning can and frequently did also become intertwined with sexist assumptions about normal sexual conduct between men and women. An example of this is when it is assumed that a woman cannot show lack of consent by simply saying no but must resist to the last, and hence lack of serious injuries is turned into evidence of consent. However, the same sort of questioning might occur in a sodomy trial with

a male complainer. Male complainers who were homosexual were liable
to be subjected to similar sorts of stories and stereotyping as female
complainers; they were presented as seeking sex, promiscuous, immoral
and vindictive.

POSSIBLE REMEDIES

Ideas for possible solutions suggested themselves from a number of
sources including the experience of court attendance, background research on other jurisdictions and informal discussion with practitioners
and legal academics. A section of the formal interviews was devoted to
asking practitioners for their responses to a range of potential recommendations. While some of these received a negative response, the ensuing
discussions were fruitful in suggesting yet other possibilities. The suggestions presented here, arise from reflection on all these various 'inputs'.
Fuller consideration of the recommendations offered in this report could
perhaps be facilitated by a process of consultation with the appropriate
bodies.

A number of factors contribute to each of the three general problems.
The first problem concerning prohibited evidence being introduced
without following the procedures is the most open to amelioration without radical changes. That is assuming that it would be possible for the
prosecution and the judiciary, without enormous upheaval, to become
much more prepared to intervene. The norm of not objecting too much
could be tackled in training. Intervention might be encouraged by guidance from the Lord Advocate and by using a Lord Advocate's Reference.
A short briefing paper giving examples of occasions where intervention
would be appropriate could be derived from this research. Further work
might be needed at the level of the Sheriff Court to persuade both the
prosecution and Sheriffs that sexual history evidence is used in their
courts and to ensure that practitioners have the legislation in mind in trials
for the full range of offences to which the legislation applies. More
radically, the legislation could be amended along the lines suggested in
the *Heilbron Report* (see Chapter 1) to include a statutory right to attack
the accused's character if the defence illegitimately attacks the character
of the complainer.

Some of the factors contributing to the second problem, the admission
of evidence which contravenes the aims of the reform, could similarly be
modified without radical change. Guidelines encouraging the prosecution to take an active, investigative and critical part in the application
dialogue could help. Furthermore it should be possible to tighten up what
is included in prosecution productions, particularly the medical report.
Police surgeons could be asked to pass on only legally relevant details in
their report and not to give a full medical history, which can expose the

complainer's pregnancy and contraceptive histories to the defence, when they have no direct relevance on the subject matter of the charge. However, it might be thought inappropriate that doctors be asked to make such a distinction between medical and legal relevance – in which case, it is only possible to urge prosecutors and judges to be especially mindful of these problems and to work against opportunistic use of such materials by the defence.

A more radical but perhaps more certain remedy would be to modify the discretionary character of the exceptions, choosing instead an 'issue-based' formulation. Clearly, general exhortations to ensure the evidence was relevant to key issues in the trial would not be adequate, since there is little consensus on the precise nature of relevance. Much more specific types of circumstances in which sexual history or character evidence would be relevant, should be specified. This could be further strengthened by specifying that probative value should be weighed up so that prohibited evidence is not admitted when its relevance is very slight. Similarly the court could be encouraged to balance the probative value of proposed questioning or evidence against its prejudicial effects.

In the re-examination of the complainer, and in summing-up, the prosecution could be encouraged to take a more active role in countering irrelevant and deliberately confusing evidence led by the defence. Also the defence might be deterred from taking complainers step by step through the accused's version of their sexual encounter, if the prosecution routinely responded by insisting that the accused provide an equally detailed account, if they chose to enter the witness stand.

While it was generally agreed that speculative questioning regarding the complainer's sexual history or sexual character should not be allowed, there is some ambiguity about what actually *counts* as speculative questioning; a directive would be helpful. If the legislation was otherwise unchanged, removal of the Crown exemption might result in a somewhat reduced incidence of sexual history and sexual character evidence, as the prosecution would also have to make an application. However, if belief in the general relevance of sexual history and sexual character evidence persists, despite the legislation, then both prosecution and defence would remain involved in some successful applications which contravene the spirit of the legislation. Removal of the Crown exemption in combination with much more specific exceptions would be a more powerful solution.

The reformers did want to tackle the third problem, namely that a complainer's sexual character can be attacked without making explicit references to sex (but the legislation was weakened by the amendment specifying in 'sexual matters', as an addition to the exclusion of evidence, that the complainer is 'not of good character'). It is possible that a more spirited resistance to such innuendo on the part of the prosecution could have an effect and this should be encouraged; just as the prosecution should be encouraged to attack routinely the character of the accused if such attacks are made on the complainer. Amendment of the legislation to remove reference to 'in relation to sexual matters' from this section of the provisions would clearly strengthen the grounds for objecting to such attacks.

However, the ease with which the defence can suggest that a complainer is of uncertain moral virtue owes much to general cultural stereotypes of women (and homosexual men). There are persisting views about women and their sexuality to which the defence can readily appeal, successfully distracting the jury from the relevant evidence.

Changes to the procedures and to the legislation could further restrict the possibility of manoeuvre by the defence and the prosecution with reference to introducing sexual history and sexual character evidence. Such changes will not however necessarily affect the susceptibility of juries to appeals for such evidence. A possible long-term solution to the problem of wrongful not-proven or not-guilty verdicts is public and jury education. Perhaps it should be generally known that the defence routinely tries to besmirch complainers, to call them liars, to bring in irrelevant evidence, to seize on any aspect of their sexuality that can be found and to construct motives for false allegation. Clearly such education would need to be carried out in a way which fostered critical listening rather than general scepticism about the whole proceedings. Again it would be possible to derive appropriate briefing materials from this research.

Given the large number of young complainers in sexual offences, the recent deliberations concerning child witnesses are highly relevant in considering how to reduce the ordeal of complainers. Given the particular nature of the ordeal of recounting a rape or sexual abuse, many of the recommendations concerning child witnesses could be usefully considered with reference to all complainers in rape and serious sexual offence trials. Any future wide ranging review might consider whether the legal definition of rape can be usefully reformed and might examine the call made by Rape Crisis Centres for a separate legal representative for the complainer in rape cases.

Furthermore, the statute ought to be amended to cover incest and clandestine injury.

Appendix 1

LAW REFORM (MISCELLANEOUS PROVISIONS) (SCOTLAND) ACT 1985

S. 36 (1) After section 141 of the Criminal Procedure (Scotland) Act 1975 there shall be inserted the following sections:

S. 141A (1) In any trial of a person on any charge to which this section applies, subject to section 141B, the court shall not admit, or allow questioning designed to elicit, evidence which shows or tends to show that the complainer:

(a) is not of good character in relation to sexual matters;
(b) is a prostitute or an associate of prostitutes; or
(c) has at any time engaged with any person in sexual behaviour not forming part of the subject matter of the charge.

S. 141A (2) This section applies to a charge of committing or attempting to commit any of the following offences, that is to say:

(a) rape;
(b) sodomy;
(c) assault with intent to rape;
(d) indecent assault;
(e) indecent behaviour (including any lewd, indecent or libidinous practice or behaviour);
(f) an offence under section 106(1)(a) or 107 of the Mental Health Scotland) Act 1984 (unlawful sexual intercourse with mentally handicapped female or with patient);
(g) an offence under any of the following provisions of the Sexual Offences (Scotland) Act 1976:
    (i) section 2 (procuring by threats, etc.);
    (ii) section 3 (unlawful sexual intercourse with girl under 13);
    (iii) section 4 (unlawful sexual intercourse with girl under 16);
    (iv) section 5 (indecent behaviour towards girl between 12 and 16);
    (v) section 8 (abduction of girl under 18);
    (vi) section 9 (unlawful detention of female); or
(h) an offence under section 80(7) of the Criminal Justice (Scotland) Act 1980 (homosexual offences).

S. 141A (3) In this section 'complainer' means the person against whom the offence referred to in subsection (2) above is alleged to have been committed.

S. 141A (4) This section does not apply to questioning, or evidence being adduced, by the Crown.

S. 141B (1) Notwithstanding the terms of section 141A, in any trial of a person on any charge to which that section applies, where the court is satisfied on an application by that person:
(a) that the questioning or evidence referred to in section 141A (1) above is designed to explain or rebut evidence adduced, or to be adduced, otherwise than by or on behalf of that person.

(b) that the questioning or evidence referred to in section 141A(1)(c) above:
    (i) is questioning or evidence as to sexual behaviour which took place on the same occasion as the sexual behaviour forming the subject-matter of the charge; or
    (ii) is relevant to the defence of incrimination; or

(c) that it would be contrary to the interests of justice to exclude the questioning or evidence referred to in section 141A(1) above, the court shall allow such questioning or, as the case may be, admit such evidence.

S. 141B (2) Where questioning or evidence is or has been allowed or admitted under this section, the court may at any time limit as it thinks fit the extent of that questioning or evidence.

S. 141B(3) Any application under this section shall be made in the course of the trial but in the absence of the jury, the complainer, any person cites as a witness and the public.

S. 346A and S. 346B cover summary procedure. The difference from S.141A and S. 141B (above) which cover solemn procedure is only in the offences covered.

S. 346A (2) This section applies to a charge of committing or, in the case of paragraphs (b) to (g), attempting to commit any of the following offences, that is to say:
(a) attempted rape;
(b) sodomy;
(c) assault with intent to rape;
(d) indecent assault;
(e) indecent behaviour (including any lewd, indecent or libidinous practice or behaviour);
(f) an offence under any of the following provisions of the Sexual Offences (Scotland) Act 1976:
    (i) section 2 (procuring by threats, etc);
    (ii) section 3(2) (unlawful sexual intercourse with girl under 13);
    (iii) section 4 (unlawful sexual intercourse with girl under 16);
    (iv) section 5 (indecent behaviour towards girl between 12 and 16);
    (v) section 8 (abduction of girl under 18);
    (vi) section 9 (unlawful detention of female); or
(g) an offence under section 80(7) of the Criminal Justice (Scotland) Act 1980 (homosexual offences).

Appendix 2

TABLE A2.1: High Court Trials by location, July 1987–May 1990.

Court Location	Number of Trials
Glasgow	102
Edinburgh	76
Paisley	9
Stirling	13
Airdrie	25
Kilmarnock	18
Jedburgh	2
Dundee	15
Perth	12
Inverness	10
Aberdeen	14
Dunfermline	4
Greenock	1
Kircaldy	2
Ayr	2
Total	305

TABLE A2.2: High Court Trials involving a single charge, July 1987–May 1990.

Charge	Number	Percentage
Rape	102	77
Attempted rape	15	11
Clandestine injury	6	5
Assault with intent to rape	4	3
Sodomy	2	2
Incest and Related Offences Act s. 2A	2	2
Sexual Offences (Scotland) Act s. 3	1	1
Total	132	100

TABLE A2.3: Sexual history evidence by charge.

Applications to introduce sexual history and sexual character evidence, and such
evidence introduced without application, by charges.

Charges	Applications	Introduced without applications		Prosecution only	All cases without applications	All cases
	(%)	(A)* (%)	(B)**			
Rape	78 (35)	39 (18)	53	8	143	221
Rape-rel.	23 (36)	9 (14)	9	3	41	64
Statutory	11 (22)	8 (16)	9	3	38	49
Homosexual offences	4 (24)	2 (12)	2	1	13	17
Indecency	6 (33)	3 (16)	3	–	12	18
Incest	3 (17)	3 (16)	4	4	15	18
Clandestine injury	1 (17)	1 (17)	1	–	5	6
All charges	98	49	64	14	207	305

NOTES

* A case is counted if it included one or more of the following with respect to the
   complainer – sexual relations with the accused before or since the occasion of
   the charge; sexual relations with others; virginity; prostitution; masturbation;
   pregnancy.
** As A, but including sexual relations with the accused on the occasion of the
   offence.

Appendix 3

TABLE A3.1: High Court contested trials attended.

Case[1]	Court[2]	Charge[3]	Outcome[4]	Sentence[5]	Application[6]
001	ED	AWIR	NG	–	No
		Rape	NP (maj)	–	
		Ass. & Robb.	NG	–	
		Perv.Just	NP (maj)	–	
001a	ED	Att.Rape	G	5 yrs	No
002	GL	AWIR	NG	–	Yes (s)
		Rape	NP	–	
		Con.Bail	NG	–	
003 (3 acc.)	GL	Rape	G	5 yrs each	Yes (s)
007	ED	AWIR	NP	–	
		Rape	G SOA 76.4	6 mths	Yes (s)
009	GL	Ass.	Wthd-		
		Rape	NG Att. Rape/	–	No
		AWIR			
011	GL	Ass., Abd. & Rape	NP	–	No
		Ass. of Police	CD	–	
		Fire 68.17	NP	–	
		CLA 77.50	G	4-yr ban	
		Fire 68.19	G	£300 fine	
		PC 53.1	CD	–	
		TA 81.25	G	4-yr ban	
013	ED	Rape	NG	–	No
019	GL	BoP	NG	–	
		Rape	NP	–	No
		Perv.Jus	G	12 mths	

Case	Court	Charge	Outcome	Sentence	Application
022	ED	Theft	G	Total	
		Att.M.,		12 yrs	
		Rape & Robb.	G del Robb	for	No
		Ass.	G	all	
024	GL	Rape	NP	–	No
026	GL	Att.M.	NP	–	
		AWIR	G	3 yrs	No
		Con.Bail	G	3 mths	
030	ED	Rape	G	8 yrs in	No
		L&L	G	total	
031	GL	Rape	Acq	–	No
(2 acc.)			L&L	NP	–
		Rape	G		
		Rape & Robb.	G	1st, 7 yrs	
				2nd 2, 5 yrs	
032	GL	SIC	G	Total	No
		Sodomy	G	30 mths	
		L&L	G	for all	
		Sodomy	G		
		Sodomy	G		

A late guilty plea was tendered after all prosecution evidence had been led, and some of the defence evidence – counted as contested trial.

Case	Court	Charge	Outcome	Sentence	Application
033	ED	Ass.	G	Adm	
		Rape	G	6 yrs	No
		Murder	G	Life	
038	ED	Rape	NP	–	No
		BoP	G	7 yrs	
		AWIR	G	in total	
		AWIR	G	for all	
043	ED	AWIR	G	4 yrs YOI	No
		Con.Bail	G	6 wks YOI	
		Con.Bail	G	6 wks YOI	
				Total 4 yrs YOI	
045	GL	Rape	G	9 yrs	No
		Theft	Wthd	–	
		Ass. & Att.M	G	9 yrs	
		Theft	Wthd	–	
		Con.Bail	G	3 mths	
				Total 9 yrs	
				and 3 mths	

Case	Court	Charge	Outcome	Sentence	Application
048	PAI	Att.M	Acq	–	
		Ass.SI	Acq	–	
049	ED	Rape	NG	–	Yes (uns)
052	GL	Rape	NP	–	Yes (ps)
		BoP	NG	–	
054	GL	L&L	Late G	15 mths	No
		SOA 76.3	Late G	for both	
058	GL	Rape	NG	–	No
060	ED	Ass. & Rape	NG	–	Yes (ps)
062	GL	Rape	G Att.Rape	2 yrs	No
		Con.Bail	G	Adm	
063	GL	Att.Rape	NG	–	No
		Att.Rape	Late G	15 mths	
065	GL	Rape	G	5 yrs	No
		Perv.Jus	Wthd	–	
		Bop	G		
		BoP	G		
		BoP	NG	–	
		BoP	G		
		Rape	NP	–	No
		Con.Bail	G	2 mths	
				Total 5 yrs	
066	GL	Rape	G I.Ass.	1 yr	No
		PA 67.41	NG	–	
069	ED	Rape	NG	–	No
070	GL	L&L	NP	–	No
		CLA 85.4	NP	–	
		CLA 22.4	NP	–	
		L&L	G	3 yrs	
		Incest	G	3 yrs	
		L&L	G	2 yrs	
		Sodomy	G	5 yrs	
		SIC	Wthd	–	
		L&L	G	2 yrs	
		Sodomy	G	5 yrs	
		SOA 76.5	G	2 yrs	
		SOA 76.5	G	2 yrs	
		L&L	G	3 yrs	
		Incest	G	5 yrs	
				Total 5 yrs	

Case	Court	Charge	Outcome	Sentence	Application
071	DNF	Rape	G Ass.	Def	No
		Rape	NG	–	
		M. Damage	NG	–	
074	GL	Rape	NG	–	No
075	ED	L&L	G	3 yrs	No
		Ass.	NG	–	
		BoP	NG	–	
		Ass.	G	3 yrs	
				Total 3 yrs	
077	KLM	Att.Rape	G	6 yrs	Yes (uns)
078	GL	Rape	G Att.Rape	5 yrs	No
079	ED	Att.Rape	G with dels	18 mths	No
080	ED	Rape/Incest	NG	–	Yes (s)
082	GL	Rape	NG	–	No
		Rape	NG	–	
		SOA 76.3	G alts	4 yrs	
		SOA 76.5	NG	–	
083	GL	Rape	NP	–	No
085	DND	Theft	Late G	Def	
		AWIR	NG (unan)	–	No
087	DND	Rape	NG	–	No
		Con Bail	NG	–	
089	GL	Rape	G (maj)	15 yrs	Yes
		L&L	G (maj)	15 yrs	
		Incest	NP(unan)	–	
		SOA 76.5	G (maj)	4 yrs	
		Rape/Incest	NG (unan)	–	
		Rape	G (unan)	15 yrs	
		L&L	G (unan)	15 yrs	
		AWIR	Wthd	–	
		Incest	NP (maj)	–	
		L&L	G (unan)	15 yrs	
		L&L	J directs NG	–	
		Rape	G (unan)	15 yrs	
		AWIR	NG (unan)	–	
		Rape	G (unan)	15 yrs	
		SOA 76.5	G (unan)	2 yrs	
		Rape/SOA 76.2	G (unan)	7 yrs	

Case	Court	Charge	Outcome	Sentence	Application
		Rape/SOA 76.2&5	NP (maj)	–	
		Rape	NP (unan)	–	
				Total 15 yrs	
090	ED	AWIR	G	2 yrs YOI	No
		Ass. & Robb.	G	2 yrs YOI	
				Total 2 yrs	
092	GL	Rape	G Att.Rape	1 yr	Yes (uns)
095	GL	Ass.	Wthd	–	
		CJ 80.78	Wthd	–	
		Theft	G	3 mths	
		Ass. & Robb.	G	3 mths	
		Rape	NG	–	No
				Total 3 mths	
098	GL	L&L	NP	–	No
		SOA 76.5	NP	–	
		Rape/Incest	NP	–	
		SOA 76.5	NP	–	
		SIC	NP	–	
		Rape	NP	–	
		SIC	NP	–	
100	ARDR	Rape	G (maj)	5 yrs	No
		CThrts	NG	–	
103	ED	I.Ass.	G	2 yrs	No
		I.Exp.	NP	–	
		I.Ass.	G	2 yrs	
				Total 2 yrs	
105	ED	Theft	NG	–	
		Rape	G (maj)	5 yrs	Yes (s)
		Thrts	NG	–	
109	DND	Rape	NP	–	No
110	GL	L&L	Wthd	–	No
		SOA 76.5	Wthd	–	
		Thrt Rape	G (unan)	10 yrs	
		Rape	G (unan)	10 yrs	
		PC 53.1	G	3 mths	
				Total 10 yrs	
111	DND	Rape	NP	–	No
		Ass.	NP	–	

Case	Court	Charge	Outcome	Sentence	Application
117	JDB	Theft	G	Acq	No
		Rape	NP	–	
		BoP	Wthd	–	
118	KLM	AWIR	NG	–	Yes
		Att.Rape	Wthd	–	
		Rape	Acq by J		
		Ass.	Wthd	–	
119	GL	Abd.	NP (maj)	–	No
		Rape	G (maj)	7 yrs	
121	GL	Ass.	Wthd	–	
		Rape	G SOA 76.4	1 yr def	No
123	GL	AWIR	G with dels	Def	No
		Robb.	G Theft	Def	
124	ED	CJ 80.80	Acq by J	–	Yes
		Sodomy	Wthd	–	
		Sodomy	Wthd	–	
		CJ 80.80	Acq by J	–	
		SIC	G (unan)	5 yrs	
		Sodomy	G (unan)	5 yrs	
		Sodomy	G with dels	5 yrs	
		Att.Sodomy	NP (unan)	–	
		Sodomy	G (unan)	5 yrs	
				Total 5 yrs	
128	GL	Rape	NP	–	No
131	DND	Ass. & Sodomy	NP	–	No
134	ED	Att.Rape	G with dels	30 mths	Yes
135	ED	Att.Rape	Desrtd		
136	ED	Rape	NG (maj)	–	No
139	ED	Rape	NP	–	No
140	ARD	Rape	NP (maj)	–	No
143	ARD	Att.Rape/ SOA 76.4	G I.Ass.	1 yr	No
145	ED	Assault	NP	–	
		Abd. & Rape	NP	–	Yes (s)
146	GL	Rape	NG (unan)	–	No

Case	Court	Charge	Outcome	Sentence	Application
156	ED	Rape	Wthd	–	Yes
158	ED	Rape	G to SOA 76.4	1 yr def	Yes
162	STR	Rape	NG	–	
167	STR	BoP	G	Adm	Yes (s)
		Ass.	G	Adm	
		Rape	NP	–	
		Ass.	NP	–	
		Per.Jus	Wthd	–	
		Theft	Wthd	–	
		Con.Bail	Wthd	–	
169	GL	AWIR	G I.Ass.	30 mths	
		Ass.	Wthd	–	
171	ED	Att.Rape	Wthd	–	
		Rape	Wthd	–	
		BoP	Wthd	–	
		Att.Rape	Wthd	–	
		Rape	Acq by J	–	
172	ED	L&L	G with dels	Def	Yes
		Incest	NG (unan)		
		L&L	G (maj)	Def	
		I.Ass	G (maj)	Def	
		CLA 22.4	G (maj)	Def	
		Incest	Wthd	–	
		L&L	Wthd	–	
		I.Ass.	Wthd	–	
		SOA 76.5	Wthd	–	
174	GL	Rape	G Att.SOA 76.3	100 hrs CS	No
		Con.Bail	G		
176 (4 acc.)	GL	I.Ass.	G (maj)	There were	No
		Theft	Wthd	4 accused	
		Rape	NG (maj)	and they	
		Theft	Wthd	received	
		Rape	G (maj)	differential	
		Rape	G I.Ass.	sentencing	
				1st acc: 5 yrs	
				2nd acc: 5 yrs	
				3rd acc: 8 yrs	
				4th acc: 6 yrs	

178	GL	Accused pleads guilty to some charges (i.e. 1, 3, 6 and 10, with deletions and as libelled to 5, 8 and 12) and not guilty to the rest (i.e. 2, 4, 7, 9, and 11). This is not accepted by the Prosecution, so a trial takes place.

Case	Court	Charge	Outcome	Sentence	Application
		L&L	Wthd	–	No
		Sodomy	G (unan)	4 yrs	
		L&L	G (unan)	1 yr	
		Sodomy	G (maj)	4 yrs	
		L&L	G (unan)	1 yr	
		L&L	G (unan)	1 yr	
		Sodomy	G (unan)	4 yrs	
		L&L	Wthd	–	
		Sodomy	NG (maj)	–	
		L&L	G (unan)	1 yr	
		Sodomy	NG (maj)	–	
		L&L	Wthd	–	
				Total 4 yrs	
179	ED	Rape	NG	–	No

TABLE A3.2: High Court application case attended by researchers.

Case[1]	Court[2]	Charge[3]	Outcome[4]	Sentence[5]	Success[6]
002	GL	AWIR	NG	–	Success
		Rape	NP	–	
		Con.Bail	NG	–	
003 (3 acc.)	GL	Rape	G	5 yrs	Partial
007	ED	AWIR	NP	–	
		Rape	G SOA 76.4	6 mths	Success
049	ED	Rape	NG	–	Refused
052	GL	Rape	NP	–	Partial
		BoP	NP	–	
060	ED	Assault & Rape	NG	–	Partial
077	KLM	Att.Rape	G	6 yrs	Refused
080	ED	Rape/SOA 76.2	NG	–	Success
089	GL	Rape	G	15 yrs	Success
		L&L	G	15 yrs	
		Incest	NP	–	
		SOA 76.5	G	4 yrs	
		Rape/Incest	NG	–	
		Rape	G	15 yrs	

Case	Court	Charge	Outcome	Sentence	Success
		L&L	G	15 yrs	
		AWIR	Wthd	–	
		Incest	NP	–	
		L&L	G	15 yrs	
		L&L	Acq	–	
		Rape	G	15 yrs	
		AWIR	NG	–	
		Rape	G	15 yrs	
		SOA 76.5	G	2 yrs	
		Rape/SOA 76.2	NG	7 yrs	
		Rape/SOA 76.2&5	NP	–	
		Rape	NP	–	
				Total 15 yrs	
092	GL	Rape	G Att.Rape	1 yr	Refused
105	ED	Rape	G	5 yrs	Success
		Theft	NG	–	
		Threats	NG	–	
118	KLM	AWIR	NG	–	Success
		Att.Rape	Wthd	–	
		Rape	Acq		
		Assault	Wthd	–	
124	ED	CJ 80.80	Acq	–	Success
		Sodomy	Wthd	–	
		Sodomy	Wthd	–	
		CJ 80.80	Acq	–	
		SIC	G	5 yrs	
		Sodomy	G	5 yrs	
		Sodomy	G with dels	5 yrs	
		Att.Sodomy	NP	–	
		Sodomy	G	5 yrs	
		Total 5 yrs			
134	ED	Att.Rape	G with dels	30 mths	Success
145	ED	Abd. & Rape	NG	–	Success
		Assault	NP	–	
156	ED	Rape	Wthd	–	Success
158	ED	Rape	G SOA 76.4	1 yr Def	Success
165	ED	Att.Rape	NG	–	Success
167	ST	Bop	G	Adm	Success

Case	Court	Charge	Outcome	Sentence	Success
		Assault	G	Adm	
		Rape	NP	–	
		Assault	NP	–	
		Per.Jus	Wthd	–	
		Theft	Wthd	–	
		Con.Bail	Wthd	–	
172	ED	L&L	G with dels	Def	Withdrawn
		Incest	NG	–	
		L&L	G	Def	
		I.Ass.	G	Def	
		CLA 22.4	G	Def	
		Incest	Wthd		
		L&L	Wthd		
		I.Ass.	Wthd		
		SOA 76.5	Wthd		

TABLE A3.3: Sheriff Solemn trials attended by researchers.

Case[1]	Court[2]	Charge[3]	Outcome[4]	Sentence[5]
010	GL	AWIR	G	18 mths
012	ED	Ass.w.i.Rob	G	3 mths
		I.ass.	G with dels	15 mths
		BoP	G	3 mths
				Total 18 mths
016	GL	AWIR	G	2 yrs prob
020	GL	AWIR	G	18 mths YOI
055	GL	L&L	G	20 mths
		Con.Bail	G	3 mths
				Total 20 mths
081	ED	L&L	G	9 mths
106	ED	SIC	NP (maj)	–
		SIC	Wthd	–
		SIC	NP (maj)	–
120	GL	AWIR	NG	–
147	GL	I.ass.	Acq by Sh	–
		I.ass.	G	9 mths
148	GL	SOA 76.5	NG	–

Case	Court	Charge	Outcome	Sentence
		Subornation	Wthd	–
152	GL	AWIR	NG	–
159	GL	I.ass.	G	Def
		I.ass.	G	Def
		I.ass.	G	Def
		I.ass.	G	Def
		I.ass.	Wthd	–
		AWIR	G	Def
		Con.Bail	G	Def
164	ED	I.ass.	Acq by Sh	–
		L&L	G	9 mths
		SOA 76.5	G	9 mths
		SOA 76.5	Acq by Sh	–
		SIC	Acq by Sh	–
166	ED	AWIR	NG	–

TABLE A3.2: Sheriff summary trials attended by researchers.

Case[1]	Charge[3]	Outcome[4]	Sentence[5]
004	L&L	NG	–
	L&L	NG	–
	L&L	Acq by Sh	–
	L&L	NG	–
	L&L	Acq by Sh	–
005	SOA 76.4	G	£50 fine
008	L&L	CD	–
015	BoP	G	£5 CO
	BoP	G	£20 CO
			£100 fine
			£100 security
	BoP	NG	–
025	I.Exp.	NP	–
036	I.Ass.	CD	–
037	I.Ass.	G	£225 fine
044	L&L	G	£120 fine

Case	Charge	Outcome	Sentence
050	L&L	NP	–
056	SOA 76.4	G	3 mths imp
064	L&L	G with dels	£150.00 fine
067	I.Exp.	NG	–
068	BoP	G with dels	£80.00 fine
088	I.exp.	G	£100.00 fine
094	SOA 76.4	NG	–
096	L&L	NG	–
112 (3 acc.)	SOA 76.4 SOA 76.10	G G	1st: 1 yr prob 2nd: 1 yr prob 3rd: 50 hrs CS
130	I.Ass. I.Exp.	G G with dels	Total 3 mths YOI
132	I.Exp. I.Exp. I.Exp.	NP G G	– security £250.00
133	SOA 76.4	Wthd	–
149	L&L L&L	G G with dels	£150.00 £150.00 Total £300.00
163	I.Behav.	Wthd	

NOTE: All above cases were heard in Edinburgh with the exception of 088 which took place in Stirling.

NOTES

1. The case number is the identification number given to the trial by the researchers. These numbers are used throughout the text to make it clear which trials are being discussed.

   When more than one accused was involved in the case the number is shown in brackets below the case number: e.g. (2 acc.), two accused.

2. The locations of the High Courts and Sheriff Courts are abbreviated as follows:
   ARD   Airdrie

DND	Dundee
DNF	Dunfermline
ED	Edinburgh
GL	Glasgow
JDB	Jedburgh
KLM	Kilmarnock
PAI	Paisley
ST	Stirling
STR	Stranraer

3. When there is more than one accused, each was charged with all charges, unless otherwise specified. The following abbreviations are used:

/	charges separated by / were specified as alternatives
Abd.	Abduction
Ass.	Assault
Ass.SI	Assault to Severe Injury and Danger to Life
Ass.w.i.Rob	Assault with intent to Rob
Att.	Attempted
Att.M	Attempted Murder
AWIR	Assault with intent to Rape
BoP	Breach of the Peace
CJ 80.	Contravention of the Criminal Justice (Scotland) Act 1980. The number after the point is the cited section of the Act. Section 78 refers to wilful damage. The relevant part of section 80 refers to procuring the commission of a homosexual act with a person under the age of 21.
CLA 85., CLA 22., CLA 77.	Contravention of the Criminal Law Amendment Act 1885, 1922 or 1977. The number after the point is the cited section of the Act. Section 4 of the 1885 Act refers to unlawful carnal knowledge of a girl under 13. Section 4 of the 1922 Act refers to lewd, indecent and libidinous practices and behaviour towards a girl over the age of 12 and under 16. Section 50 of the 1977 Act refers to reckless driving.
Con.Bail	Contravention of the Bail etc. (Scotland) Act 1980
CThrts	Criminal Threats
Fire 68.	The Firearms Act 1968. The number after the point is the cited Section of the Act. Section 17 refers to unlawful possession of a firearm and Section 19 to having a loaded gun in a public place.
I.Ass.	Indecent Assault
I.Behav.	Indecent Behaviour
I.Exp.	Indecent Exposure
L&L	Lewd, Indecent, Libidinous Practices and Behaviour

M.Damage	Malicious Damage
Perv.Just	Attempt to Pervert the Course of Justice
PA 67.41	Contravention of the Police (Scotland) Act 1967. Section 41 refers to resisting arrest.
PC 63.	Contravention of the Prevention of Crime Act 1953. Section 1 refers to carrying an offensive weapon in a public place.
Robb.	Robbery
SIC	Shameless and Indecent Conduct
SOA 76.	Contravention of the Sexual Offences (Scotland) Act 1976. The number after the point is the cited section of the Act. Section 2 refers to incest. Section 3 and 4 refer to unlawful sexual intercourse with a girl under the age of 13 and aged 13 to 15. Section 5 refers to lewd, indecent and libidinous practices and behaviour towards a girl age 13 to 15. Section 10 refers to allowing premises to be used for unlawful sexual intercourse.
TA 81.25	The Transport Act 1981. The relevant section refers to failing to take a breath test.

4. There are three possible verdicts for a jury: Guilty (G), Not Guilty (NG) and Not Proven (NP). Where possible, whether the verdict was reached by a majority (maj) or unanimously (unan) is shown in brackets. When the accused is found guilty to a reduced charge, the new charge is shown immediately after the 'G'. When the accused was found guilty with the deletion of some specific part of the charge this is indicated by the abbreviation 'with dels'. Other outcomes have been abbreviated as follows:

Wthd	charges withdrawn or deserted by the prosecution
Acq by J	the judge has instructed that the accused must be acquitted
Acq by Sh	the sheriff has instructed that the accused must be acquitted.

5. Unless otherwise specified, a number of years or months indicates a sentence to imprisonment. The following abbreviations are used for other types of sentence:

Acq	Acquitted
Adm	Admonished
CS	Community Service
CO	Community Order
Def	Sentence was Deferred
Prob	Probation
YOI	Young Offenders' Institution

The Sentence may be defered to a later date to allow reports to be prepared on the accused which the judge or sheriff has requested to inform sentencing. However, if a specific period of imprisonment has been defered then this means that the sentence will not be served if the accused can claim good conduct when the case is reviewed by the court.

6. Whether or not an application was made to introduce prohibited evidence is indicated by a Yes or No in each case in Table A3.1. The outcome of an application is indicated by:

(s)   successful
(un)   unsuccessful
(ps)   partially successful

This is written more fully in Table A3.2, which deals only with cases containing an application. Since no applications were observed by researchers in the Sheriff Courts, this column is dropped from Tables A3.3 and Table A3.4.

Bibliography

Adler, Z. (1982), 'The Reality of Rape Trials', *New Society*, 4 February.

Adler, Z. (1982), 'Rape Law – The Latest Ruling', *New Law Journal*, 5 August, pp. 746-47.

Adler, Z. (1982), 'Rape: The Intention of Parliament and the Practice of the Courts', 45, *Modern Law Review*.

Adler, Z. (1985), 'The Relevance of Sexual History Evidence in Rape: The Problems of Subjective Interpretation', *Criminal Law Review*.

Adler, Z. (1987), *Rape on Trial* (London and New York: Routledge & Kegan Paul).

Atkins, S. and Hoggett, B. (1984), *Women and the Law* (Oxford: Basil Blackwell).

Berger, V. (1977), 'Man's Trial, Women's Tribulation', *Columbia Law Review*, Vol. 77, No. 1, p. 1.

Brown, B., Burman, M. & Jamieson, L. (1992), 'Sexual History and Sexual Character Evidence in Scottish Sexual Offence Trials' (Edinburgh: HMSO, Scottish Office Central Research Unit Papers).

Chambers, G. and Millar, A. (1983), *Investigating Sexual Assault* (Edinburgh: HMSO, Scottish Office Central Research Unit Study).

Chambers, G. and Millar, A. (1986), *Prosecuting Sexual Assault* (Edinburgh: HMSO, Scottish Office Central Research Unit Study).

Clark, A. (1987), *Men's Violence: Women's Silence* (London: Pandora).

Cross, R. and Tapper, C. (1985, sixth edition), *Cross on Evidence* (London: Butterworth).

Dickson, W. G. (1887), *Treatise on the Law of Evidence in Scotland* (as updated by S. J. Hamilton Grierson) (Edinburgh: T&T Clark).

Edwards, S. (1986), 'Evidential Matters in Rape Prosecutions from "First Opportunity to Complain" to Corroboration', *New Law Journal*, 28 March, pp. 291–3.

Elliot, D. W. (1983), 'The Young Person's Guide to Similar Fact Evidence – I', *Criminal Law Review*.

Elliott, D. W. (1984), 'Rape Complainants' Sexual Experience with Third Parties', *Criminal Law Review*.

Estrich, S. (1987), *Real Rape* (Cambridge, Mass: Harvard University Press).

Field, D. (1988), *The Law of Evidence in Scotland* (Edinburgh: W. Green & Son).

Gane, C. H. W. and Stoddart, C. N. (1980), *A Casebook on Scottish Criminal Law* (Edinburgh: W. Green. and Son).

Gane, C. H. W. and Stoddart, C. N. (1983), *Criminal Procedure in Scotland:*

Cases and Materials (Edinburgh: W. Green & Son).

Garfinkel, H. (1956), 'Conditions of Successful Degradation Ceremonies', *American Journal of Sociology*, Vol. 61, March.

Harper, R. and McWhinnie, A. (1983), *The Glasgow Rape Case* (London: Hutchinson).

Heidensohn, F. (1986), 'Portia or Persephone', *International Journal of the Sociology of Law*, Vol. 14.

Heilbron Committee, The (1975), *Report of the Advisory Group on the Law of Rape* (London: HMSO) Cmnd. 6352.

Hume, Baron (1844, 4th edition), *Commentaries on the Law of Scotland Respecting Crimes*.

Kalven, H. and Zeisel, H. (1966), *The American Jury* (Boston and Toronto: Little, Brown).

Kelsen, H. (1991), *General Theory of Law and State* (Oxford: Clarendon).

Lees, S. (1989), 'Trial by Rape', *New Statesman and Society*, 24 November.

McBarnet, D. (1983), 'Victim in the Witness Box – Confronting Victomology's Stereotype', *Contemporary Crises*.

MacKinnon, C. (1987), *Feminism Unmodified: Discourses on Life and Law* (London: Harvard University Press).

MacPhail, I. D. (Unpublished), 'Research Paper on the Law of Evidence'.

MacPhail, I. D. (1987), *Evidence* (Edinburgh: Law Society of Scotland).

Marsh, J. C., Geist, A. and Caplan, N. (1982), *Rape and the Limits of Law Reform* (Boston: Auburn House).

Moody, S. R. and Tombs, J. (1982), *Prosecution in the Public Interest* (Edinburgh: Scottish Academic Press).

Naffine, N. (1990), *Law and the Sexes: Explorations in Feminist Jurisprudence* (Sydney, Melbourne, Wellington and London: Allen and Unwin).

Norby, V. W. (1980), 'Reforming Rape Laws – The Michigan Experience', in J. Scutt, *Rape Law Reform*.

Pattenden, R. (1986), 'The Character of Victims and Third Parties in Criminal Proceedings Other than Rape Trials', *Criminal Law Review*.

Renton R. W. and Brown H. (1983), 'Criminal Procedure According to the Law of Scotland', in G. H. Gordon, J. Maclean and C.H.W. Gane (eds), *Title* (Edinburgh: W. Green and Son, 15th edition).

Scottish Law Commission (1983), *Evidence. Report on Evidence in Cases of Rape and Other Sexual Offences* (Edinburgh: HMSO).

Scottish Law Commission (1980), *Consultative Memorandum No. 46*.

Scutt, J. A. (1980), *Rape Law Reform* (Canberra: Australian Institute of Criminology).

Smart, C. (1989), *Feminism and the Power of Law* (London: Routledge).

Smith, J. C. (1976), 'The Heilbron Report', *Criminal Law Review*.

Temkin, J. (1984), 'Evidence in Sexual Assault Cases: The Scottish Proposal and Alternatives to it', *Modern Law Review*, Vol. 47, No. 60.

Temkin, J. (1984), 'Regulating Sexual History Evidence - The Limits of Discretionary Legislation', *International and Comparative Law Quarterly*, Vol. 33.

Temkin, J. (1987), *Rape and the Legal Process* (London: Sweet & Maxwell).

Walker, A. G. and Walker, N. M. L. (1964/1986), *The Law of Evidence in Scotland* (Glasgow: Bell and Bain).

Williams Report on Obscenity and Film Censorship (1979), (London: HMSO) Cmnd. 7772.

Index

Index of Cases